Using New Technologies to Enh
and Learning in History

Nearly all history teachers are interested in how new technology might be used to improve teaching and learning in history. However, not all history departments have had the time, expertise and guidance that would enable them to fully explore the wide range of ways in which ICT might help them to teach their subject more effectively.

This much-needed collection offers practical guidance and examples of the ways in which new technology can enhance pupil engagement in the subject, impact on knowledge retention, get pupils learning outside the history classroom, and help them to work collaboratively using a range of Web 2.0 applications.

The chapters, written by experienced practitioners and experts in the field of history education and ICT, explore topics such as:

- how to design web interactivities for your pupils;
- what you can accomplish with a wiki;
- how to get going in digital video editing;
- what to do with the VLE;
- making best use of the interactive whiteboard;
- designing effective pupil webquests;
- digital storytelling in history;
- making full use of major history websites;
- using social media.

Using New Technologies to Enhance Teaching and Learning in History is essential reading for all trainee, newly qualified and experienced teachers of history. It addresses many of the problems, barriers and dangers that new technology can pose, but it also clearly explains and exemplifies the wide range of ways in which ICT can be used to radically improve the quality of pupils' experience of learning history.

Terry Haydn is Professor of Education at the University of East Anglia, UK.

Using New Technologies to Enhance Teaching and Learning in History

Edited by Terry Haydn

Routledge
Taylor & Francis Group

LONDON AND NEW YORK

First published 2013
by Routledge
2 Park Square, Milton Park, Abingdon, Oxon OX14 4RN

Simultaneously published in the USA and Canada
by Routledge
711 Third Avenue, New York, NY 10017

Routledge is an imprint of the Taylor & Francis Group, an informa business

British Library Cataloguing-in-Publication Data
A catalogue record for this book is available from the British Library

Library of Congress Cataloging-in-Publication Data
Using new technologies to enhance teaching and learning in history / edited by Terry Haydn.
p. cm.
Includes index.
ISBN 978-0-415-68837-6 (hardback) -- ISBN 978-0-415-68838-3 -- ISBN 978-0-203-07559-3
1. History--Computer-assisted instruction. 2. History--Study and teaching. 3. Educational technology. I. Haydn, Terry.
D16.255.C65U85 2013
907.0785--dc23
2012026090

ISBN: 978-0-415-68837-6 (hbk)
ISBN: 978-0-415-68838-3 (pbk)
ISBN: 978-0-203-07559-3 (ebk)

Typeset in Galliard
by GreenGate Publishing Services, Tonbridge, Kent

Printed and bound in Great Britain by
TJ International Ltd, Padstow, Cornwall

Contents

List of figures and tables

Figures

Tables

Notes on contributors

Johannes Ahrenfelt is Co-Director of 99SQUARED Ltd and works as an independent consultant helping schools use ICT effectively. He has also written books and various digital resources on learning and teaching as well as ICT in education. Johannes worked as Subject Leader of History for several years as well as County Advisor for Learning and Teaching with ICT.

Doug Belshaw currently works at JISC infoNet where he researches digital literacies, mobile learning and open education. Prior to this he was Director of e-Learning at a large, multi-site, all-age Academy, and taught history and ICT for seven years.

Janos Blasszauer, MEd in ELT, is a high school teacher at Batthyany Lajos Grammar School, Nagykanizsa, Hungary. He has attended and delivered presentations and workshops at national, regional, and international events on ICT in education. He was an associate member of the e-help project.

Arthur Chapman is Reader in Education at Edge Hill University, Lancashire. He taught history for 12 years in Surrey and Cornwall and worked on the PGCE Secondary History courses at the University of Cumbria and the Institute of Education, University of London prior to taking up a post at Edge Hill. *Constructing History, 11–19*, edited with Hilary Cooper, was published by Sage in 2009.

Nick Dennis has taught history throughout the age and ability range in the state and independent sector and is Deputy Head (Academic) at Berkhamsted School. Nick is a board member of the Independent Schools Council ICT Strategy Group and provides advice to schools in the strategic development of ICT. As an Apple Education Mentor, Nick is a strong advocate of using mobile technologies in the classroom with a strong focus on the pedagogical benefits.

Terry Haydn was a history teacher in a Manchester comprehensive school for 20 years before moving to work in teacher education. He is currently Professor of Education at the University of East Anglia. He has a long-standing interest in the use of ICT in history teaching and has written widely about history education.

Richard Jones-Nerzic teaches history at the European School Brussels III and runs the website *International School History*. He was coordinator of the European History e-Learning Project (e-help). He has recently co-authored a series of textbooks for students of International Baccalaureate history.

Dan Lyndon is an Advanced Skills Teacher and Head of History at Broomfield School, Enfield with nearly 20 years of experience teaching history in schools across London. He is also a published author of books for KS2, KS3 and GCSE and the webmaster of two websites: blackhistory4schools.com and comptonhistory.com.

Ali Messer is Programme Convener for Secondary PGCE, and tutor for History PGCE and MA Education students at the University of Roehampton. She was a history teacher and Head of Faculty in schools for 20 years, where she became interested in exploring e-learning in history.

John Simkin runs the Spartacus Educational website. He worked as a history teacher in comprehensive schools for many years and in the early 1980s was involved in producing history computer programs and teaching packages for Tressell Publications (Attack on the Somme, Into the Unknown and Wagons West) and Spartacus Educational (Wall Street and Russian Revolution).

Ben Walsh has been involved in history education for over 25 years as a teacher and head of department. He is a well known author of textbooks and electronic resources for history teaching. His time is now divided between writing, running training courses for history teachers, examination work and research into the use of technology in history teaching.

Neal Watkin is an Advanced Skills Teacher working within and across schools in Suffolk. He has a particular interest in using ICT within the classroom, thinking skills, and curriculum planning. In the aspects of ICT and e-learning, his work focuses on utilising ICT as a way to motivate students and draw out key historical skills. He is also the co-author of three books on teaching and learning.

Alf Wilkinson taught history and was ICT coordinator in London, Bedfordshire and Lincolnshire for many years. He devised and ran the Historical Association's New Opportunities Fund ICT training and is an experienced CPD provider. He now works part time for the Historical Association as their Professional Development Manager.

Acknowledgements

I would like to thank all the contributors to this volume, for fitting this in on top of everything else. I would also like to thank all those in the e-help project who were such an inspiration to work with, and Joe Haydn for doing the graphics for the book. Thanks also to LK.

Introduction

Terry Haydn

Things change quite quickly in the field of education and new technology. A previous volume on history and ICT (Haydn and Counsell, 2003) was written when Wikipedia had only recently been launched, and had under 200,000 entries. MySpace and Skype were not yet online, Facebook and YouTube had yet to be launched, Twitter, iTunes and the iPhone did not exist. The term 'Web 2.0' had only recently been coined, and was in its infancy. Few history classrooms were equipped with a data projector, had internet access, interactive whiteboards or access to a VLE (Haydn, 2004). Data were often stored on what was called a 'floppy disk'; something I now use as an artefact to help illustrate the increase in the pace of change occasioned by improvements in communications technology (see Google ngram for an illustration of the life-cycle of the floppy disk compared to the blackboard – www.google.com/ngrams).

There has also been a radical change in teacher and student teacher *attitudes* to the use of computers in history teaching in recent years. From a situation where many history teachers were sceptical about the potential benefits of ICT (Easdown, 2000),[1] recent research suggests that most teachers and student teachers are generally positive about ICT, keen to explore its use, and feel hampered more by lack of time to explore and develop ICT use, rather than lack of interest (see, for example, Haydn and Barton, 2008; Beacham and McIntosh, 2012).

The proliferation of new developments in technology, particularly in terms of Web 2.0 applications, has made it increasingly difficult to keep up with what is 'out there' which might be of use for teaching history. Given the range of applications that one might explore and attempt to make use of, there are hard choices to be made in terms of which applications to pursue and invest time in.

It is also hard to find time to disentangle and assess the myths, hype, misconceptions and misjudgements that influence discourse about education and ICT. UK Politicians have generally been unreservedly enthusiastic about the use of ICT in education, and have tended to see ICT as a sort of unproblematic educational miracle (Haydn, 2003), and conferences with titles such as 'The future of technology in education' are often dominated by speakers from companies trying to sell technology to schools, rather than teachers and researchers (see, for example, the list of speakers at the Westminster Education Forum Keynote Seminar, 13 September 2011). Terms such as Prensky's (2001) 'digital natives' (cited in over 4,000 studies) have sometimes been accepted as unexamined assumptions, rather than tested against reality, and there has been little research on which ICT applications are most useful if you are a history teacher, in relation to cost, time invested and impact on learning (see Chapter 1 for further discussion of these points).

Figure 0.1 'Hard choices...'

Given that there are many demands on their time, how much time should history teachers invest in their understanding of ICT, and which ICT 'avenues' should they pursue in terms of 'pay-off' for the time and effort invested in ICT? Hadfield *et al.* (2009) make the point that with student teachers, it is sometimes necessary to move them on from thinking about the 'social status' of some facets of ICT (such as being expert at using the interactive whiteboard), and the 'learning status' of ICT applications (i.e. which applications have most potential for improving pupil learning).

How essential is it that history teachers use ICT in their teaching? Way back in 1995, Cochrane argued that 'in future, there will be two sorts of teacher; the ICT literate and the retired' (Cochrane, 1995), and more recently, it has been suggested that teachers who do not use technology should be dismissed (Thompson, 2012), and that the use of ICT is 'essential' to effective learning[2]:

It is time to shift our mindsets away from the notion that technology provides a *supplemental* teaching tool, and assume, as with other professions, that technology is *essential* to successful performance outcomes (i.e. student learning). To put it simply, effective teaching requires effective technology use.

(Ertmer and Ottenbreit-Leftwich, 2010: 256, emphasis in original)

I have some reservations about such claims, and what might be termed 'technology fundamentalism'. When I think of the outstanding teachers who do sessions at the main history education conferences in the UK, or who do sessions as visiting speakers for my PGCE students, many of them make little or no use of ICT. However, as I argue in Chapter 1, history teachers who do not make any use of ICT are perhaps missing out on some opportunities to make particular points in a more vivid and effective way, and ways of getting pupils to learn history outside the confines of the taught sessions.

This also raises interesting questions about what it means 'to be good at ICT' as a history teacher or student teacher. In Chapter 1 I will argue that there are different ways of being 'good at ICT' and that there are different pathways that teachers might take towards this end, depending on aptitude and interests. There are 'hi-tech' and 'low-tech' routes that might be pursued, which is not to say that 'hi-tech' applications necessarily deliver better learning outcomes for pupils. As one history teacher educator respondent suggested in a 2009 survey:

Some projects have perhaps tended to overemphasise the hi-tech and quite complex aspects of ICT and that puts some people off ... They think they are going to lack the technological expertise to do things well and it will expose them as being not quite up to date.

(OECD, 2009)

As Chapman, Walsh and Prior, and John have pointed out, even the simple word processor is a very useful tool for teaching history, given the facility it provides for sorting, editing and manipulating information – and yet how many teachers are aware of the range of ways in which the word processor might be of use in helping pupils to do well in history? Used in the right way, the word processor can be a way of getting pupils beyond what Walsh terms 'Encarta Syndrome' (the unthinking use of copy and paste from websites) and ensuring that pupils have to think about, work on and deploy the information they have accessed on the internet (Walsh, 1998; Prior and John, 2000; Chapman, 2003).

Gillespie (2011) suggests that teachers fall into different categories in terms of their attitudes to ICT, with a (roughly) 10/80/10 split: around 10 per cent of what she terms 'early adopters', keen to develop new applications that come to their attention, 10 per cent who are a bit reticent and hesitant about exploring ICT, and who tend to stick to 'tried and tested' traditional modes of teaching, and then around 80 per cent of teachers who are somewhere 'in the middle' – interested, but balancing time investment in ICT with many other competing professional agendas. In a project designed to give dedicated time to teachers to explore the use of ICT in their subject teaching, some departments went down the route of creating departmental revision websites, or experimenting with the use of Adobe Flash animations, others spent the time building up collections of high-quality digital resources on particular topics. Nearly all the teachers involved in the project reported that the ICT developments had been helpful in improving learning outcomes for pupils, and they nearly all volunteered to be involved in 'Phase 2' of the project the following year (Haydn and Barton, 2008). New Technology rarely provides 'shrink-wrapped' and teacher-proof solutions to the challenges of teaching topics and ideas effectively. It usually takes time and thought to consider exactly how best to deploy new technology applications.

Even in a book with 14 chapters, it is not possible to cover the full range of ICT applications and developments that have the potential to improve teaching and learning in history. For readers who are interested in a wider range of ICT applications, the e-help website (see Figure 0.2) has text and video versions of 40 seminars that were part of the e-help project (European History E-Learning Project), an EU-funded project that brought together a group of teachers from across Europe who were interested in the use of new technology in history teaching. Over a period of five years, between 2003 and 2008, the core group and a number of invited experts in the field of history and ICT met for a number of weekend seminars, to consider developments in ICT that might have the potential to improve teaching and learning in history. Most of the contributors to this volume were involved in the project. The seminars on the website detail many ideas and applications that are not contained within this volume.[3]

However, as I argue in Chapter 1, 'being good at ICT' as a history teacher is less about having encyclopaedic knowledge of such applications, and advanced technical expertise in ICT, and more about focusing on one or two applications and thinking of interesting and worthwhile things to do with them.

A history teacher education respondent in the survey cited earlier in this chapter suggested that 'There are good and helpful things that teachers can do with ICT, but teachers and student teachers need a knowledgeable guide to provide a quick way in to easy-to-use and high impact resources and ideas.' All the contributors to this volume gave up their time in the hope that this book would provide such a guide. Whether you are interested in 'hi-tech' or 'lo-tech' ways of using ICT; whether you are an 'early adopter', a 'traditionalist' or, like most teachers, somewhere in the middle, I hope that there are things that you will find of interest and use in the book.[4]

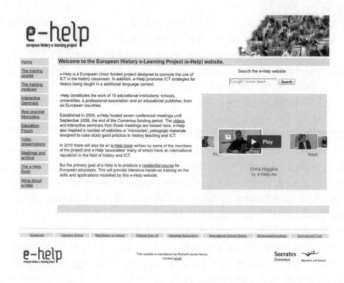

Figure 0.2 The e-help website

Video and text versions of the e-help seminars can be accessed at www.e-help.eu.

Notes

1 In a seminar reporting his research, Easdown noted that when a student teacher expressed the view that ICT had absolutely nothing to offer teachers of history, an assembled group of history mentors applauded the statement.
2 It is interesting to note that, whereas previous versions of the standards necessary to qualify as a teacher in the UK included extensive reference to the ability to use ICT in subject teaching – in the case of the 1998 version of the Standards for Qualified Teacher Status, over 17 pages of specific competence statements, requiring over 100 ICT 'capabilities' (DfEE, 1998), the most recent version of the Standards makes no mention of the ability to use ICT (DfE, 2011).
3 The e-help website which has videos and transcripts of all the seminars presented in the course of the e-help project can be accessed at www.e-help.eu. The majority of the participants in e-help were from a background in secondary teaching, so most of the examples in terms of 'content' pertain to the secondary history curriculum. However, we hope that many of the ideas and applications discussed will also be of interest and use to those teaching history in primary schools.
4 Because web addresses sometimes change or disappear, and things change quite rapidly in the field of ICT and education, updated links and updates can be found at either the ICT section of my website (www.uea.ac.uk/~m242/historypgce/ict/welcome.htm), or on my (embryo) wiki at http://historyandict.wetpaint.com).

References

Beacham, N. and McIntosh, K.J. (2012) 'Student teacher attitudes and beliefs towards using ICT as part of inclusive practice: a 2008–2009 pilot survey', *Tean Journal*, 4 (2), online at http://bit.ly/AtMwtr, accessed 28 February 2012.

Chapman, A. (2003) 'Conceptual awareness through categorising using ICT: using ICT to get Year 13 reading', *Teaching History*, 111: 38–43.

Cochrane, P. (1995) Quoted in *Times Educational Supplement*, 23 June.

Department for Education (2011) *Teachers' standards*, London, DfE.

DfEE (1998) *Teaching: High Status, High Standards. Requirements for courses of Initial Teacher Training*, Circular 4/98, London, DfEE.

Easdown, G. (2000) 'History teachers and ICT', in G. Easdown (ed.) *Innovation and Methodology: Opportunities and constraints in history teacher education*, Lancaster: HTEN, pp. 19–35.

Ertmer, P. and Ottenbreit-Leftwich, A. (2010) 'Teacher technology change: how knowledge, confidence, beliefs and culture intersect', *Journal of Research on Technology in Education*, 42 (3): 255–84.

Gillespie, H. (2011) *Cross-disciplinary applications of ICT to support student learning*, seminar, University of East Anglia, 1 November.

Hadfield, M., Jopling, M., Royle, K. and Southern, L. (2009) *Evaluation of the Training and Development Agency for Schools for Schools' funding for ICT in ITT projects*, London: TDA.

Haydn, T. (2004) 'The use of ICT in history teaching in secondary schools in England and Wales, 1970–2003'. Unpublished PhD thesis, University of London.

Haydn, T. and Barton, R. (2008) '"First do no harm": factors influencing teachers' ability and willingness to use ICT in their subject teaching', *Computers and Education*, 51 (1): 439–47.

Haydn, T. and Counsell, C. (eds) (2003) *History, ICT and Learning*, London: RoutledgeFalmer.

OECD (2009) *Case studies of the ways in which initial teacher education providers in England prepare student teachers to use ICT effectively in their subject teaching*, Paris: OECD. Online at www.oecd.org/dataoecd/42/39/45046837.pdf.

Prensky, M. (2001) 'Digital natives, digital immigrants', *On the Horizon*, 9 (5), MCB University Press, October, online at www.marcprensky.com/writing/prensky%20-%20digital%20natives,%20digital%20immigrants%20-%20part1.pdf, accessed 14 November 2011.

Prior, J. and John, P. (2000) 'From anecdote to argument: using the word processor to connect knowledge and opinion through revelatory writing', *Teaching History*, 101: 31–4.

Thompson, V. (2012) 'The digital age is now, so embrace it', letter to *Times Educational Supplement*, 20 January.

Walsh, B. (1998) 'Why Gerry likes history now: the power of the word processor', *Teaching History*, 93: 6–15.

Chapter 1

What does it mean 'to be good at ICT' as a history teacher?

Terry Haydn

Introduction

There are several strands or facets of capability in the use of ICT in subject teaching (see Box 1.1), and most teachers are stronger in some strands than others. There are different ways of being 'good at ICT', but it is certainly not just a case of being accomplished in terms of technical capability, range of applications used, or amount of ICT use. In terms of a 'bottom line' in response to the question posed by the title, it might be the extent to which teachers exploit the potential of new technology to improve teaching and learning in history.

In a survey of the views of experienced teacher educators and mentors, only one out of 52 respondents defined competence in ICT in terms of a list of technical things that teachers should be able to do. In the words of one teacher educator:

> It's funny because in a skills set sense, I don't have a list... I don't think, they must be able to do PowerPoint, they must be able to upload a YouTube video and so on. It's more that when we cover things... particular concepts... we consider how various bits and pieces of ICT might help to get the idea or concept across more effectively and they just bump into lots of ICT things along the way.
>
> (OECD, 2010: 11)

Although awareness of the existence of ICT applications and basic technical competence in them were seen as 'entry level' factors to developing the capability to use ICT effectively in subject teaching, these factors were deemed less important than teachers having good ideas about 'what to do' with ICT applications once they had learned how to use them:

> It's about them thinking about what sorts of things you can do with Twitter, or PowerPoint or whatever.
>
> It's certainly not about how much they use ICT – PowerPoint and whiteboards often don't add value to pupils' learning... it's about them coming up with some good ideas that work to improve lessons.
>
> It's not good enough to put a tick, can use PowerPoint, tick, can use moviemaker... it's about how well they can use it... whether they can use it in a powerful and effective way.
>
> It's actually about creativity and flair in thinking of how best to deploy ICT.
>
> (OECD, 2010: 24)

Box 1.1 What does it mean 'to be good at ICT' as a history teacher?

- You're pretty good 'technically'; you are relaxed and reasonably adept at working out how to use new applications and fix 'glitches'/minor or straightforward technical problems.
- You are knowledgeable and up to date in your awareness of the range of ICT applications and programs which can be used to enhance teaching and learning in history.
- You are accomplished in your use of the interactive whiteboard and PowerPoint; your use of these applications usually engages and motivates pupils.
- You are well organised and efficient in terms of using ICT to save time in planning and assessment and to organise your personal 'archive' of resources effectively, clear emails, etc.
- You are good at using ICT to build up really good 'collections' of powerful impact resources on a wide range of topics. You are familiar with and make use of many of the 'gems' that are available on good history websites.
- If you have got access to the internet and a data projector in your teaching sessions, you take full advantage of the wealth of resources on the net to improve the impact of your lessons.
- You are able to deploy these resources to construct well designed and intellectually rigorous pupil tasks using ICT – you can think of good ideas for deploying digital resources and structuring good activities for pupils using ICT resources and applications.
- You are an 'early adaptor', quick to pick up on new developments and applications in ICT and work out ideas for doing something useful with them in the history classroom.
- You make good use of ICT (websites, discussion groups, Blogs, Twitter, etc.) to develop your use of ICT in history by being a proactive and diligent part of the 'community of practice' of history teachers in the field of ICT.
- When you use ICT in your teaching, it usually works well.
- Your use of ICT improves the quality of your lessons.
- Your pupils use ICT to learn history outside taught sessions.
- Your pupils are good at 'expressing themselves digitally'.

As I have argued elsewhere, becoming good at ICT is partly about discerning which applications seem likely to have the potential for high 'pay-off' in terms of enhancing learning in history, and which are tangential or irrelevant – and then having the intelligence and application to go on to devise or acquire worthwhile things with ICT (Haydn, 2011).

One caveat with respect to technical 'fluency' in ICT applications is that it is helpful if teachers are sufficiently confident in their use of a program or application that they can involve pupils in using the technology independently and purposefully. This not only opens up the possibility of pupils learning history outside taught sessions, it also provides the sense of agency and responsibility that Carr (2008) argues is so crucial to pupil engagement in learning. When using Web 2.0 applications, it also provides a means of 'activating learners as instructional resources for one another' (Wiliam, 2011: 46), in terms of promoting 'dialogic' learning – getting pupils to talk, discuss, argue and develop their thinking with each other.

In terms of a framework for progression in the use of ICT, Table 1.1 suggests the steps towards a situation where the 'communications' strand of new technology (the 'C' in ICT), enables the development of a 'community of practice' where teacher and pupils can work collaboratively on enquiry questions in history outside the confines of classroom time.

Box 1.1 lists some statements that teachers might reflect on in terms of thinking about the extent to which they are exploring the potential of ICT to improve their teaching, and pupils' learning. I am not suggesting that the list is a comprehensive one, but it might serve as a starting point for teachers or student teachers who are interested in developing their ability to make effective use of ICT.

As you can see, a range of attributes are involved here, some related to technical skills and abilities, some to initiative with resources or organisational skills, and others involving creativity and imagination and 'networking' skills. As well as reflecting on how strong you are in these facets of ICT capability, and which would be the most propitious areas for development, given your situation and 'strengths and weaknesses', it can also be interesting to think about which of these areas are most influential in terms of improving pupil learning, and where we might develop expertise in ICT and share high-quality ICT resources through collaborative and peer-teaching approaches.

Table 1.1 A model for progression in the use of ICT applications

Level 1	Awareness of the application and of the fact that it might be used in some way to develop pupil learning in history.
Level 2	Ability to use the application to find out or do something 'useful'.
Level 3	Ability to use the application (to some good learning purpose) in the classroom, with pupils.
Level 4	Ability to get pupils using the application autonomously and usefully so that they can continue to work on enquiry questions outside the classroom and in collaboration with other pupils.

Some myths and misconceptions about ICT (and learning)

One of the causes of disappointment in the extent to which new technology has brought about radical and evenly spread improvements in education is the tendency of those who have not been teachers (and novice teachers) to underestimate the difficulties and complexities involved in learning.[1] In the early stages of their school placements, student teachers sometimes assume that 'because they have taught it, the pupils have learned it', and write lesson evaluations that suggest that all the pupils learned everything they were trying to teach. I have heard it said that good teaching is 'just common sense'. Given that only a very small proportion of what is taught to learners is remembered and understood, it would seem that effective teaching is anything but 'just common sense'.

If you believe that learning is primarily about the transfer of information, ICT would appear to have a lot to offer, given the increases in the speed and volume of information transfer that it makes possible (see Box 1.2).

As well as the problem that information is not the same as knowledge, there is the problem that not all pupils are trying desperately hard to learn. Fullan argues that even when students *do* want to learn, teaching something to another person is actually quite difficult: 'Even when people are sincerely motivated to learn from you, they have a devil of a time doing so. Transferability of ideas is a complex problem of the highest order' (Fullan, 1999: 63).

Box 1.2 The information transmission theory of learning

It's not every day you encounter a member of the government who appears to understand the net. Most politicians (Clinton, Blair, Blunkett to name but three) see it as a pipe for pumping things into schools and schoolchildren.

(Naughton, 1998: 19)

There is also the problem that sometimes pupils do not fully understand what we are trying to teach and are confused by our teaching. Lightman and Sadler's research (1993, 1994) revealed that, after a series of lessons on a topic, fewer pupils grasped the concepts in question than before the lessons. There is also the problem of knowledge retention (Willingham, 2009; Shemilt, 2009): why does so much of the learning 'slip away' over time, and what can we do to reduce this slippage? Desforges (2002) argues that knowledge application (in the words of Wineburg, 'the chasm between knowing X and using X to think about Y' – Wineburg, 1997: 256), is an even bigger problem, particularly in the UK system. To add to these problems, there is also the issue of not having enough curriculum time to teach all that has to be covered in the National Curriculum or examination specifications. This emerged as a major worry for history teachers in a recent Historical Association survey of the concerns of UK history teachers about current arrangements for the teaching of history in schools (Burn and Harris, 2011).

All these problems or 'deficits' between what the teacher is trying to teach, and how much learning results from this teaching, raise the question of how various functions and attributes of ICT might help to solve the problems and reduce the deficits. In what ways does ICT have the potential to improve pupils' desire to do well in history and get better at it? How might it help teachers to explain things in a more powerful and effective way – and in a way that pupils are more likely to remember and understand? Can it be used to help pupils make connections between the abstruse and abstract concepts that pervade the history curriculum (to be able to understand, for example, that revolutions have some things in common but can take very different forms)? And in what ways might ICT help us to get pupils to continue with their learning beyond the confines of taught classes?

Another misconception that has hampered ways of exploring how new technology might enhance teaching and learning is what Mishra (2012) terms 'technocentrism'; the tendency to look mainly or exclusively at what the technology can do, in generic and technical terms, rather than what it offers for particular subject disciplines (data logging software, for example, is very useful for science teachers but of no interest to history teachers). There has also, until recently, been a tendency to look at the effect of the technology 'in isolation', rather than thinking about how the affordances of the technology interact with teachers' substantive subject content knowledge and their pedagogical subject knowledge.[2] For example, a teacher might be an absolute wizard in terms of their ability to do dazzling things with an interactive whiteboard, but if they don't know much about the causes of the English Civil War (or whatever), or how one might make the topic meaningful and accessible to pupils, it is unlikely to result in a successful lesson.

In other words, it is the teacher's awareness and understanding of the ways in which various strands of new technology might enable him or her to provide 'the most powerful analogies, illustrations, examples, explanations and demonstrations' (Shulman, 1986: 9) that will make their teaching more effective, when used in combination with their expert subject knowledge and sophisticated pedagogical skills. Mishra and Kohler's idea of 'Technological Pedagogical Content Knowledge' (sometimes abbreviated to 'TPACK') has been very influential in getting educators to move away from 'technocentric' explanations of the effective use of technology in education, by getting teachers to think about how the technology might work in combination with their content and pedagogical knowledge (Mishra and Kohler, 2006).

For those who are 'novices' in the field of ICT and history education, there are three other misconceptions or misrepresentations which it is helpful to be aware of. The first is that becoming good at using ICT as a teacher is dependent on having advanced techno-logical expertise and a 'tekkie' sort of mind. An OECD survey of the use of ICT in teacher education in the UK suggested that some student teachers regarded the ability to be good at using ICT as almost 'genetic' (i.e. you have either got the ICT gene or you haven't, and there is not much you can do about it). Experienced teacher educators pointed out that there are now so many templates and models available to set up a wiki, a blog or a website, that it is a fairly simple thing to do, compared to the days when setting up a website required quite expert knowledge of html coding (OECD, 2010). As one mentor remarked to me, 'If you can use Word, you can set up a blog or a wiki, and play around with most Web 2.0 applications.' As a person who is not technically minded, I firmly believe that anyone (or any department) can become good at using ICT to enhance their teaching, as long as they are willing to put some time, thought and effort into it.

A second misconception is that 'being good at ICT' is about possessing advanced levels of expertise in the use of expensive and sophisticated 'kit', such as interactive whiteboards, e-portfolio software and response systems (voting software). Although it is possible to do interesting and useful things with interactive whiteboards (see Chapter 11), research evidence suggests that they have not had the same transforma-tional impact on practice as more prosaic (and cheaper) developments (Ofsted, 2011). As I argue in Chapter 7, being good at ICT is in practice more about the quality of the ideas and resources you incorporate into ICT applications, rather than the level of technical expertise in using the application.

Not all history teachers possess advanced skills in using interactive whiteboards or e-portfolio software, but there will not be many people reading this chapter who do not possess a memory stick, who do not use history websites to augment their resources, and who do not use the data projector in their teaching. These are what are sometimes termed the 'killer applications' that have had a radical influence on how teachers work. Many of the 'experts' in the educational use of ICT interviewed in the OECD study cited above made the point that Web 2.0 applications have considerable potential for improving teaching and learning (particularly in terms of getting pupils to learn outside the classroom), and for the most part, they cost nothing.

A third misconception is that some new technology applications, such as interactive whiteboards and hand-held or 'palmtop' computers, have not had the transformative impact hoped for because teachers have 'Luddite' tendencies, and lack the ability to make use of the technology. A DfEE official described teachers as 'a hurdle to be overcome' in integrat-ing technology use (quoted in Haydn, 2004), and other studies have suggested that it is teachers rather than technology who are to blame for ICT applications not fulfilling their potential (see, for example, Perry, 2003).

Convery points out that research into ICT is often conducted by researchers with an interest in and a positive view of the potential of new technology, and suggests that together with hyperbolic claims by policymakers and those selling the technology, this created an inflated technological rhetoric and unrealistic expectations 'which inhibit teachers' prag-matic attempts to integrate technology in classroom contexts, and the teachers subsequently become blamed for the failure of the technology to fulfil its promise' (Convery, 2009: 25).

The vast majority of teachers want to do their best for their pupils and to teach well. It seems implausible that they would choose not to use something that was useful in helping them to do this. Davis *et al.* (1989) argued that if an ICT application was useful, and was easy to use, then teachers would use it. The almost universal adoption of the use of the video recorder and data projector to play moving image extracts in history lessons is one illustration of this (Haydn, 2004). However, there is evidence to suggest that it often takes time for teachers to work out how to make best use of newly emerging technologies, and some forms of new technology require some investment of time before the teacher becomes accomplished in their use, and completely confident about integrating them into their classroom practice. I have argued elsewhere, that more than anything, teachers need someone to 'model' effective use of technology, to show what it can do, and then time to work out how to use it in their own teaching (Haydn and Barton, 2010). There is, of course, the danger that teachers may be 'settled' in their teaching habits: although I now have wireless access to the internet in my teaching sessions, I suspect I don't always take full advantage of the not inconsiderable advantage of having access to the riches of the internet in my teaching sessions, because I have operated for many years without this luxury. I have to make a conscious effort to remember to think about how I might use it to improve teaching sessions that I have done previously without access to the internet.

Two further points might be made in terms of having a well-founded understanding of the potential of ICT for improving teaching and learning in history. It is an oversimplification to assume that all young people are active in using social media and use it in sophisticated ways. Prensky's (2001) idea that all young people are 'digital natives' and most adults are 'digital immigrants' has been widely cited (in 4,342 other studies at the time of writing this chapter), leading to calls for teachers to 'tune in' to social networking and adapt it for educational purposes. Drawing on studies of young people's use of social media by Hargittai (2008), Van Diyck (2009) and Margaryan *et al.* (2011), Selwyn concludes that, although there are many 'dabblers' and 'joiners', only a small minority of young people actively create content through social media, or critique the work of others. He warns against assuming that because many young people use social media for 'day to day' things, this will automatically translate into high-quality educational use:

> This is not to criticise social media based actions as worthless or without merit. However, these issues do point to the difficulties of assuming social media to be ready sites of educational empowerment, democratisation and enhanced freedom. As such, it is important for educationalists to begin to understand social media use and social media users in more realistic – rather than idealistic – terms.
>
> (Selwyn, 2012: 13)

Buckingham (2007: 136) also warns of the danger of attempts to 'jazz up' formal education with a superficial gloss of kid-friendly digital culture.

This is not to suggest that history teachers do not need to think about how to use social media and Web 2.0 applications to improve their practice, 'shared community spaces and inter-group communications are a massive part of what excites young people and therefore should contribute to their persistence and motivation to learn' (Mason and Rennie, 2007: 199). But we must not assume that all pupils are 'digital natives', or that they will *necessarily* be keen to use social media for educational purposes. As Arthur Chapman argues in Chapter 4, it is actually quite challenging to construct an online discussion task that will get all learners to contribute to enthusiastically. Several of the chapters that follow offer suggestions and examples of how history teachers might exploit Web 2.0 applications to good effect in their teaching.

Finally, it is important to be aware of some of the ways in which the use of ICT can make teaching less effective. An earlier Ofsted report into the use of ICT in history classrooms found that lessons where technology was used were on average less satisfactory than lessons without ICT (see Harrison, 2003). The dangers include overuse and ineffective use of PowerPoint or the interactive whiteboard, which can lead to an increase in pupil passivity and disengagement, setting tasks which allow pupils to copy and paste information without reading or understanding it, the distracting influence of multimedia effects, slowing down of content coverage, overemphasis on presentation and 'effects' rather than content, unfocused and time-wasting pupil use of the internet, overuse of poorly designed unchallenging 'comprehension type' whiteboard activities, showing overly long moving image extracts to 'pass the time until the bell goes', and the potential loss of narrative compared to book and textbook sources (Laurillard, 1998; Tufte, 2006; Walsh, 1998, 2006).

This section in not designed to discourage you from further exploration of ICT to see if it can improve learning in history, but it can be helpful to have a sound awareness of the limitations and dangers of ICT, and some of the myths and misunderstandings that have arisen about it in recent years.

Why invest time in becoming 'good at ICT'?

In spite of the caveats expressed in the previous section of the chapter, and for all the reservations and frustrations about unreliable equipment, overblown expectations, and inchoate 'hype' about ICT (OECD, 2010), most people reading this chapter will have seen or experienced at least some occasions where the use of ICT has enabled the history teacher to teach something in a more effective way, or made the experience of learning history more stimulating and more productive for learners. Most people who have worked in teacher education have encountered some departments that have managed to transform pupils' attitude to learning through the use of ICT, pupil take-up of ICT beyond KS3, and pupils' ability to learn for themselves, and to learn collaboratively using ICT. Other departments have focused on enabling pupils to express themselves digitally in a fluent, powerful and accomplished manner (see the pupil-made film about 'The British Schindler' for a good example of this – www.internationalschoolhistory.net/BHP/index.htm). Many history teachers will have used ICT to make a particular teaching point in a more powerful and effective way.

In terms of which facets of new technology have had the most helpful impact on history teaching, there has been a tendency for 'cutting-edge' technological developments to receive more publicity and attention than innovations that are used 'day in, day out' to enhance learning in history. I still see voice recognition software as a sort of technological miracle – but rarely see it used in schools. Newspaper articles about 'the twenty-first-century classroom' showing video conferencing, *Skype* or *Elluminate* being used to 'beam' expert historians into the classroom to talk to your sixth formers about their essays paint a rosy picture of how ICT will transform learning, but such applications are not yet routinely used in UK schools. Even indisputable advantages of the computer, for example databases that enable us to manipulate, interrogate and test hypotheses on historical data much more quickly than sifting through all the records by hand (see Martin, 2003 and NCET, 1998 for some examples of this), are not used on a daily basis by history teachers. I would argue that the applications and developments that have done most to improve history teaching over the past two decades are not in the area of sophisticated and expensive 'kit', but cheaper and simpler applications.

The data projector

How many history teachers would prefer *not* to have a data projector in their classroom? As recently as 2003, when asked to choose what was the most helpful ICT application, the majority of history teachers chose the combination of video recorder and data projector (Haydn, 2004). Compared to the blackboard, chalk and textbooks, the facility to project images and moving images in colour to the whole class at any point in any lesson (rather than having to march the class down to the ICT suite for the once a term 'ICT special') revolutionised history teachers' practice. The question is, of course, how well do history teachers use the data projector? To introduce pupils to a stunning range of high-impact resources that make them think about historical content in a more profound and thoughtful way, or to feed pupils on a staple diet of low grade PowerPoints?

'Impact resources'

One of the 'variables' with my student teachers, in terms of being or becoming 'good at ICT', is the degree of resourcefulness that they devote to using ICT to get hold of what I call 'impact' resources.

By 'impact resource', I mean something that makes a particular teaching point in a vivid and powerful way; something that stays in learners' minds long after the lesson has gone (what Heath and Heath, 2008 term 'stickiness'). It is often something that disturbs learners' previous understandings, or which 'problematises' the issue or concept in a way that makes learners think further about it. It also encourages 'dialogic' learning, whereby learners are sufficiently interested by the resource that they are willing to clarify and modify their understanding through discussion with others. It intrigues learners to the extent that they are prepared to play an active part in constructing meaning themselves. It becomes part of learners' 'historical consciousness': what Rusen (1993: 87) refers to as 'playing a role in the mental household of the subject'.

Copyright considerations place some constraints on providing examples of 'impact' resources within this book (although a few examples are given in Chapter 7), but they can take various forms. They can be images, graphs, moving image clips, 'mysteries',[3] pieces of prose, maps,[4] newspaper articles, metaphors and roleplays – all 'gatherable' through use of the internet.

An extract from the BBC documentary *QED: Armageddon* (www.youtube.com/watch?v=7AYMS1po0L8) can convey an understanding of the gap between a large conventional bomb (www.liveleak.com/view?i=08f_1215297182) and an atomic blast, which would be difficult to convey as vividly, however good the teacher's skills of exposition. The Fry and Laurie 'In the library' clip (www.youtube.com/watch?v=ZwB4Bps3pT4) powerfully makes the point that history (and newspapers, the news, etc.) is edited, it is a construct (teachers need to see the clip first before deciding whether to edit it for use with pupils). The moving image clip of the 'Blue eyes, brown eyes' experiment, from '5 steps to tyranny' (www.youtube.com/watch?v=68GzOJQ8NMw) is much more powerful than just telling pupils about the experiment. It can have even more impact when used with the Hitler quotation from Greyling's (4 March 2000) newspaper article, 'The last word on racism' (www.guardian.co.uk/books/2000/mar/04/books.guardianreview8),[5] and, if time permits, appropriate extracts from the Adam Curtis documentary *The century of the self* (Curtis, 2002, www.youtube.com/watch?v=lhxfArTAcfM). The Wikipedia entry for Fritz

Fischer and the causes of World War One (http://en.wikipedia.org/wiki/Fritz_Fischer) can also help to reinforce the point that sometimes politicians create 'outsider groups', or foreign threats, to divert attention from domestic problems. (I am aware that history teachers have different views about the use of Wikipedia. I would argue that the important thing is that the uses and dangers of using Wikipedia – and Google – should be part of pupils' historical education – see Walsh, 2009 for further development of this point.)

Image libraries give easy access to many of the iconic images of the past century: the boy standing in front of the tank, the little girl burning from napalm, Tommie Smith's black power salute, Kohl and Mitterand holding hands at a memorial ceremony, the executed Vietcong soldier… All these images are ways into powerful and important stories about history (which can also be accessed on the internet). Most newspapers now archive their articles on the internet and at the time of writing this chapter, most of them are still 'free access'. Newspapers are an excellent source of high-quality writing about history, and can often provide useful homework or 'pre-reading' for teaching sessions (see below for further development of this point).

Many pupils often say that roleplays help them to learn history in a way that they remember, and the internet can also be a useful way of accessing ideas for roleplay. Some of Ian Luff's ideas for roleplay and practical demonstration can be accessed at www.uea.ac.uk/~m242/historypgce/drama/welcome.htm.

'Building learning packages'

Ben Walsh (2003) makes the point that one of the biggest advantages of ICT is the facility it offers to quickly and easily build up, store and organise a range of resources that will give them a rich archive of high-quality materials on whatever topics they are teaching. It is also much easier to share 'collections' with fellow history teachers. The 'keepvid' site (www.keepvid.com) makes it easy to 'capture' moving image extracts from the internet, so that they can be securely stored on to a hard drive or memory stick, and used whenever needed; sites such as Evernote (www.evernote.com), Dropbox (www.dropbox.com) and Skydrive (www.skydrive.com) make it easy to store, organise and share digital resources (see Chapter 2). Although many people use sites such as Delicious (www.delicious.com), YouTube (www.youtube.com) and Slideshare (www.slidshare.com), to bookmark and collect resources, not all of them take advantage of the facility to offer access to other people's collections.

One of the most precious resources in education is teachers' time; I suspect there are not many people who work longer or harder than teachers who are regularly teaching 20 odd lessons a week, in addition to all the other aspects of their job. The 'communications' strand of ICT can drastically reduce the amount of time that teachers have to spend collecting resources and ideas for their lessons. Many history teachers spend considerable amounts of time building up 'niche' collections of resources on particular topics or what the Hampshire History Centre terms 'De luxe' lessons (www3.hants.gov.uk/education/hias/curriculum-resources/curriculum-resources-centres/history-centre.htm). Simon Harrison has spent hours of his time putting together (what I think is) a brilliant package of resources on Battalion 101, which is available free at www.keystagehistory.co.uk/free-samples/battalion-101.html; Russel Tarr has a useful collection of links at www.delicious.com/russeltarr, and Russel Tarr and Dan Moorhouse have interesting collections on YouTube (www.youtube.com/user/russeltarr, www.youtube.com/user/

dmoorhouse1973). One of my sad little hobbies is collecting quotations about the differing views that historians, politicians and educators have about the purposes and benefits of school history (www.uea.ac.uk/~m242/historypgce/purposes/purposesquotesintro.htm). It can also be helpful to 'sub-contract', building up collections between groups of learners. I encourage my students to build up a collection of images on particular topics over the course of the PGCE year, and then share them at the end of the course. This makes it much easier to build up a collection of rich, in-depth resources, rather than having a lot of rather thin and anaemic collections. Professor Stephen Heppell argues that the practice of teachers sharing their resources and ideas with each other offers one of the most powerful ways of improving practice in education (Heppell, 2011).

In addition to teachers' 'collections', there are also a number of archives and databases that are now online. It is not possible to list all of them, but a few that are worth exploring are listed below:

- *Lessons from the Past* (http://lessonsfromthepast.co.uk): Lindsey Johnstone's pupils interviewed a number of women in the local area about their experiences, leading to the construction of a database recording their findings and unearthing shocking findings on the implications of the 1915 Mental Deficiency Act for single mothers and 'ordinary' working-class people. The project is in several respects a model of intelligent enquiry, and had a big and positive impact on the pupils' conducting the interviews (Graham, 2012).
- *The Commonwealth War Graves Commission* (www.cwgc.org): A really useful way to 'localise' aspects of World War One.
- *Letters of Note* (www.lettersofnote.com): A collection of interesting letters, postcards, telegrams, faxes and memos; see, for example, 'To my old master' (www.lettersofnote.com/2012/01/to-my-old-master.html).
- *The Listening Project* (www.bbc.co.uk/radio4/features/the-listening-project): The BBC/Radio 4's oral history archive; see, for instance, the intergenerational conversation 'Destiny: Chick and Lindsay' (www.bbc.co.uk/radio4/features/the-listening-project/conversation/p00r3j80).
- *My Time Machine* (www.mytimemachine.co.uk): An archive of eyewitness history, including 'Karl Marx goes on a pub crawl' (www.mytimemachine.co.uk/pubcrawl.htm).
- *WiseArchive* (www.wisearchive.co.uk): The working lives of older people.
- *Google ngram* (http://books.google.com/ngrams): An interesting app from Google labs, which can be used to search Google's digitised collection of books (now around 5.2 million, estimated at around 4 per cent of the books that have been published) for the frequency of appearance of particular words and terms. You can either just put in one word and it will graph it over a selected time span, or you can input up to five words, separated by a comma, to see the changes in the prevalence of the words over time. It can be used to gain insight into cultural change over time. For example:
  - To find out about the comparative frequency of occurrence of words describing some left-wing movements over the course of the twentieth century, choose the time span 1900–2008 and input socialism, communism, anarchism and syndicalism.
  - 'Equality' has become an important and high profile concept in recent years, but how has its popularity or influence as a concept fluctuated over the past few centuries (say, from 1600–2008)? (Note the interesting fluctuations within the seventeenth century.)

- To what extent has the phenomenon of the 'takeaway' meal become more prevalent over the past century? (Just input 'takeaway' and the date span 1900–2008.)
- Have there been any cultural changes in terms of what *types* of takeaway have become more popular over the past century? (Input 'fish and chips', ' pizza', 'curry', 'chinese' and 'burger'.)
- Do books mainly tell the history of males or females: have there been any changing trends in this area? Type in 'he said' and 'she said' and the timespan 1700–2008 to find out.
- Has there really been a shift from a culture of responsibilities and duty, to one of hedonism and 'I want it now' over the past century? Type in 'I must' and 'I want' and see if there appear to be any changes over the course of the century.
- When did 'boredom' start to be a problem for the human race?

This is in addition to the existence of a range of excellent museum websites (see www.muse-umwebsites.co.uk for a guide), and major history websites (see www.uea.ac.uk/~m242/historypgce/ict/welcome.htm for my students' views on the ten most helpful history websites).

Ofsted also offers a range of resources that are digitally available. Even apart from their digitally available report on current strengths and weaknesses of current provision (see *History for All*, www.ofsted.gov.uk/resources/history-for-all), we cannot say that Ofsted have not been clear about what they think constitutes good practice in history, or that they have not suggested examples and models of good practice. The subject-specific criteria used on subject inspections can be found at: www.ofsted.gov.uk/resources/generic-grade-descriptors-and-supplementary-subject-specific-guidance-for-inspectors-making-judgemen. The good practice website can be found at: www.goodpractice.ofsted.gov.uk/searchSch.php?searchTerms=history&show=case&sort=dateZ&search=Search. The professional development resources can be found at: www.ofsted.gov.uk/resources/subject-professional-development-materials-history.

Another important collection is the digitally available (to subscribers) archive of *Teaching History* articles on the Historical Association's website. *Teaching History* is the profession's equivalent of the *British Medical Journal* for doctors. If you are a history teacher, you should read it, and digital access to the archive makes it much easier to do this. The 'e-cpd' section of the website (www.history.org.uk/resources/secondary_resources_11.html), and the web trails (www.history.org.uk/resources/secondary_resources_61.html) focusing on the key concepts and processes outlined in the National Curriculum (such as interpretation, significance, change and continuity, etc.) are particularly useful features.

Finally, two sites that offer striking ways of presenting information graphically: *Gapminder World* (www.gapminder.org); particularly good for showing change over time (see for example 'the wealth and health of nations'), and *Information is Beautiful* (www.informationisbeautiful.net); some stunning (and idiosyncratic) ways to show information on screen (see for instance, 'Left versus right', and 'Every country in the world is best at something').

Getting pupils to do history outside the classroom

The internet has extended the range of ways in which history teachers can get pupils to learn history beyond the confines of taught classes. Of course, it has always been possible for history teachers to set homework, but Web 2.0 developments in particular have radically increased the range of things that history teachers can ask pupils to work on outside class. There are now some history departments where most pupils probably do more learning outside the classroom rather than in taught classes. Two examples from my own teacher education partnership spring to mind. One involved a class producing a GCSE revision DVD as a class project. Revision for examinations can sometimes be difficult to make interesting for pupils, given that they are of course going over the same content for a second time. The DVD project created a different format for doing revision, which required a degree of creativity, imagination and commitment from the pupils. All the pupils became enthusiastic about the project (of course, this does not happen as an automatic consequence of such an approach), and even pupils outside the class who had heard about the project asked to be involved. The final product was very impressive and was 'showcased' by the school, and the head of history told me that because they had made the DVD, they did use it to revise and it drastically improved their attitude to the subject. This would appear to bear out Papert's call for pupils to sometimes be asked to be involved in extended projects 'with enough duration for the child to become personally, intellectually and emotionally involved', as longer projects enabled learners to try out ideas and put 'something of themselves' into the work (Papert and Harel, 1991: 4). The same effect can be seen in the documentary about Nicholas Winton, produced by the pupils at British International School Bratislava (www.internationalschoolhistory.net/BHP/index.htm).

A second project asked pupils to prepare a *Dragons' Den* case for a local firm, drawing on the historical roots and development of the company, as part of work on the Industrial Revolution. As someone asked to judge the 'final', it was apparent that many of the pupils had spent many hours outside class time, interviewing relatives or former employees, putting together a film about the company using Windows Moviemaker, getting hold of samples of the product, putting together a presentation for 'the Dragons' and producing a glossy brochure to accompany the presentation. The work produced by pupils of all abilities was very impressive. Nearly all these year 8 pupils (12–13 year olds) had made short films (as well as brochures and PowerPoint presentations) with an apparently effortless fluency that continues to elude me. One pupil was so excited on the day of the final that he had to take some time out as he had become over-excited. (For readers outside the UK, this is not a common problem when teaching the Industrial Revolution to year 8 pupils.)

Russel Tarr's wiki is a good example of how a wiki can be used to get pupils to work outside the classroom, and to 'sub-contract' different elements of a topic to groups of pupils, who then make digital contributions to the wiki in response to their section of the topic. Topics vary from 'Who was the most important person in history?' and 'Who was the most important contributor to the Renaissance? for younger pupils, to quite erudite and scholarly extended work on different cultural facets of Weimar Germany, or Civil War-era Spain (http://history-wiki.wikispaces.com). Richard Jones-Nerzic has also used a range of extended 'out of classroom' activities in this way (www.internationalschooltoulouse.net/igcsehistory/home.htm).

Using ICT to 'open up' topics and link the past to the present and the future

The internet makes it easy to 'tune in to' current debates about historical and present day issues and controversies. The combination of YouTube, history and current affairs blogs and wikis, and digital access to newspaper archives makes it easy to draw on materials that consider 'persistent issues in history' (see the *Persistent issues in history* website for further explanation of this term – http://pihnet.org), and enable pupils to see the 'big picture' of the past over extended periods of time in context, from ancient history, right up to the present day.

One example of this can be related to the Agrarian Revolution; sometimes taught in schools as a period in the seventeenth and eighteenth centuries where there were some important developments in agriculture (Tull's seed drill, 'Turnip' Townshend, Malthus, Bakewell and Young, and selective breeding, enclosures…). Treatment of this topic sometimes stops at this point as if the production and consumption of food was no longer an important issue in human affairs (in the same way that 'Women in history' sometimes stops at women getting the vote in 1918). Web-based resources provide easy access to resources that demonstrate to pupils that these issues were not confined to particular periods in the past, and are relevant to the lives they will live when they leave school (see, for example, YouTube videos on *The History of Food*. Google ngram (see below) can help history teachers to show that problems and issues relating to food production and consumption have changed over time. (Although it is not digitally available, pages 162–4 of Denis Shemilt's (2009) 'Drinking an ocean, pissing a cupful' is also a helpful resource).

Newspaper articles are particularly helpful in this respect. Although they might seem colourless, long and devoid of images compared to present-day textbooks, newspapers often contain high-quality pieces from some of the world's greatest writers (and historians), including reviews of the most recent historical scholarship. Introducing pupils to quality writing from the broadsheet newspapers, and getting pupils to read some of these articles can be an important step in moving from the 'bite-size' and 'picture' mentality that prevails in many textbooks, to being able to sustain concentration and persevere with longer and more challenging sections of extended writing. Any time you read a good article about history in a newspaper (with the exception of the few that are behind 'Paywalls'), it is very easy to use the 'Search' or 'Archive' feature of the newspaper's website to locate the URL for the article, so it can be used by pupils at the click of a mouse (see Box 1.3).

Box 1.3 Some examples of digitally available newspaper articles that can be useful to teach history

'The day the East End said "No pasaran" to Blackshirts', www.guardian.co.uk/uk/2006/sep/30/thefarright.past?INTCMP=SRCH.

- 'Report highlights golden future of history graduates', Donald Macleod, *Guardian*, 19 July 2005: Highlights the wide range of careers that history graduates go into and the fact that 'History graduates are found in disproportionate numbers on the boards of the UK's top 100 companies', www.guardian.co.uk/education/2005/jul/19/highereducation.workandcareers.
- 'War within war' (account of Black Americans' experience of the Vietnam War), www.guardian.co.uk/weekend/story/0,,551209,00.html.
- Linda Colley, *Guardian*, 7 September 2001 (letters page) 'Slaves to history', www.guardian.co.uk/letters/story/0,,547950,00.html.
- 'The Great Queen: Parts 1 and 2', Ian Mortimer's article (*Telegraph Weekend*, 31 March 2012): compares the reigns and situations faced by Queen Elizabeth I and Queen Elizabeth II, www.telegraph.co.uk/history/9176453/The-Great-Queen-parts-1-and-2.html.
- Other newspaper articles which are digitally available, and suggestions for how newspapers might be used in history teaching can be found at http://historyandict.wetpaint.com/page/Newspapers.

Using ICT to develop pupils' digital literacy

Thomson (1999) argues that one of the most important and least studied aspects of world history is the many examples of how easily led human beings can be. In a sense this problem has become worse as techniques and technologies for the manipulation and distortion of information have become more sophisticated. Eason writes of 'the problem of the net. The sum of human knowledge is there, but so is the sum of human ignorance, misinterpretation and malice' (Eason, 2000).

Recent research by Ofcom suggests that many young people are not careful and discerning users of the internet:

> They are unable to find the information they are looking for or trust the first thing they do... They are unable to recognise bias and propaganda... as a result they are too often influenced by information they should probably discard. This makes them vulnerable to the pitfalls and rabbit holes of ignorance, falsehood, cons and scams. Inaccurate content, online misinformation and conspiracy theories... are appearing in the classroom.
>
> (Bartlett and Miller, 2011: 3)

The study found that teachers considered that:

- only a third of 9–19 year olds had been taught how to judge the reliability of online information;
- only 16 per cent had a 'good or better' understanding of the difference in quality of information between statistics or anecdotes;
- only 15 per cent were 'good or better' at recognising bias or propaganda.

A JISC Study also found that the speed of young people's web searching means that little time is spent in evaluating information, either for relevance, accuracy or authority (JISC, 2006).

This is clearly a massively important issue for history education, and perhaps constitutes one of the most powerful arguments for ensuring that all young people receive a full and rigorous historical education, and one that is appropriate for the twenty-first century. In an excellent article on how to use the internet to teach historical interpretations, Moore (2000: 35) points out that

> all adults, no matter what they do with their lives, need to be able to see how and why the historical interpretations that bombard them were constructed. Otherwise they are prey to propaganda and manipulation, not to mention cynicism or a lack of regard for truth.

In another very useful article, Ben Walsh argues that this is not a reason for not using the internet in our teaching, just because it is full of 'dodgy' sites: young people need to be educated in a way that equips them to deal with such hazards, and 'good historical knowledge and sound historical practice are by far the best defences against websites which seek to promote an extreme point of view by using history as a vehicle to carry it' (Walsh, 2008: 9).

Wineburg and Martin (2004) warn of the dangers of just 'leaving them to Google' for information:

Try typing 'Holocaust' and 'crematorium' as keywords, and your surfing will eventually take you to an official looking website for the *Institute for Historical Review*, its home-page proclaiming 'truth and accuracy', with a dedication to 'promoting greater public awareness of key chapters of history, and a dispassionate statement of its '501(c)(3) not for profit tax exempt status'. Follow a few lines and you'll soon learn that contrary to what you might have believed, the Holocaust never happened. In our age of new technologies, every crackpot has become a publisher. The ability to judge the quality of information can no longer be considered 'extra credit'.

(The website www.martinlutherking.org is another example of website which can be used to alert pupils to the dangers of accepting websites at 'face value'.)

The implications of these developments mean that we must ensure that our teaching of 'provenance' goes beyond the traditional points about 'unwitting testimony', 'corrobora-tion' and 'position', and extend to educating pupils to understand that because something is on the internet, this does not guarantee its reliability. They should also be educated to understand some of the techniques that are used to manipulate information, and how historians attempt to ascertain the reliability of information, including 'peer review', 'com-munities of practice', web syntax (for example that '~' means 'personal site' even if it has an 'edu' or 'ac' suffix), and an understanding of terms such as 'reverse searching' (seeing which other sites a website links to), 'astroturfing', 'trolling' and 'blackhatting'. Ofsted has identified the development of young people's ability to handle information intelligently and become intellectually autonomous as perhaps the most important function of school history; the ability 'to use evidence critically and with integrity, and present differing views. Above all else, history needs to provide young people with the ability to make up their own minds' (Ofsted, 2006: section 4.2.7).

Using Web 2.0 and social media to get pupils to participate actively in learning

One of the most revolutionary changes in ICT over the past decade has been the move from websites (sometimes termed a 'one to many' application), to the era of Web 2.0 ('many to many'). In the 1990s and early 2000s, educators used the internet to 'broadcast' to learners (Selwyn, 2012: 3). Web 2.0 and social media applications are much more participatory in nature. Users do not simply receive information – they can share and pass on information, form groups, comment and critique the contributions of others, and recreate, re-edit or respond to other people's contributions.

Many of these applications and developments offer learners the opportunity to make active contributions and responses to the learning they are involved in, to work collabo-ratively, and to develop their work and ideas iteratively, in response to their interactions with others. Not only can this increase their motivation and commitment to learning, it can enable them to learn from each other as well as from the teacher. It also offers them the opportunity to carry on working outside the confines of taught sessions.

Some of these applications, particularly wikis (Chapter 3), discussion forums (Chapter 4) and blogs (Chapter 5), offer considerable potential for encouraging the dialogic and con-structivist approaches to learning that are seen as helpful to learning by the contributors to this volume. This is the idea that learners remember and understand best what they have to some extent had to work out for themselves; had to think about and mull over, and actively participate in; they have had in a sense 'to go 10 rounds with the information'. Dede (1995: 12) provides a useful summary of 'the constructivist case' on learning, and makes the important point that providing access to information is often only a first step in learning:

> We have found that learner investigation and collaboration and construction of knowledge are vital, and these things don't follow teaching by telling, and learning by listening. It isn't that assimilation of knowledge isn't a good place to start, because it is hard to investigate something unless you know a bit about it. But assimilation is a terrible place to stop. The excitement about access to information is that it is the first step to expertise, to knowledge construction. Only if access to data is seen as a first step- rather than as an end in itself, will it be useful.

As I have argued elsewhere (Haydn, 2003), we must be careful not to overstate this position; there are times when it is possible to learn from simply receiving information, as when we learn from reading books. The internet is useful partly because it provides access to some high-quality writing. But sometimes, the amount of learning that takes place is dependent on what the learner does with the information; whether they integrate it into what they already know, and how they relate it to contingent aspects of their knowledge. It can also depend on the skill with which the ICT elements of learning are integrated with the teachers' knowledge of the topic, the quality of their exposition and questioning, and their other pedagogic skills.

Other Web 2.0 applications may be less significant in terms of their potential for encouraging 'active learning', but they can nonetheless help teachers to vary their teaching approaches and the format of pupil activities. This can be helpful when teachers teach a class over several years – it is not always easy to keep coming up with new ideas for pupil activities week after week, and the plethora of Web 2.0 applications can help in this respect. Table 1.2 gives details of a few Web 2.0 applications that might be used to teach history; a more extensive list can be accessed at http://historyandict.wetpaint.com.

Using ICT to increase pupil motivation and engagement

There is some evidence to suggest that skilful use of ICT can increase pupils' motivation and self-esteem (see, for example, Passey *et al.*, 2004). As early as 2002, evidence was emerging that students in the USA were starting to choose course options that had a reputation for high frequency use of ICT (Phillips, 2002), and a more recent UK study suggested that there were some history departments that attributed increased take-up of the subject at Key Stage 4 to high level teacher expertise in using ICT (Harris and Haydn, 2009). In the words of one respondent in the study:

> We have got some teachers who make good use of the internet, who can use the interactive stuff on School History, Active History and so on creatively, and who can use PowerPoint well... We are starting to see a difference in terms of take up at Key Stage 4... We are all pretty good with technology, the kids use moviemaker to make their own films and presentations... which they really enjoy... we have a revision website which we launched with t-shirts and publicity posters... the pupils use it a lot, our take up is very healthy, we are one of the biggest option groups in the school now. It's not just about ICT but ICT has helped.
>
> (Harris and Haydn, 2009: 32)

Table 1.2 Some examples of Web 2.0 applications that might be used to teach history

Pinterest www.pinterest.com	Allows pupils (or teacher) to set up a 'digital pinboard' and 'pin' images, videos and other objects to their pinboard. Includes standard social networking features. Interesting to compare pinboards that have been made previously – striking differences between pinboards on the Tudors and the Stuarts, Victorians and Edwardians.
Museum Box http://museumbox.e2bn.org	'This site provides the tools for you to build up an argument or description of an event, person or historical period by placing items in a virtual box. What items, for example, would you put in a box to describe your life; the life of a Victorian Servant or Roman soldier; or to show that slavery was wrong and unnecessary? You can display anything from a text file to a movie. You can also view and comment on the museum boxes submitted by others.'
Slideshare www.slideshare.net	Gives you access to thousands of other people's PowerPoint presentations which you can search by topic, keyword etc. Can be great for getting ideas. There are some really interesting ones on Web 2.0.
Timerime www.timerime.com	A template that enables pupils to construct their own timelines, including text, images and links to music and YouTube clips.
Bubbl.us https://bubbl.us/	Free mindmapping software.
Wallwisher www.wallwisher.com	Enables pupils to contribute a 'digital post-it' before or after a lesson, for example, to say what they thought was 'the golden nugget' of the lesson, or to answer a question posed for a homework.
Wordle www.wordle.net	Enables you to analyse texts in the form of 'tag clouds' to show which words and ideas are most prominent in text extracts, such as comparing US presidents' inaugural addresses. A form of content analysis but presents outcomes in a visually accessible way.

Part of this has been the skilful interplay between 'high' and 'low' value activities (Heafford, 1990); where teachers use quizzes and games to make at least some part of the lesson 'fun', and pupils become more 'biddable' to engaging with 'the hard stuff' in exchange for this. Andy Walker's use of interactive games led to a substantial increase in GCSE pass rates, and Walker argues that as well as 'fun', the activities brought significant increases in pupils' understanding of historical language and concepts (Walker, 2005). But ICT can also lure pupils into what Papert (1970) sometimes termed 'hard fun'. ICT often enables pupils to present their work in a way that 'looks better' than handwritten stuff, and some ICT-based tasks can be intellectually intriguing and challenging, while being less physically laborious. Counsell makes the point that 'It is not just about technology replacing effort, but technology helping to persuade pupils that intellectual effort can be stimulating' (Counsell, 1999).

Accomplished use of ICT to fashion a task that intrigues and challenges pupils can make all the difference between desultory compliance and what Dewey described as 'the giving of the mind without reserve or qualification to the subject at hand' (Dewey, 1910: 317–18). Of course, there is no automatic 'pay-off' in terms of pupil engagement (see Figure 1.1).

Figure 1.1 No automatic pay-off in terms of using ICT to improve pupil engagement

A dreary and unimaginative PowerPoint presentation can be just as boring as textbook and worksheet, but although not all pupils are driven scholars, many of them are 'biddable' to learning if the task is well designed. Sometimes we can get people to do difficult things if we make the task attractive (www.youtube.com/watch?v=2lXh2n0aPyw), and there is some evidence that ICT can help to make learning more enticing and attractive to learners.

Conclusion

Recent inspection findings suggest that there are quite wide variations in the degree to which history teachers and departments are making the most of the potential of ICT to improve pupils' learning in history (Ofsted, 2011). In the words of William Gibson (1984), 'The future is already here, it is just not very evenly distributed.'

Progress in making effective use of ICT is to a large degree a function of how much time and thought goes into exploring what ICT might add to school history. One teacher–educator offered the following explanation of the disparity between student teachers' ability to use ICT at the end of their course of training:

> They all get pretty much the same input... at least in the taught course at the university... and yet some of them get much further in their use of ICT than others and it doesn't seem to be just about which schools they have gone to for their placement.

There are psychological and attitudinal factors at work here... it's about attitudes to risk and new experiences, about initiative and perseverance. Some of them are full of good intentions but don't stick at it and move on with things... They say 'That's great... that's really interesting...', and then go away and forget all about it... Some of them are full of good intentions but never get round to it... others are very dogged and persevering... 'I'm going to stay behind in school every night this week until I can do this'... you need to get across to students these points or they think of it just in terms of being good or bad at ICT as a sort of genetic thing.

(OECD, 2010)

I would encourage you to explore ways in which ICT might enhance your teaching. I have found it very rewarding and worthwhile when I have learned to do something with ICT that improves one of my teaching sessions. Although ICT is not the unproblematic educational miracle proclaimed by politicians and those selling expensive kit to schools, I believe that it has a lot to offer those who teach history in schools.

Notes

1 An example of this tendency can be found in a Daily Telegraph editorial (7 March 2003) which stated that 'As any good teacher knows, the way to drum something into a dim child's head is to repeat it.' It is worth noting that several initiatives to raise attainment in the UK over the past decade have been 'quantitative' in approach – more homework, longer school day, shorter holidays (assuming a sort of *pro rata* increase in 'learning productivity), rather than focusing on how we might make teaching more effective. It can be salutary to think about what proportion of what you were taught has been retained, understood and applied. I learned maths for 11 years and can only do addition, subtraction, multiplication and on a good day, percentages. Algebra, Geometry, trigonometry mean nothing to me. I could do the first four things when I was six. The last ten years were not very productive. I did not understand, or forgot, most of what I was taught.

2 'Pedagogic subject knowledge' is the idea that in addition to having sound knowledge of the topic to be taught, the teacher needs to organise and present the topic in a way that is adapted to the understandings and abilities of the learners in the class, by knowing the most powerful and effective analogies, illustrations, examples and explanations, so that the topic is represented to learners in a way that makes sense to them, and they are not 'lost' or 'baffled' by the process (Shulman, 1986).

3 I work in Norwich and sometimes use a Steve Bell cartoon of a giant sheep destroying Norwich cathedral (*Guardian* Archive); I ask learners what the cartoon is about/what it means. After they have discussed it and made attempted explanations, I give them Bell's explanation which was given in an article in the *Eastern Daily Press*.

4 See, for example *Timemaps*, at www.timemaps.com/history, *The map as history*, at www.the-map-as-history.com, an animated map of Europe, 1–2006 at www.youtube.com/watch?v=QC1l6XaGI3I. There are also animated maps on a range of wars and campaigns (see for instance, the Dunkirk Campaign, www.youtube.com/watch?v=IlRne0xO-Ew). I sometimes use a map with the MacDonald's logo printed to show store locations across the midlands, to demonstrate the concept of 'cultural imperialism'.

5 'I know perfectly well... that in a scientific sense, there is no such thing as race... but I, as a politician, need a conception which enables the order which has hitherto existed to be abolished... And for this, the conception of race serves me very well.'

References

Bartlett, J. and Miller, C. (2011) *Truth, Lies and the Internet: A report into young people's digital fluency*, London: Demos, online at www.demos.co.uk/files/Truth_-_web.pdf, accessed 18 January 2012.

Buckingham, D. (2007) *Beyond Technology's Promise*, Cambridge: Polity.

Burn, K. and Harris, R. (2011) 'Historical Association Survey of History in Schools in England 2011', online at www.history.org.uk/resources/secondary_news_1290.html, accessed 18 January 2012.

Carr, M. (2008) 'Can assessment unlock the doors to resourcefulness and agency?', in S. Swaffield (ed.) *Unlocking Assessment: Understanding for reflection and application*, London: David Fulton, pp. 36–54.

Convery, A. (2009) 'The pedagogy of the impressed: how teachers become victims of technological vision', *Teachers and Teaching: Theory and Practice*, 15 (1): 25–41.

Counsell, C. (1999) Paper presented at the SCHTE Conference, University of Keele, 6 July.

Curtis, A. (2002) *The Century of the Self*, documentary, BBC 4.

Davis, F., Bagozzi, R. and Warshaw, P. (1989) 'User acceptance of computer technology: a comparison of two theoretical models', *Management Science*, 35 (8): 982–1003.

Dede, C. (1995) 'Quoted in Technology Schools', *Educational Leadership* (USA), ASDC. October: 7–12.

Desforges, C. (2002) *On Teaching and Learning*, Cranfield: NCSL.

Dewey, J. (1910) 'Science as subject matter and as method', in R. Archembault (ed.) *John Dewey on Education: Selected writings* (1974), Chicago, IL: Chicago University Press, pp. 313–38.

Eason, J. (2000) 'Weblife: urban myths', *Guardian Online*, 20 July.

Fullan, M. (1999) *Change Forces: The sequel*, London: Falmer.

Gibson, W. (1984) Quoted in *Media Guardian*, 21 September: 3.

Graham, H. (2012) 'No more role models: using oral history to find your own way', *Oral History*, Spring: 111–17.

Hargittai, E. (2008) 'Whose space?', *Journal of Computer Mediated Communication*, 13 (1): 276–97.

Harris, R. and Haydn, T. (2009) 'Factors influencing pupil take-up of history post Key Stage 3: an exploratory enquiry', *Teaching History*, 134: 27–36.

Harris, R. and Haydn, T. (2009) '"30% is not bad considering…": factors influencing pupil take-up of history post Key Stage 3: an exploratory enquiry', *Teaching History*, 134: 27–36.

Harrison, S. (2003) 'The use of ICT for teaching history: slow growth, a few green shoots. Findings of HMI Inspection, 1999–2001', in T. Haydn and C. Counsell (eds) *History, ICT and Learning in the Secondary School*, London: Routledge, pp. 38–51.

Haydn, T. (2003) 'Computers and history: rhetoric, reality and the lessons of the past', in T. Haydn and C. Counsell (eds) *History, ICT and Learning in the Secondary School*, London: Routledge, pp. 11–37.

Haydn, T. (2004) 'The use of ICT in history teaching in England and Wales 1970–2003', unpublished thesis, University of London.

Haydn, T. (2011) 'History teaching and ICT', in I. Davies (ed.) *Debates in History Teaching*, London: Routledge, pp. 236–49.

Haydn, T. and Barton, R. (2010) 'Getting teachers to use new technology by just giving them more time', in B. Olaniran (ed.) *Cases on Successful e-Learning Practices in the Developing and Developed World*, New York: IGI Global, pp. 29–41.

Heafford, D. (1990) 'Teachers teach but do learners learn?', in C. Wringe (ed.) *Language Learning Journal 1*, quoted in Pachler, N. and Field, C. (1997) *Learning to Teach Modern Foreign Languages in the Secondary School*, London: Routledge.

Heath D. and Heath, C. (2008) *Why Some Ideas Take Hold and Others Come Unstuck*, New York: Random House.

Heppell, S. (2011) 'Quoted in the "Connecting Learning" blog', 16 November, online at www.connecting-learning.co.uk, accessed 18 February 2012.

JISC (2006) 'Information behaviour of the researcher of the future: a ciber briefing paper', online at www.jisc.ac.uk//media/documents/programmes/reppres/gg_final_keynote_11012008.pdf, accessed 18 January 2012.

Laurillard, D. (1998) 'Multimedia and the learner's experience of narrative', *Computers and Education*, 31 (2): 229–42.

Lightman, A. and Sadler, P. (1993) 'Teacher predictions versus actual student gains', *Physics Teacher*, 31 (3): 162–7.

Margaryan, A., Littlejohn, A. and Vojt, G. (2011) 'Are digital natives a myth of reality? University students' use of digital technologies', *Computers and Education*, 56 (2): 429–40.

Martin, D. (2003) 'Data handling and historical learning', in T. Haydn and C. Counsell (eds), *History, ICT and Learning in the Secondary School*, London: Routledge, pp. 134–51.

Mason, R. and Rennie, F. (2007) 'Using Web 2.0 for learning in the community', *Internet and Higher Education*, 10: 196–203.

Mishra, P. (2012) *Creative Teaching with Technology: Introducing the TPACK Framework*, Keynote address at the TIES Conference, University of Barcelona, 1 February, online at http://ties2012.eu/en/pg-videos.html, accessed 19 February 2012.

Mishra, P. and Koehler, M. (2006) Technological pedagogical content knowledge: a framework for teacher knowledge, *Teachers College Record*, 106 (6): 1017–54, online at http://punya.educ.msu.edu/publications/journal_articles/mishra-koehler-tcr2006.pdf, accessed 18 November 2011.

Moore, R. (2000) 'Using the internet to teach interpretations in years 9 and 12', *Teaching History*, 35: 35–9.

NCET (1988) *History Using ICT: Searching for patterns in the past using databases and spreadsheets*, London: BECTa/Historical Association.

Naughton, J. (1998) *The Observer*, 22 March, p. 19.

Ofsted (2006) *Annual Report of Her Majesty's Chief Inspector for Schools*, London: Ofsted.

Ofsted (2011) *History for All*, London: Ofsted.

OECD (2010) *Case Studies of the Ways in which Initial Teacher Education Providers in England Prepare Student Teachers to Use ICT Effectively in their Subject Teaching*, Paris: OECD, online at www.oecd.org/dataoecd/42/39/45046837.pdf.

Papert, S. and Harel, I. (1991) 'Situating constructionism', in S. Papert and I. Harel, *Constructionism*, New York: Ablex, pp. 1–9.

Passey, D., Rogers, C. G., Machell, J. and McHugh, G. (2004) The Motivational Effect of ICT on Pupils: A Department for Education and Skills Research Project 4RP/2002/050-3, London, DfES, online at http://eprints.lancs.ac.uk/3691.

Perry, D. (2003) *The Use of Handheld Computers (PDA's) in Schools*, Coventry: DfES/Becta.

Phillips, J. (2002) 'The dinosaurs didn't see it coming, but historians had better: computer aided activities in the history classroom', *History Computer Review*, 18 (1): 27–36.

Prensky, M. (2001) 'Digital natives, digital immigrants', *On the Horizon* (NCB University Press, 9 (5), October, online at www.albertomattiacci.it/docs/did/Digital_Natives_Digital_Immigrants.pdf, accessed 18 January 2012.

Rusen, J. (1993) 'Experience, interpretation, orientation: three dimensions of historical learning', in P. Duvenage (ed.) *Studies in metahistory*, Humanities Sciences Research Council.

Sadler, P. (1994) *Simple Minds*, BBC 2 television broadcast, 19 September.

Selwyn, N. (2012) *Social Media, Social Learning? Considering the limits of the 'social turn' in contemporary educational technology*, Keynote address at the Third European Conference on Information technology in Education and Society, University of Barcelona, 1 February.

Shemilt, D. (2009) 'Drinking an ocean and pissing a cupful', in L. Symcox and A. Wilschut (eds) *National History Standards: The problem of the canon and the future of teaching history*, Charlotte, NC: Information Age Publishing, pp. 141–210.

Shulman, L. (1986) 'Those who understand: knowledge growth in teaching', *Educational Researcher*, 15 (2): 4–14.

Thomson, O. (1999) *Easily Led: A history of propaganda*, Stroud: Sutton Publishing.

Tufte, E. (2006) *The Cognitive Style of PowerPoint: Pitching out corrupts within*, Cheshire, CT: Graphics Press.

Van Dijck, J. (2009) '"Users like you?" Theorising agency in user-generated content', *Media, Culture and Society*, 32 (1): 41–58.

Walker, A. (2005) 'Using ICT to break down barriers to learning', paper presented at an 'e-help' seminar, Toulouse, 18 February, online at www.e-help.eu/seminars/walker.htm, accessed 18 January 2012.

Walsh, B. (1998) 'Why Gerry likes history now: the power of the word processor', *Teaching History*, 93: 6–15.

Walsh, B. (2006) 'Beyond multiple choice'. Online at http://e-help.eu/seminars/walsh2.htm, accessed 18 December 2011.

Walsh, B. (2008) 'Stories and sources: the need for historical thinking in an information age', *Teaching History*, 133: 4–9.

Wiliam, D. (2011) *Embedded Formative Assessment*, Bloomington, IN: Solution Tree Press.

Willingham, D. (2009) *Why Don't Students Learn?* San Francisco, CA: Jossey-Bass.

Wineburg, S. (1997) 'Beyond breadth and depth: subject matter knowledge and assessment', *Theory into Practice*, 36 (4): 255–61.

Wineburg, S. and Martin, D. (2004) 'Reading and rewriting history', *Educational Leadership* (USA), 62 (1): 42–5.

Chapter 2

The history utility belt

Getting learners to express themselves digitally

Neal Watkin

Robin: Where'd you get a live fish, Batman?
Batman: The true crimefighter always carries everything he needs in his utility belt, Robin.

Introduction

Batman's utility belt is a marvellous piece of kit, he always seems to have exactly what he needs to defeat the villain he is facing or get himself out of a precarious situation. For me, this is the perfect analogy for using ICT in the classroom. Technology has taken massive strides forward in the last decade and it has changed our perceptions of what it can do and how it should be used. We have seen a shift away from technology being under lock and key in the 'Computer Room' and a move into people's pockets. The fact that students carry with them, every day, the technology equivalent of a Swiss Army knife should not frighten us, we should embrace it and load up our own utility belt to assist us in the classroom.

Below is a discussion about the ICT tools that have made the most difference to my practice and why I feel they are essential in the modern classroom.

Beyond PowerPoint

Like many history teachers, I regularly make use of the internet, the data projector and PowerPoint in my teaching, but I have also found it interesting and useful to experiment with other new technology applications that go beyond teacher led and teacher controlled uses of ICT. In particular, I have tried to explore ways of getting pupils to express themselves 'digitally', in order to explore and develop their own ideas about history and to respond to my input to the lesson, rather than being primarily the recipients of content and ideas that I have provided. This does seem to have had the effect of increasing their commitment to learning in history, their willingness to 'do history' outside the confines of taught sessions, and to learn from each other, as well as from me.

These experiments have raised interesting questions about how we as teachers can fully exploit the use of new technology to enhance pupil learning and show them what they are capable of achieving. Although we must be careful about accepting at face value the idea that all pupils are 'digital natives' (Bennett *et al.*, 2008; Crook, 2012; Selwyn, 2012), there is some evidence to suggest that active involvement in learning can improve pupil motivation, and that ICT can play a part in this (QCA, 2005; Harris and Haydn, 2009). As Rosen rightly points out in his seminal study of the iGeneration:

> So, what's the problem? *They hate school.* Why? Education has not caught up with this new generation of tech-savvy children and teens. It is not that they don't want to learn. They just learn differently. Gone are the days when students would sit quietly in class, reading a book or doing a math worksheet. Literally, their minds have changed – they have been 'rewired.' With all the technology that they consume, they *need more* from education.
>
> (Rosen, 2010: 3)

For me, the content of lessons is not the issue, it is the way that we deliver it and the processes we use that need a radical rethink. Students need engaging in a way that we are not necessarily used to and we need to work hard to ensure that we understand the learning styles of the young people in front of us.

Activities that engage students are easy to identify, but those that also unlock potential are more problematic. This is where I find the Puentedura's SAMR model[1] really useful. If the tasks that you ask students to do simply substitute or augment what could be done with paper then they will provide little more than passing amusement, but if they transform an activity, by modifying or redefining a process you are more likely to draw out of students a response not possible with other, more traditional, approaches.

One of my favourite approaches is audio blogging. I use Audioboo (http://audioboo. fm) in the classroom on a regular basis and I have found that it can have a transformational effect on students. Recording your thoughts verbally and publishing them is more than a substitute for writing. First, it is quicker and uses the form of communication that most people are confident with. This in itself can increase participation in an activity. Second, it encourages redrafting: people care what they sound like and about the impression this creates. After recording initial thoughts, students can listen back and easily record a new version. It is a less permanent form of communication and controlled by the individual rather than the teacher. There is also evidence to suggest that pupil talk can consolidate pupils' understanding of what has been taught, and aid retention of what has been learned (Alexander, 2004; Willingham, 2009).

As an example of this approach, I recently worked with a mixed-ability Year 7 class on the question 'Why doesn't Thomas Clarkson get the credit he deserves?' As part of the answer students were looking at the evidence Clarkson found to discredit the slave trade and the arguments put forward by its main supporters. Their main task at this stage was to create a speech that Clarkson could have delivered at one of the many meetings he held to gather support for his cause. As a class, we identified seven factors and therefore divided into seven groups to produce solid arguments against the slave trade. Each group produced an audio response, after carefully drafting the work on paper. We listened back to each of the sections and critiqued the work for both content and style. We then produced second drafts and published them live on the Audioboo site. Although the lesson ended with us summing up the arguments and writing a class conclusion, the work continued to live: at lunchtime the next day three members of the class came to my room and asked if they could record their section again, because they were still not happy with the way it sounded towards the end. After a quick rehearsal we made another recording and deleted the old one. As a class we had created an excellent speech and we enjoyed listening to it the following lesson. It also meant that students had something to refer to when completing their assessment later in the scheme.

Both my students and I found the process an interesting one. The use of audio blogging had made students more engaged in the work and they were happy to create three or four drafts of work (something that would have been hard to convince them to do if it was writing). I think there are two reasons why this happened: the use of audio makes the drafts more accessible and the public nature of the product makes them care more about the quality. The public element also helped establish more effective Assessment for Learning (AfL). As Berger states in his incredible book, *An Ethic of Excellence*:

> Critique in most classroom settings has a singular audience and a limited impact: whether from a teacher or peer, it is for the edification of the author; the goal is to improve that particular piece. The formal critique in my classroom has a broader goal. I use whole-class critique sessions as a primary context for sharing knowledge and skills with the group.
>
> (Berger, 2003: 93)

'Critiquing' has changed my attitudes and transformed the quality of work in my classroom. Asking students to put their work up for public scrutiny is a bold move. Asking pupils to listen patiently as others coolly dissect their work is difficult for some. It is difficult for teachers too, relying on a whole class to come out with quality comments with just a few prompts from you. However, it does work if approached in the right manner, and some students are used to this kind of approach. They hardly think twice about posting a video to YouTube, or a song on Soundcloud. Instant feedback is now part of their learning vocabulary for a growing number of learners; the trick for educators is to find ways to make this process work in the classroom setting. I believe that the example given above comes somewhere close to emulating the 'upload for public comment' culture currently dominating the web, but it happens in a way that is not threatening to the students. It is a way of developing the resourcefulness and sense of 'agency' of pupils; getting them to take ownership and responsibility for their work (Carr, 2008). This can make all the difference between pupils just 'going through the motions' with a piece of work, and trying hard to do it really well. I have used the same audio blogging technique with a range of groups from Year 7–13 and the outcomes are always the same: greater engagement, willingness to redraft work and better end products. This often involves willingness to continue with the work outside the taught sessions.

Using audio blogging may seem like a simple and effective way to harness the technology students have with them on a daily basis; after all, most phones have some method of voice recording included as part of their software. However, mobile phones and mobile devices in the classroom can be controversial. Some schools and individual teachers talk about the potential dangers in terms of child protection and equality of access, and, these concerns can't be ignored. However, as long as we address them head on and deal with them appropriately at the point when we use mobile devices then the issues are limited to a point of irrelevance.

Having conducted some research within my own school, I found that 71 per cent of Year 7 students don't possess the technology to access the internet or smart applications on their mobile devices. This is a real problem if you want to push instant technology and to utilise the latest resources. The percentage was almost reversed when students reached

Year 11 (68 per cent had internet and application access), but there is a real issue here for those teachers who want to use technology and don't want some members of the class to feel uncomfortable. One solution is to stick with the technology that they do have. Most students have phones (in my school, 88–100 per cent) and most phones have a camera. Cameras may seem a little old hat these days, but they do make for a powerful learning tool when harnessed properly.

With Year 10 I have been working on a 'live storyboard' project connected to the Wild West. Learning about the Wild West was completed through the question 'Why was the Wild West so Wild?' and by looking at five case studies, some of (in-)famous individuals such as Billy the Kid, others on places or groups (such as the Chinese communities). As the class learned about each case study they used the cameras on their phones to take a series of still images to represent the key points in the story that might help them to answer the question. The images were shared using Bluetooth on my laptop or via email and stored in a file on my hard drive. I ensured that students worked in friendship groups and that images were deleted afterwards. When all the evidence was analysed I asked students to think as if they were going to make a documentary to answer the key question and we created a class storyboard using the images created by students in the previous lessons. These were then annotated (using Publisher) and printed out. The use of cameras allowed us to create an effective storyboard within 30 minutes, including image manipulation and added effects. This timescale would not have been possible with pen and paper.

The topic could have ended there, but I wanted students to fully demonstrate that they understood the complexities of the Wild West and how factors interacted to cause some of the issues seen in towns such as Abilene. To do this I used the fantastic PEEL (point, example, evidence and link) procedure 'Fact into Fiction' and got students to create a giant comic book that had an original story, but used real characters, places and events from their learning.[2] The story had to be historically plausible (no alien invasions or anachronistic super tools), but incorporate the key elements of what made the Wild West so wild. Students had access to the digital scenes they had already shot in order to think through what they could include and were able to mock up new ones using their mobile devices. They even brought in props such as guns and beards to get a greater realism. The digital images served as a blueprint for a more authentic hand-drawn final copy which stands 125 cm high.

The purpose of creating a new and fictional account is to anchor the learning by making fresh and novel connections to the main points gained from the history.[3] The use of digital images works in a similar way and allows students to creatively explore a topic in a time-efficient way.

Cameras can also be a great way of capturing the process of learning in class. With my Year 9 classes I have completed several project-based learning units and this involves extensive use of independent learning and group activities. Allowing students to take images of the key moments in their learning journey means that a more effective discussion can be had with students about HOW they went about the task and WHY they made the decisions that they did. The process has even more impact if the images are printed out and annotated and a dialogue is started between the teacher and student. For example, the Year 9s completed an information piece to display at Poperinge New Cemetery that will raise the profile of a forgotten Jamaican soldier, Herbert Morris. The work went through three drafts and students digitally recorded their work at each stage. At the end of the process students stuck an image of each draft side by side, followed by an image of all the work by the soldier's gravestone. This allowed them to clearly see how much their work had changed and why they needed to make improvements. The ability to visibly account for the development of a piece of work gives the student a better chance of understanding how their skills have developed – it demystifies the nature of learning and provides progression and thinking with an actual language that is often just implicit.

Film can be used in exactly the same way as photography, with students collecting their own pieces of film and emailing them to the teacher. Filming used to be a rare treat for students, but now it is something that is almost part of their daily lives and most of them have the technology in their pocket to be able to do it. An added benefit with filming is that it covers a longer period of time and therefore stands up to more detailed analysis. I am a great fan of allowing students to film an early draft of a film 'off the cuff', without a script or rehearsal. It means that a substantial dialogue can then be had about where improvements can be made. It reveals, through practice and real examples, the need for planning and careful structure. I used this technique with my Year 12 students when they were looking at the motives of Henry VIII at the time of the Break with Rome. In pairs, students recorded an initial draft of their early thoughts. This was completed in a Big Brother style piece to camera, with one student talking and the other asking relevant and prompting questions. We then played the video back to the class and analysed the content. Students soon realised that unstructured talk did not sound convincing and neither did it make good history. So, notes were written, cue cards created and recording started again. After three drafts, the quality was there. Pupil discussion was not limited to 'production' issues, but included thoughtful discussion of substantive historical content.

With both film and photographs, ground rules need to be set and adhered to by all. I make it clear to students why we are working in this way and the potential benefits to them, but also the steps we will have to take if someone decides to break the rules. Very rarely have students overstepped the boundaries, but the 'etiquette' for this way of working does need spelling out to pupils. There are occasions when teachers who will painstakingly go over the rules for creating an exam answer, simply assume that students somehow innately know what is needed for successfully using ICT within a group. Just like any activity, it needs careful structuring and students need ground rules for its use.

I appreciate that some teachers and schools would be deeply uneasy about students filming each other. If that is the case, simply substitute real people for children's' toys and the same effect can be gained. In fact, it is a technique that carries its own benefits. When teaching interpretations of Henry VIII's government to Year 12, I borrow my daughter's Playmobil and allow students to create scenes that demonstrate the viewpoint they are examining. The toys often lead to a deeper level of analysis because it removes students from acting in the scene and allows them to see the topic from the outside – they become directors rather than actors. Playdoh and stick puppets work equally well.

Engagement from blogging or using cameras is really useful for creating energy in the classroom, but teachers also want students to be reflective and take a step back to consider the significance of what they have done. Capturing this reflection can be a challenging issue. This is especially true of exam groups where you want something for students to refer back to when revision time and exams close in. Summing-up, reinforcing and recapping the learning is vital and Twitter can be a valuable tool for doing this. The virtues of social networking have been covered elsewhere in this book, but the process of writing the key message from the lesson (the 'golden nugget' my PGCE tutor used to call it) in 140 characters is both interesting and mentally taxing for students. If students contribute each lesson to a class Twitter account, the timeline can be saved or reviewed at regular intervals to show how learning builds up. I also used it as part of the Summer School that I helped to run. Here, it was a useful way to give parents and colleagues a flavour of the learning that we engaged in, but was also a vital part of our idea collecting and a way of setting targets for the next phase of learning. What I have found when using Twitter is that in a short space of time students are asking to attach photographs and links to the tweets to further assist with consolidation of learning.

So far I have opted for a collaborative approach where I moderate the account and the class contribute by taking it in turns to add tweets. I would love each student to have an individual account, but while access is still patchy, this feels like the most sensible option. There are other ways of achieving this kind of outcome, such as the excellent Wallwisher website (www.wallwisher.com). An example of the sort of 'post-it' comments that pupils can contribute can be accessed at http://wallwisher.com/wall/icttrip.

Wallwisher did a good job of capturing their thoughts and needs for that particular moment in time, but it does not allow a dialogue to form, or any movement of ideas or comments that could strengthen the learning – two things that Twitter does really effectively.

As mentioned above, capturing learning has become relatively easy, but being able to capture the dialogue that normally occurs after students present their media creations to their peers is harder. This was a real problem for me because the discussions that resulted from digital content were always intriguing and often very insightful. For months I was troubled by the fact that students were able to create digital content, but the conversations that they were having about the work were not being captured within the content itself. I wanted to find a way to make comments part of the digital content we created in class, because this seemed both neat and more in tune with the behaviours that many iGeneration students displayed when they uploaded material to a video or music site.

I started to play around with YouTube annotations and Soundcloud (http://soundcloud.com) and discovered that a wealth of opportunities opened up. YouTube annotations are a really useful tool. They allow the user to effectively write on top of a movie clip that has been uploaded. This means that a group of students can watch the video created by another group and add reminders and comments, or pause the film to allow proper consideration of an issue. The annotations are then saved along with the movie. The benefit of this approach is that all the learning experience can be captured, not just the end product. Students can ask clarifying questions of others and suggest improvements and these can become part of the work, rather than something that is stored separately. Annotations can be added to over time and edited so that dialogue can be ongoing. The beautiful thing is that annotations can be clicked on and off in play mode so that you can view the film in its original state or see what comments have been added. This further enhances discussion in class.

I recently used this approach to extend an activity developed for Year 9 by Dale Banham. He designed a sequence of lessons that gets students to look at a number of interpretations of JFK using mainly still images and film clips. In the final lesson students have to select images and then use MovieMaker to create a short piece about one of three different interpretations (positive, negative and balanced). The task seems to work really well because it asks students to grapple with the idea of what each interpretation looks like – the images they use both help them to understand their interpretation and prompt a rich vocabulary for their voiceover. The useful end point for the work is to play the movies in class and ask students to compare the three approaches. We can then discuss why these three interpretations are possible given that the same events were analysed. However, recently I have added an extra step using the YouTube annotations facility.

The class were divided into small groups and given someone else's work to look at. They were also given a specific focus. Some were asked to check the level of historical detail in the work and add caption boxes as annotations to show where the film could be given more depth. Other groups were asked to use annotations to comment on the style and flow of the film – did it have enough variety and energy, were the images carefully chosen, was colour used with effect? The last groups were asked to add speech bubbles to the characters that appeared in the film so that extra information was made available to support the interpretation. Each group also had to add a positive comment to the section of the movie that they thought most effective and all students were free to post questions at any point. What emerged was a lively commentary that analysed interpretations in a deeper way than had been possible through the original activity. Students were able to demonstrate just how much they understood about how interpretations are created and also learned valuable lessons about how to strengthen their work. Once all the annotations were complete, we watched the movies again and drew up a list of key advice that could be followed next time we had to grapple with interpretations. We took a photo of the whiteboard and tweeted it. (You need to have a YouTube account to use the annotations facility; this is free.)

Soundcloud does a similar job with audio. I have been uploading some of the Audioboo files we have been creating on Great War ghosts to the site so that students can comment on the content and tag it to a specific part of the audio. What is great about Soundcloud is that it allows conversations to develop as students respond to the comments left. This gives it a really authentic feeling of collaboration.

Nothing I have found deals with collaboration better than Google Docs (https://docs. google.com). Google Docs has revolutionised the way that I approach A Level teaching. The flexibility of the system and the ability for all people to collaborate and share resources makes it such a powerful tool. Although I have only used this post-16 (they are the only students who currently have access to Google Docs) I am convinced that it is an approach that can be developed with all year groups.

One of the main issues that Year 13 face with their coursework is the daunting task of critiquing the work of professional historians. They seem timid when confronted with extended accounts and words, but above everything else, deference stops them from making comments that are too negative. In order to encourage them to engage with this skill I decided to demystify the process of creating historical interpretations and then analysing them. First, I gave each member of the group a pair of sources about attitudes to early policing. They were tasked with using just these sources to answer the question 'How effective were the New Police before 1865?' Each student completed their analysis of the sources and then used Google Docs to write their answer, including as many quotes and opinions as they could. Each student then shared their document with the other members of the class. The next stage was to introduce students to the 'Copleston Doctorate'. I told students that they were going to write an essay that replicated some of the characteristics present in a PhD essay. Their work needed to use a range of source material and the work of five other 'Historians'. They were only allowed to use the work of other people from the group. They were allowed to agree or disagree with any of the 'Historians', but the rule was that if they did use the work of someone else it would be fully analysed and evaluated. If any of the students had their name used by five other people they could be eligible for the Copleston Doctorate, providing their own final essay was of a sufficient standard (see Figure 2.1).

Copleston History University

Institute for Advanced Studies

Greeting to all to whom these Letters shall come:
The Copleston History University Council of Directors
by virtue of the authority vested in it by law and
On recommendation of the Faculty elders does hereby confer on

Who has satisfactorily completed the Studies prescribed therefore
The Degree of

Doctor of History

With all the rights, Privileges and Honours appertaining thereto.
In witness Whereof the Seal of the University is hereto affixed.
Granted at Copleston History University, this year of 2011

Tutor   Chair

Figure 2.1 'The Copleston Doctorate'

I set up a few ground rules about referencing (e.g. 'Quote from Primary, Paraphrase from Secondary') and let them loose on the essay question 'How effective were the New Police before 1865?', giving them two weeks to complete the assignment. Using the school VLE I set up a league table so that students could see who was using their work and in what context. It wasn't long before students started messaging each other with convincing reasons why their opinions should be included in someone else's essay. Since everyone was openly sharing their work with the rest of the group, the process took on a much more competitive edge and sparked more debate than I had seen over a single essay than ever before.

Once the results were in, six students had achieved five citations by others and produced a quality essay as well. They were awarded their doctorates at a special ceremony (yes, we really did have a graduation ceremony complete with scrolls and hats) and they were given the privilege of being referred to as 'Doctor' in all future lessons.

Once the ceremony was over we sat down as a group and debated the process. We unpicked the learning and how they might now go on and develop critical analysis of academic Historians. So, I gave them a section from two texts on the development of the Police, one by the renowned Cambridge Historian V.A.C. Gatrell and the other by Clive Emsley of the Open University.[4] The reading was by no means an easy read and the two pieces contradicted each other and challenged some of the primary evidence they had previously gathered. Once again, we used Google Docs to collect thoughts and the students worked in three research groups of 3–5 people to come up with an effective critique of the two Historians. I asked them not to delete any conversations for amendments so that we could see HOW they arrived at their answer. The result was a fascinating presentation from all groups that led to a shared document on how to tackle the critical analysis of Historical interpretations. This was created by sharing slides using Google Present.

I now ask my A Level students to complete all presentations using Google Present. This, I believe, has three benefits: it cuts down on the amount of 'fluff' included (Google has fewer options than PowerPoint), it is easier to share with others this way, and it cuts down on the amount of time it takes for each student to log off and then the next to log on (a real pain when learning time is at a premium).

Google Apps in general allow students to collaborate and work with people outside of the normal friendship groups. It helps them to get instant feedback and makes the process of learning a highly social activity. Above all, it puts ownership of the learning in the hands of students and allows them to access it whenever they like.

However, if students are creating a wealth of digital content, they need an easy way of storing and managing it. I would briefly like to mention two tools that have become a regular feature in my classroom, especially with exam groups: Dropbox (www.dropbox.com) and Evernote (www.evernote.com).

Dropbox is simply a place that students can store and share content. It works across platforms and is available for web, desktop and smartphone use. In the classroom it makes it easy to share resources with students as I can drop a file (for example, a screenshot) into a shared folder and everyone can access the information at any point. This means that students will instantly know where the key documents are and where to find the latest files that were part of the class. Many students have used Dropbox to assist them in developing their coursework, creating a folder structure to divide up large topics and slotting research into the relevant section. Since a growing proportion of research is completed online it makes sense to have a recording system that also utilises the internet.

However, I also encourage students to use Evernote, particularly at A Level. Evernote shares many principles with Dropbox, except that it is for notes rather than whole files. You can upload a text, photo or voice note instantly and at any point. The great advantage of Evernote though is tagging. Evernote allows you to attach multiple tags to your notes and store them along with the information. For Year 13 students completing their coursework assignment this is a very quick, easy and practical way for them to organise their research. They can write a text note and then 'tag' it with the relevant factor that it relates to, ready for use later. Once a section of research is complete, students can call up all the notes relating to a single factor by searching their Evernote account for that tag. Students have found it a really useful tool in helping them to navigate what is a complex piece of work.

I have no doubt that developing the use of these applications, and going beyond 'teacher-use' of ICT has improved the quality of pupils' work and increased their commitment to learning in history. It has also increased the amount of time that pupils spend learning history outside the classroom, and the extent to which they learn from each other, as well as from me.

We have also found it useful to develop an ICT 'suitcase' for departmental use. This is just a container that houses digital cameras, voice recorders and camcorders, and that makes it logistically very quick and easy to use these devices in any lesson. All the tools mentioned above are easy to access and run – that is what technology should be about. To create good digital content, students need technology that is more efficient and smarter than simply getting it down on paper. For the vast majority of students technology comes easily and they take it in their stride, but as educators we need to help them create something meaningful from the device that sits in their pocket or the website that is just a click away.

Notes

1 For a wealth of useful resources on SAMR model see Ruben Puentedura's blog www.hippasus. com/rrpweblog.
2 Ian Mitchell (ed.), *Teaching for Effective Learning: The Complete Book of Teaching Procedures* (2009): 139–140. Alternatively, visit and register with the PEEL website, www.peelweb.org/ index.cfm?resource=about.
3 For the purpose of modelling the process of 'Fact into Fiction' there is a splendid IOS app called Sparklefish – www.sparklefishapp.com.
4 The sources were taken from V.A.C. Gatrell, 'Crime, Authority and the Policeman-State', in F.M.L. Thompson (ed.), *The Cambridge Social History of Britain, 1750–1950, Vol. 3: Social Agencies and Institutions* (Cambridge, 1990): 243–310, and Clive Emsley, *Crime and Society in England: 1750–1900*, third edition (Harlow, 2005).

References

Alexander, R. (2004) *Towards Dialogic Teaching: Rethinking classroom talk*, York: Dialogos.
Bennett, S., Maton, K. and Kervin, L. (2008) 'The digital natives debate: a critical review of the evidence', *British Journal of Educational Technology*, 39 (2): 775–86.
Berger, R. (2003) *An Ethic of Excellence: Building a culture of craftsmanship with students*, London: Heinemann.
Carr, M. (2008) 'Can assessment unlock and open the doors to resourcefulness and agency?', in S. Swaffield (ed.), *Unlocking Assessment: Understanding for reflection and appreciation*, London: David Fulton, pp. 36–54.
Crook, C. (2012) 'The "digital native" in context: tensions associated with importing Web 2.0 practices into the school setting', *Oxford Review of Education*, 38(1): 63–80.
Harris, R. and Haydn, T. (2009) 'Factors influencing pupil take-up of history post Key Stage 3: an exploratory enquiry', *Teaching History*, 134: 27–36.
Mitchell, I. (ed.) (2009) *Teaching for Effective Learning: The complete book of PEEL teaching procedures*, Sydney: Peel Publications. Alternatively, visit and register with the PEEL website, www.peelweb.org/index.cfm?resource=about.
QCA (2005) 'Pupil perceptions of history at Key stage 3', London: QCA.
Rosen, L. (2010) *Rewired*, Basingstoke: Palgrave Macmillan.
Selwyn, N. (2012) 'Social media, social learning: considering the limits of the "social turn" in contemporary educational technology', keynote address at the *Third European Conference on Information Technology in Education and Society*, Barcelona, 1 February.
Willingham, D. (2009) *Why don't students like school?* San Francisco, CA: Jossey-Bass.

Chapter 3

History wikis

Ali Messer

Introduction

This chapter provides guidance on how to set up your own history wiki and ideas from a range of history wikis on the web. We will look at the possible benefits of this kind of software for teachers: at the time of writing any teacher can set up a wiki instantly, for nothing. It will also look at how user-generated content such as Wikipedia has begun to change the ways in which students study outside of school, and some principles for making the most of the opportunities presented, while remaining aware of some of the issues. We will then look at the benefits for learners in understanding how wikis are created and from participating in wiki creation as critical readers and reflective writers. It will include practical advice about how working with wikis can help us to develop in our students a deeper understanding of historical enquiry, enable them to enter into debates about interpretation and significance in history, and see how accounts of the past are constructed by amateur and professional historians alike.

What is a wiki?

A wiki is a website where users can create and edit content, by adding, removing and changing content quickly. It is based on software that makes the editing process as easy as working with an Office document. Unlike many websites, it is designed to be created by many people through an edit link to the source document, available over the web. It has been described as: 'A book we can all share in reading. But in addition we can make corrections, add new pages... links... [and] multimedia...' (Hendron, 2008: 35). Everyone will be familiar with Wikipedia, launched formally in 2001 by Jimmy Wales and Larry Sanger, using ideas pioneered by Ward Cunningham. By November 2011, Wikipedia included over 20 million articles in 282 languages, written by over 31 million registered users and many anonymous contributors worldwide. When you read this chapter, the dominance of Wikipedia in search engine results may have faded. The need to be able to evaluate information on the web for 'relevancy and credibility' will not (Howland *et al.*, 2012: 31). This means that it will still be useful to use wiki-based websites as a way to enable students to see for themselves how accounts of the past are constructed. Reuben Moore's prophecy at the beginning of the new millennium in *Teaching History* has been fulfilled:

> The Internet is not a passing trend. Our young people will use it in their daily lives... they will continue to confront interpretations and representations of history. All adults... need to be able to see how and why the historical interpretations that bombard

them were constructed. Otherwise they are prey to propaganda and manipulation, not to mention cynicism or a lack of regard for truth.

(Moore, 2000: 35)

His view has since been echoed in the wider world: 'In an era where digital technologies are increasingly embedded in the everyday... effective and successful economic and civic participation are crucially tied to mastery of digital technologies and engagement with participatory culture' (Carrington *et al.*, 2009: 70).

Why should history teachers care about wikis?

The central argument in this chapter is that, for students in schools to be able to engage with history online, they need to understand how both history, and 'information' on the web, is constructed. In the process of getting to grips with online history-making through wikis, they can see the warp and weft of history-making itself. There is debate about the craft of history:

> Has the digital revolution transformed how we write about the past – or not? Have new technologies changed our essential work-craft as scholars, and the way in which we think, teach, author, and publish? Does the digital age have broader implications for individual writing processes, or for the historical profession at large?
>
> (Dougherty and Nawrotzki, 2011/12: 1)

Reuben Moore claimed that, however historians might choose to work,

> pupils do need to understand the process of construction and, where appropriate, to attempt some construction for themselves. We history teachers, collectively, have a wealth of experience of giving pupils strategies and criteria for reaching their own historically valid decisions. We must teach our students to bring these skills to the ICT lab, instead of leaving them festering in the history classroom like forgotten games kit.
>
> (Moore, 2000: 37)

ICT has long escaped from the lab, and as de Groot has argued, 'Popular culture is in a state of constant contention and evolution, and the representation of the historical is part of that development' (de Groot, 2009: 5). This makes it ever more important that we strive to enable our students to make sense of the past as it is represented digitally online, in games and in film outside the history classroom.

Inspired in part by Moore's article, Counsell argued that it might be possible to categorise progression in historical learning using technology into type A, where increasing sophistication in using technology is 'intrinsic to history's purposes' (Counsell, 2003: 62), or type B where it is used to achieve goals that could be reached by traditional methods. This chapter will try to show how active participation in wiki creation can offer type B activities that remain essential to history such as reading critically and developing structured writing. Investment on the part of teacher and student in wiki editing is likely to be most worthwhile, however, if we also seek out type A activity in which 'Full interactivity involves critical thinking on the part of the learner' (Haydn, 2003: 220). Evaluating a history wiki created by others is likely to be type A, and we can prepare students for this kind of evaluation in many ways, including creating their own wiki pages. Haydn argued that:

The full potential of ICT for providing worthwhile interactive learning in history will only be realised when instructional design consistently takes into account the nature of history as a subject discipline, and requires learners to apply, amend, revise, compare, interpret, analyse, select and make judgements on the information they access.

(Haydn, 2003: 221)

If wiki activities are designed with this advice in mind, they have the potential to support many different kinds of progress in historical thinking.

How to set up a wiki

There are currently many free and hosted wiki providers used by educators, so first find a wiki provider. These sites make the process easy; current examples include:

www.wikispaces.com/content/for/teachers

http://pbworks.com

http://wikisineducation.wetpaint.com

www.mediawiki.org/wiki/MediaWiki

Having set up a wiki you have a major decision to make: will this be a public wiki from the start that any web user can see, assuming that they can find it? If your focus was a local history project this could be a practical way to draw in community or local museum staff involvement, because many people can edit the wiki from different locations. You could include student created content, because a significant feature of the software is that unhelpful edits (vandalism) can always be reversed. Your students might find the idea of creating public content engaging as many of them are confident creators of online content within social networks, but it may also have a more powerful impact: 'When learners use technologies to represent their actions and constructions, they understand more and are able to use the knowledge they have created in new situations' (Howland *et al.*, 2012: 4). Sixth-formers at Esher college found the editing required in preparing a website for others to be challenging and motivating, 'it mattered to them that [their work] … would be on public view to their peers, to another college and to a "real" historian' (Chapman and Facey, 2009: 116). It seems that, for a wiki-based website to work best, it needs to have a genuine audience and involve students who are creating pages in the 'discussion, debate and argument that are the essence of history as an interpersonally constructed form of knowledge' (Cooper and Chapman, 2009: 4). In practice, this probably means that some lesson as well as homework time would need to be devoted to the process, especially at the start and end of a project. What the wiki might offer, then, is a scaffold through the development stages of the project. To ensure that this works as you intend, you will need to find out what editing permissions you can assign to your students (Malaga, 2009). On many wikis, users who are writers and not editors cannot create or delete pages. This could be a significant safety feature, or with older students, a limitation. It is easy to upgrade user permissions, but it needs to be done with forethought.

If you are leading a school trip and you want staff and students to be able to edit an account of your visit, a wiki could be very powerful; see this example suggested by my colleague at Roehampton, Bridget Middlemas: http://historicalissuesinhumanrights.pbworks.com/w/page/18426419/FrontPage. Figure 3.1 shows a screenshot.

Historical Issues in Human Rights Field Trip April 20th – 25th 2009

5 students and 2 members of staff from the Human Rights programme at Roehampton University travelled together across Europe to Auschwitz via Paris, Berlin, Wannsee and Krakow between the 20th and the 26th of April 2008. This wiki attempts to create a virtual field trip that maps our journey and our learning – Paris by train on the first day, then a night flight to Berlin, for two days (also visiting Wannsee), then another train journey to Krakow in Poland, for another two days, spending one of them at Auschwitz–Birkenau.

We all kept learning diaries of our experiences. We have tried to utilise the <u>multimedia capabilities</u> of Wiki technology to the best of our ability, using video, photos, poems, and links to other applications to complement our personal diary entries.

Jo Doumuyah

I am a first year Human Rights student at Roehampton University. The history of the Holocaust history is a part of my nationality as a Pole. Before World War II, in my city Warsaw where my father's family comes from, Jewish and non-Jewish Polish families lived together. My Grandad was living in Pl.Grzybowski– today known as Jewish street– sharing everyday life with a different religion and culture before the war. I knew the place called Auschwitz–Birkenau from my childhood years, however I did not understand the real meaning of it until the day my eyes have seen the camp on 24th of April 2009.
I said to myself: *"it is good to see the camp only one time and just forget it! To forget only the place, but to remember them.* <u>I will never forget you ...</u> "

Alexia Hudson

View Larger Map

<u>Facilitating your own field trip or offsite visit</u>

<u>Build your own Wiki</u>

<u>Planning meeting Thursday 2nd April 1430 Belfry Bar</u>

<u>What to bring checklist</u>

<u>Itinerary</u>

Figure 3.1   Making a wiki about a field trip. You can start with a protected wiki visible only to invited users, but then make it public at the end of a project to act as an exemplar for other projects or visits

Teachers using wikis as public websites

Some history teachers use public wikis as an easy to make platform for homework and revision guides, and this might help you if your school's virtual learning environment does not match your creativity. Take a look at this school wiki: http://sawtryhistory.wikispaces.com.

Darryl Tomlin and colleagues show an awareness of ways in which students search the web, and in a page about picture libraries they emphasise the importance of considering the provenance of the images to be found online. It also invites students to become curators using a template. It has been argued that digital history: 'has its own vocabulary and requires different skills sets (emphasising, for example, curation as opposed to detective work)' (Dougherty and Nawrotzki: 2011/12: 1). This is interesting. As teachers we may have seen the web initially as a highway to *discovery*. It turns out that the more traditional but also deeper thinking of the museum curator, showing concern about provenance and making informed selection, may be as important as the skills of exploration. This approach makes a great deal of sense to history teachers already using a range of other e-learning strategies with sixth-formers:

> We can help students to rise to the level of advanced-level historical thinking by scaffolding student experiences in ways that build on what they already know and can do and by encouraging them to think metacognitively about what they are doing and about the demands of the subject they are studying.
>
> (Chapman and Hibbert, 2009: 121)

The selection, editing and curating processes that can be built into wiki tasks are ideal candidates for enabling this kind of deep learning.

Another example of a teacher's public wiki leading to student-created content (in wiki-based e-portfolios) can be seen in Figure 3.2. In the screenshot shown here, the teacher creating the wiki also encourages students to use the discussion forum provided, and anyone viewing the site can look at the history pages to see how the content developed.

This is teaching as embroidery: where the students and others can see how the pages are stitched together. Not only can colleagues be invited to edit pages, so can students. Any invited participant can use the discussion to comment on content, or to ask questions. This makes wiki-based websites very flexible for teachers in a way that virtual learning environments and other websites may not be.

Laurillard argued that for any teaching strategy in an academic context to be successful, 'There is no room for mere telling, nor for practice without description, nor for experimentation without reflection, nor for student action without feedback' (Laurillard, 2002: 71). In history, the use of technology that encourages students to create their own understandings of the world, making their ideas available for debate, discussion and revision, is beginning to approach the ways into learning articulated in Laurillard's 'Conversational Framework'. Her ideas are relevant to History as a subject in school as well as university where learning from experience and experiment, as in Science or Physical Education, for example, is rarely possible. In the Pilgrim Fathers lesson sequence analysed by Ashby *et al.* (2005) in *How Students Learn*, we see Peter desperate for eyewitness or archaeological evidence of the Mayflower before being willing to draw conclusions about 19 images of the ship. In the lesson sequence it becomes evident that many images on the web are better evidence of the *significance* of the Mayflower than direct evidence of its condition on arrival in Cape Cod. This is not an easy idea to grasp, as the chapter shows with telling examples of student thinking. We can now see how Darryl's use of a wiki-based website to develop student skills as curators is not at all trivial but may be essential to the development of historical thinking in the twenty-first century. This is especially the case if we accept that there is the possibility that the 'skills of judgement and decision-making, which students continually employ in online activities' (Walker *et al.*, 2010: 217) can be transferred to historical activities.

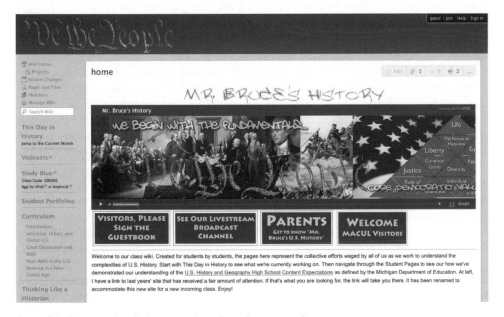

Figure 3.2 An example of a history wiki with student-created content

It seems very likely that as teachers we will need to plan explicit opportunities for this transfer to take place, through 'explicit mentoring into the practices associated with digital texts' and participatory culture (Carrington, 2009: 77; Jenkins, 2009). This may be more easily achieved within a wiki than a VLE or MLE where in many cases it is the *teacher's* role to make significant decisions about content, not the students' role, as in a wiki.

Teachers using wikis as protected websites with invited users

It could be wise, however, to start with a protected wiki, viewed only by you, colleagues and a few students, while you explore with them the best ways to use wiki software in your context (Wheeler *et al.*, 2008). Staff and students alike might find the idea of producing public content intimidating, and be more willing to participate in being part of a knowledge-building community, consisting of people they know well. If you are using a protected wiki, you can then just invite the members of a class, or course, or year group, to view it. You can also control who does the editing, by choosing selected students as writers or editors.

Libby Bond from Lampton School has been using wiki with her A level students in this way to boost their confidence as they make transitions from GCSE to A level and from school to university. She wants them to see that interpretations of the past can be evaluated and critiqued, for example because they are 'one sided', in the sense of being based on selective and dubious use of evidence. There are connections to be made here with the use of online discussion explored by Arthur Chapman (this volume) with sixth-formers needing to understand that: 'History… progresses through dialogue in disciplined communities of practice rather than through bravura performance' (Megill, 2007). She has noticed that in using their wiki they 'get anxious about editing anything… that is considered to be an authority, even if it is Wikipedia, which we all know is problematic…', (interview, November 2011). To boost their confidence, in one task she copied extracts from Wikipedia into a protected wiki, for her students to edit. She argued that: 'I think [the wiki-editing] works really well, it encourages them to question it, pick it apart, say what is missing…' (ibid.). She also sets the creation of revision pages within the wiki as independent homework tasks, with a view to giving her students 'a sense of ownership… a place where they can share ideas and their understanding of the course' (ibid.). Her students also completed a wiki task at the end of the course where they created a guide to answering one of the [A2] questions: 'this was edited by lots of different students, they… added to it, edited it, changed it, and distilled it down to "when you open the question paper, what *exactly* is it that you need to do?"' (ibid.). Libby argued that, although there are times when the wiki format was useful for extending text, it has possibly greater value in encouraging students to 'strip it away to the essence' of the matter (ibid.). As Shemilt (2009) reminds us through the words of Flaubert, 'Writing history is like drinking an ocean and pissing a cupful'; arguably this is never more the case than when writing under examination conditions. In the longer term, the aim is that, as more students create additional pages on related topics, layers are created through links, and for subsequent users of the wiki, a big picture can emerge more easily. As a teacher, Libby has found another way to achieve what history teacher Robert Bain described as the crucial tasks of the history teacher, to: '1. Externalize all the thinking in the classroom and 2. Create cultural supports for disciplinary thinking' (Bain, 2000: 335). With appropriate guidance and direction for students, this type of task can go beyond simple morale-boosting and knowledge accretion to involve 'a high degree of critical analysis... as students evaluate the ideas being co-constructed, make decisions regarding their accuracy and validity, and participate in a knowledge-building community' (Howland *et al.*, 2012: 138).

The positive outcomes of Libby Bond's work are supported by Russel Tarr, well known for his expertise and creativity in using many forms of e-learning (see www.activehistory.co.uk for a wide range of examples). He uses wikis for ongoing writing tasks:

> Another benefit is that students can see each others' work progressing, which tends to provide a spur to achievement. I also make a point of keeping the best examples of the previous year's studies available on the wiki as model examples for the students to use as guidance.
>
> (Tarr, 2011)

With many wikis you can start with a protected wiki visible only to invited users, but then make it public at the end of a project. This would make it much easier for you to manage; the completed work could then be used as an exemplar for another year, class or group as Tarr suggests, possibly with a link posted on your school's VLE (virtual learning environment). As Terry Haydn points out in Chapter 1 of this volume, he also adapts the wiki to 'sub-contract' strands of historical topics so that pupils work on different aspects of a topic and then share, discuss and collectively evaluate and assess their work.

Using wikis for historical enquiry online

A wiki itself can be used as a template with criteria given for resource selection, based for example, on an enquiry question. This example was used with PGCE students. It is based around an enquiry question very similar to many used in schools in England, which we then discuss and critique as a group. It models an approach to historical enquiry using a wiki, building in an opportunity to reflect on perennial issues, such as: what makes a good enquiry question? How do we teach students to think about usefulness as well as reliability? Can we model the researching, reading, writing and thinking processes central to enquiry? Although this activity was designed for adults on a PGCE course, the resources could be adapted for other topics and age groups. It is important to note that, as a spur to discussion, the activity includes references to National Curriculum levels encountered by student teachers on placement in English schools. The obligation to monitor the progress of students using school assessment practices can be challenging for beginning teachers, who may assume that levels capture progression in thinking about evidence in a straightforward way. The editing of the wiki pages makes explicit some of the evidential thinking required in a more nuanced way. See Figure 3.3.

The possible benefits of conducting an online enquiry, with a wiki page as the outcome, are as follows. The end product can be viewed as if it were a Wikipedia entry and wiki tools can be used, for example to look at the page history: who contributed to the page, and how did the story or account develop as different sources were used? The discussion or comment tabs can be used for other students or classes to comment on the outcome: does it show Cromwell as heroic or villainous or *something else entirely*?

Wikipedia says it is *not* democratic and seeks to achieve consensus instead through editing, not voting. Nevertheless readers are invited to rate pages, for trustworthiness, objectivity, completeness and written style (see http://en.wikipedia.org/wiki/Wikipedia:What_Wikipedia_is_not). See Figure 3.4.

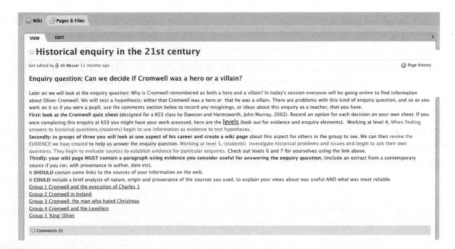

Figure 3.3 Using a wiki to explore an enquiry question

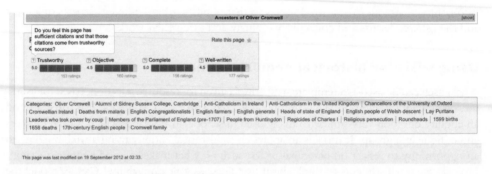

Figure 3.4 Evaluating the reliability and authority of online material

What would students make of the votes about the main Oliver Cromwell page regarding its trustworthiness, objectivity, completeness and written style (accessed on 16/1/2012)? You could use any or all of these criteria for peer assessment in an enquiry about Cromwell. If a group created a wiki page provided with the heading: *Cromwell and Christmas*, you could ask other students to make a judgement about the page: how trustworthy and objective is it? Is it a complete account and well written? They could add their ideas to the comments box or discussion tab.

It would work best if you could encourage students to discuss and debate what words such as objective and trustworthy mean in this context before they add their posts: and the discussion might take your students towards what Peter Lee calls historical literacy (Lee, 2011). Does trustworthy simply mean well supported by trustworthy citations as the Wikipedia rating suggests? This is beginning to sound like a circular argument, and counting sources is insufficient. Lee's historical literacy includes: 'A disposition to produce the best possible arguments for whatever stories we tell relative to our questions and presuppositions, appealing to the validity of stories and the truth of singular factual statements' (Lee, 2011: 65). As Chapman argues, based on the ideas of Allan Megill, claims made in interpretations differ, and 'explanatory claims… differ from descriptive claims and are validated in different ways' (Chapman, 2011: 103). Ros Ashby gives examples of how teachers might address these issues by asking students to examine the different kinds of thinking involved in testing hypotheses, simple factual statements and explanations (Ashby, 2011: 143–44). For Ashby: 'Teaching complex ideas in simple ways needs to replace the teaching of simple ideas in complex ways' (Ashby, 2011: 145). Asking students to create a wiki page, and peer assess these by first identifying the claims made, and then assessing them for evidence relevant to the claim, might offer a simple way into some advanced thinking. A singular factual statement might need one or two trusted sources in support, a hypothesis would need weightier evidence for or against, an explanation would require more powerful supporting evidence that could not easily be used to argue another way. In the Cromwell and Christmas example, students might decide that they can depend on suggestions that there were MPs willing to pass laws against celebrating Christmas, but that there is insufficiently strong evidence to support the claim that this was just the work of Cromwell, as is often claimed in popular accounts. It might also prepare them better for GCSE.

Wikis and critical reading: historical representations and debates about significance

In the GCSE course currently designed for 14–16 year olds in England by Edexcel, students are required to compare representations of history using criteria such as accuracy, comprehensiveness and objectivity. This takes students into exciting territory: historical accounts as interpretations of the past. If students tend to dismiss Wikipedia as always unreliable because 'user-generated', or alternatively authoritative for anything, they are less prepared than they could be. We need to ask them when they research online: what is the entry useful for? The answer might well relate to issues of significance and interpretation, rather than simply matters of fact.

Before referring briefly to other examples, it is instructive to return to Oliver Cromwell for a moment. For students who assume that history is only of interest to history teachers, the number of Wikipedia entries and other websites about Oliver Cromwell is remarkable. Many of the Wikipedia entries have multiple contributors, some pages edited on a daily basis. Editors include those reading academic work on Cromwell taking issue with others with those for whom Cromwell has cultural and political significance. A debate on the discussion tab about how an entry should start included the comment:

> I wasn't suggesting that an Irish view, per se, be first – rather his major legacy – what is [he] most notable for? What was the enduring effect of his life? You mention major impacts on the British makeup, however you accept that he was just part of such influences. His British legacy was blunted by the restoration. Whereas in Ireland his actions left permanent scars.
> (Irish Wikipedian, 13:45, 15 February 2011)

An editor's response is:

> It's too Hiberno-centric to say that that's Cromwell's lasting legacy – I know it is in Ireland… but in mainland Great Britain… he's most remembered for his role in the Civil War and contributions to the development of constitutional monarchy and limiting the role of the King.
> (Wikipedian who we can infer is likely to be English, 07:25, 16 February 2011)

This makes the point very neatly that significance, like reliability, is not a fixed property of a source of information (Counsell, 2004). Academic historians and Wikipedians alike agree that Cromwell is significant. What the discussion tab reveals to our students is that the nature of his significance is a matter for debate, and that the positions we adopt in this debate depend not only on evidence, but also on who we are, who we are writing for, and when we are writing.

Another fascinating way to use Wikipedia is to compare entries on controversial topics, for example discussing the sensitivities around the images used and titles chosen by academic historians, documentary makers or student accounts themselves. Laffin's (2009) ideas (inspired in part by Roy Rosenzweig, 2006) about using the editing history tab for this purpose will be examined shortly in the context of the Armenian genocide. Now that Google Translate is developing so fast, it is temptingly easy to compare the titles of entries such as Kristallnacht, rendered as Night of Broken Glass (Polish page, late 2011), and November Pogrom (German page, same date). If you are concerned about depending on an unreliable translator, consider what your students could learn by comparing entries on the death camp Treblinka by simply comparing the images, length of text, types of references provided in the Polish, German and Hebrew entries. You could look at Spanish, Danish and German accounts of the Falklands War, or the Simple English version of the Partition of India. What makes these accounts different? Wikipedian policy is designed to ensure that all editing is done from: 'a neutral point of view... representing fairly, proportionately, and as far as possible without bias, all significant views that have been published by reliable sources' (Wikipedia, accessed December 2011). Is neutrality possible? As Laffin has argued, it may not be desirable as it leads to dull writing. A comparison of entries for caste system in India, Dalit and Harijan might suggest that neutrality might not just be dull but also a misplaced objective. Would your students be impressed with accounts that did not mention discrimination and prejudice (unlike the well-referenced Dalit entry that does)? Working with wikis in these ways can be an important part of moving pupils forward from the idea of 'bias', to that of 'position'.

A current example of a Wikipedia page undergoing daily development as a result of public debate about a figure of historical significance is the entry for Alan Turing. The year 2012 is a hundred years from Turing's birth (www.mathcomp.leeds.ac.uk/turing2012/give-page.php?13), with events occurring throughout the year celebrating his life and work as a mathematician, cryptographer and all-purpose hero for those interested in the history of computing. It is interesting to note that in February 2012 the French Wikipedia entry concludes its account with a section headed: '*Persécution et mort*'. The equivalent English heading is: 'Conviction for indecency'; the Simple English version offers a remarkably different and affirming interpretation with the heading 'private life' and a presentist view of the conviction issue. Despite a well-publicised public campaign to have the conviction overturned, it still stands (http://en.wikipedia.org/wiki/Alan_Turing) at the time of writing. The Wikipedia entry has in February 2012, however, 423 people watching edits, up five from January 2012 when there were 418. The debate in the media appears to be fuelling changes in assessments of Turing's life, death and work on Wikipedia. The value of watching this type of activity for students in school is that they can see a form of public history in the making, happening online. There are historical debates about Turning's conviction; Leavitt is an example of a biographer who argues that there was injustice in the form of a conviction for indecency when Turing had gone to the police to report a burglary: 'instead of arresting the thief, they arrested his victim' (Leavitt, 2006: 168). It could be worthwhile asking older students to create their own wiki entry about Turing. Would you ask them to do this during Lesbian Gay Bisexual Trans History month (http://lgbthistorymonth.org.uk/about/lgbt-history-month)?

Another step would be to apply what has been discussed to the creation of student wiki pages on a selected topic relevant to the students and their personal histories. What title will they use? What images will they select, and why? Will you ask them to edit a page that already exists on Wikipedia (possibly pasted into a school wiki) OR an academic text that you want them to challenge? As Doug Belshaw has argued, digital literacy, however it is defined, is subjective; needing to be created and developed rather than delivered (Belshaw, 2012: http://dougbelshaw.com/ebooks/digilit). For further ideas about teaching significance using your own wiki, the ideas of Brown and Woodcock (2009) in *Teaching History* are particularly relevant. The decision-making involved would be non-trivial: as Rosenzweig argued in relation to Wikipedia, 'It is considerably easier to craft a policy about "verifiability" or even "neutrality" than about "historical significance" (Rosenzweig, 2006). It is also worth remembering at this point how Jon Simkin's remarkable website for school students began.

Jon Simkin has argued persuasively that above all we must find ways to enable our students to believe that they too can be historians and create historical content:

> I never liked history until I became a historian. That might seem a strange thing to say but I believe this view is held by hundreds of thousands of people... The people who email me with the claim that they now love history are invariably historians. Not in the sense that they earn a living from writing or teaching about history... In all cases, this research is linked to their own lives... It has enabled anyone with access to the internet to become involved in historical research. Therefore, what I am particularly interested in is providing materials that will encourage pupils to become historians.
>
> (Simkin, 2005)

Wiki-based sites for budding historians provide a place where the research into the motivating topic (family, football, war, the local area, or whatever it might be) can be displayed, and an understanding of the relevance of history can be developed. Above all:

> [I]t is... important that history teachers give some thought to pupils' understanding of *why* they do history at school. It is possible that teachers may be making assumptions about pupils' grasp of the purposes and benefits of studying the past, and that there is a need to be more explicit about these, 'feeding in' comment, quotations and information about why history is helpful, important and relevant to their lives outside and after school... Curriculum time is precious at Key Stage 3...[this can] make all the difference between desultory compliance on the part of pupils, and wholehearted and enthusiastic commitment to wanting to do history, to do well in it, and to do it for as long as possible.
>
> (Harris and Haydn, 2008: 48)

Using wikis to create critical readers: historical interpretation

In an excellent chapter in her recent book about A Level History teaching (with 16–19 year olds), Diana Laffin explores a number of ways in which to use Wikipedia and wiki tools to develop student thinking, reading and writing. She takes the view that many students find Wikipedia reassuring because it tries to be neutral, and asks her students to examine the idea of neutrality first by examining a contentious issue to uncover aspects of the topic that are more contentious (revealed through the editing history) than others. Having established that even an apparently neutral source 'varies in its supposed objectivity' (Laffin, 2009: 62), her students are now better prepared for a wiki creation task designed to create a reference guide to Nazi society, completed in a group. It is significant that Laffin argues strongly for 'peer editing and checking to develop group ownership'(Laffin, 2009: 62), as this produces a powerful learning experience, drawing on the arguments of Cohen about group work: 'It is of critical importance to let them make decisions on their own. They even need to make mistakes on their own' (Cohen, 1994: 107). Using wikis for collaborative writing enables mistakes to be made, for critical mistakes to be addressed through editing, and encourages students to pay attention to the writing of others, and gives them an audience for their own writing. By asking them to begin by producing wiki pages that are 'on the bottom end of the contentiousness scale' (Laffin, 2009: 62) there is a better chance that students will have the confidence to participate.

She then develops their use of wikis in a very powerful way, drawing on other work by Nick Dennis and Doug Belshaw, and the arguments of Rosenzweig: 'Although Wikipedia as a *product* is problematic as a sole source of information, the *process* of creating Wikipedia fosters an appreciation of the very skills that historians try to teach' (Rosenzweig, 2006: 25). Students need to understand that history is rewritten for many reasons, not least because the archives accessed by historians change over time. Students use selected sources from historians of Nazi society writing from 1945–65 to create a base wiki page about the role of fear in Nazi society. This page is then edited by later groups; with group 2 using selected historians of everyday life (1966–89), and group 3 using historians in the 1990s able to draw on new archives opened after the fall of the Berlin Wall in 1989. By looking back at the editing history, it becomes clear how the narrative changes as the use of accounts by historians from different times, places and perspectives alter the wiki entry. Laffin argues that her students are now better prepared to evaluate historical interpretations. Accounts do not change simply as a result of 'academic warfare' (Laffin, 2009: 69). Laffin has used wiki editing to make concrete the abstract idea, that the past and history – as it is written – are two separate things.

Another teacher, Annabelle Dobson from the Moat School in Leicester, adapted Laffin's wiki lesson sequence with a GCSE class. In this sequence, the historical accounts from three different eras were again used as part of preparation for a GCSE essay on Nazi methods of control. Inspired by Laffin's work to try an alternative to the teacher-led story by PowerPoint approach, Annabelle enabled her students to see that there were a number of methods of control, that historians have argued over time about which were most significant, and that they can create their own response to the issues by thinking it through using the wiki task as a scaffold. Annabelle argued that: 'The idea of the wiki is interesting, [because] the editing feature of a wiki not only allows students to reflect on the different interpretations they read but also their own interpretations' (post to MA discussion forum, 2011). This reflection has the potential to enable students to see that history is an argument (Arnold, 2000).

Using wikis to develop writing in history: the importance of argument

If wikis can be used to develop critical reading, they can also have value in scaffolding critical writing. Examples at A level will be examined here but also issues relevant to younger and less able students. Libby Bond from Lampton argued that for her A level students:

> Part of the challenge for me is for students to engage with historians..., they can evaluate historians' arguments, they can weigh into this conversation, interpretation as a conversation, having a voice and... feeling empowered to have a voice... I think that any activity that turns having a voice, and evaluating historians into having a bit of fun can only be a good thing... it breaks the illusion that the historian is infallible... and creates the idea that [history is] is a discourse, a dialogue...

This is significant because as soon as her students see a published text, even if it is Wikipedia it 'seems authoritative to them' and even the writing of other students can 'freak them out'. She wants them to believe that they are able to 'see through the academic language' so that they can 'break down the arguments': 'The last thing I want is for students from Lampton to go off to university feeling de-skilled'. Some universities are themselves using wikis for similar purposes with undergraduates: 'Students reported that they were able to develop their critical thinking skills through shared spaces... [a student said]... looking at other people's opinions and findings has helped me to question what's in front of me' (Wheeler *et al.*, 2008: 993).

One possible route to greater confidence that could be pursued with students from backgrounds where English or academic language may be used with limited confidence, is to use wiki pages for textual analysis based on the ideas explored by Arthur Chapman (2011) in *Teaching History*, and applied by Helen Hedges in work with The National Archives at Kew (www.nationalarchives.gov.uk/education/cpd/india-1857.htm).

One of Chapman's aims in creating an historical dartboard was to: 'help students evaluate the claims contained in differing interpretations of past action' (Chapman, 2011: 33). Historical claims may be based on the actions of people in the past, but as we move into an examination of their beliefs and aims (the bull's eye), 'interpretive controversies arise' (Chapman 2011). A student could be asked to examine an extract from an interpretation of the past pasted into a wiki page and highlight the claims that have been made. In discussion with another student, the status or 'strength' of the claim – from certainty to remote possibility – could be examined. If the claim made by the historian was very strong and certain – brooking no other possible alternative interpretation, for example – the students could then examine the evidence presented: is it compelling? If it is not, they could be asked to edit the page with further evidence, because 'weighty claims will need thick legs' (Chapman, 2011: 35). If further evidence cannot be established with the sources available, then the claim can be attacked: the wiki edit would then be to modify the claim. In this way students would be getting practice in evaluating claims and learning how to edit an account so that the claims are supported by appropriate evidence, while gaining expertise in using the sophisticated nuances of language relating to 'claims' and 'evidence' that may be helpful when undertaking external examinations.

As Rachel Foster has argued, in the writing of a professional historian, such as Daniel Goldhagen or Christopher Browning, 'The intensity and immediacy of the prose inescapably draws the reader into the argument' with which we want students to engage (Foster, 2011: 206). In Foster's example, Browning's account of a Police Battalion action is contrasted with Goldhagen's. The problem is that the reader can be hypnotised or even overawed by the prose, unless they are encouraged to think about how it works. We want them to be motivated by powerful writing but not paralysed by it, as Libby Bond's students were before their wiki experiments. Foster's argument that students are helped to think historically by activities such as 'reading for different purposes, extracting... claims and evidence... modelling their writing on the style of another writer' (Foster, 2011: 210) seems relevant here.

Using wiki editing to experiment with Foster's ideas would be another interesting way to develop the writing of students if invited to analyse the persuasive language used by one author and rewriting it in the style of another.

The research of Caroline Coffin suggests that to develop essay-writing skills across the age range 11–18, we need to think about genres specific to history rather than depending upon generic literacy strategies. She identifies a range of genres from the autobiographical recount (a first-person narrative) to explaining and arguing genres needed for GCSE and A Level essays of the 16–18 age range. This research suggests that students need to be presented with examples of writing in the chosen genre and focus on its grammatical features. She gives nominalisation as one example when thinking about younger students: 'When writing about history, *action words* often become *things* or events' (Coffin, 2006: 425). Her example is: 'The European settlers *arrived* [verb] in 1788. Two years after *their arrival* [nominalisation], conflict between blacks and whites began' (Coffin, 2006). For those students who find reading textbooks a struggle it isn't just the reading age that is an issue. Nominalisation has the effect, for weaker readers, of *hiding* those responsible for a development.

Coffin gives a cloze exercise as a way of showing students how nominalisation works; a wiki version of this activity could work in two ways. A teacher could place a text with nominalisations included and ask students to edit it in pairs into a simpler text, with the first example completed *using wiki editing*, so students could track back through the page history and see how the changes were made. In the second instance, the teacher could take a simple paragraph and ask students to edit it with nominalisations added. Coffin argues that:

> [W]hereas initially many teachers were concerned that valuable time needed for teaching content would be lost, there was an increased recognition, as the project developed, that an attention to language and writing is integral to learning and attaining the objectives of the history curriculum.
>
> (Coffin, 2006: 426)

Coffin makes clear that explaining genres in history requires the use of these kinds of grammatical features in essays designed to explain causes and evaluate developments. She replaces the sentence '(a) Australia *was involved* in the Second World War for 6 years and *so* things *changed* economically, politically and socially' with '(b) The *reason* for economic, political and social *changes* was Australia's 6 years of *involvement* in the Second World War' (Coffin, 2006: 421). She explains that sentence (b) 'gives greater emphasis to the causal dimension of past events' (2006: 421), and this is exactly what we need to see in the writing of our students. As a history teacher you may often see sentences like (a) in your students' writing, and you may have found yourself writing 'narrative' in the margin. Until now, writing frames have been popular as a solution, but they are no panacea (Evans and Pate, 2007). Coffin's work suggests that we now have another strategy: using wiki to turn writing like an historian into process they can see *developing on screen*.

Coffin also noticed that students want to tell stories in essays written in chronological order. As soon as we ask them to write essays such as 'Why did William win the Battle of Hastings?' we expect them to be able to privilege reasons rather than events as a focus for each paragraph. In Coffin's analysis they have gone from recounts (still in time order) to explaining genres, possibly too soon. One possible way to use a wiki would be to take examples from past students' work written in chronological order, and use wiki editing to show how the same key events become the supporting details in a PEEL (point, example, evidence and link) structure. Arguing genres also requires the use of tentative and evaluative language such as 'might, seemed, perhaps' to answer questions such as: 'To what extent was the First World War an unnecessary and tragic conflict?' and 'Why do some historians agree with this judgement?' Once again students could be invited to edit a weaker answer and to improve it using more appropriate vocabulary, possibly drawing on the work of James Woodcock (2005).

It could be that you have one class working on an essay or enquiry, creating content in pairs for homework; another class might be the audience for the pages they make and involved as commentators on the results. You could include a formative assessment task, where students create pages, receive peer (or teacher) feedback and edit the pages further in the light of the advice given. Research has indicated that 'Students often communicated complex ideas in a language that was different from... the teacher... but appeared to be more easily assimilated' (Black, 2003: 77). In addition, this approach is potentially powerful as research also suggests that peer assessment 'may even be a prior requirement for self assessment' (Black, 2003: 50), and that self assessment (based on the ideas of Sadler, 1989) 'is essential to learning' (Black, 2003: 49). The point to note here is that an edited Word document showing tracked changes can look less than impressive; when changes are accepted the journey taken by the writer is lost. The risk is that the writer fails to internalise the lessons learned through the editing process. In an updated wiki the 'final' page could look impressive but the editing history would still show the progress made and the journey taken. Students could use the editing history, see a chronological narrative turned into an explanation (or even vice versa). 'By looking at superlative student work, a teacher can use the open, editable format of wiki pages to organise further classroom discussions and activities' (Hendron, 2008: 185). If we believe in history for all (Ofsted, 2011) as Mike Maddison says we should, then we need to pay greater attention to the specific literacy burdens imposed by writing in historical genres, and Coffin's research shows us a way forward.

Using wiki in schools: conclusions and some important caveats

You may already be able to design web-based activities using an online learning environment in your school, but it is rare for you to have the greater degree of control offered by using a wiki. This is a responsibility and should be taken very seriously. You must make sure your wiki meets your school's cyber-safety requirements, and you could consider setting ground rules, perhaps based on those outlined by Andrew Church on his wiki:

The Digital Citizen will follow six tenets of citizenship.
1 Respect yourself
2 Protect yourself
3 Respect others
4 Protect others
5 Respect intellectual property
6 Protect intellectual property

(Church, http://edorigami.wikispaces.com/The+Digital+Citizen, accessed 20/1/2012)

There is no doubt that 'One of the most difficult roads to navigate in the Read/Write Web is how to balance the safety of the child with the benefits that come with students taking ownership of the work they publish online' (Richardson, 2010: 14). The solution is to consider carefully 'ways to set the size and shape of the intended audience' (ibid.). Nevertheless,

> an authentic activity requires a genuine audience – either of the producers themselves or a wider public audience... For students to care... [about the wiki editing they did] would require them to perceive it as an authentic, relevant and worthwhile practice.
>
> (Grant, 2006)

The point of using wikis is to give writers in a history classroom an audience that includes the teacher, but also peers, and possibly the wider community within the school or on the web. Enabling your students to write for a wider audience safely means that you will also need to learn how to use features alerting you to changes, and you will need to model digital professionalism. It will be important to know, and to consider how to include students who do not have unlimited access to the web at home, or who prefer to work in the real and not virtual worlds, as an informed choice or perhaps owing to specific access issues. Younger or less confident students new to using wikis might also be intimidated by their peers, reluctant to see their work changed and afraid of editing the work of others (Grant, 2006). In this situation, 'The teacher may also be able to play a role by modelling a collaborative process through participating in the students' wikis as an equal, although more experienced, group member' (Grant, 2006). This means, in my view, that although you are encouraging collaborative creativity (Miell and Littleton, 2004) in your students, they still need your guidance, in terms of social interaction, just as they might face to face. Others have argued that care needs to be taken with this, however: 'Teachers who impose a lot of right and wrong... can undermine the effectiveness of the tool' (Richardson, 2010: 61). A useful site to enable you to consider research into issues of interplay between social and teacher presence is http://communitiesofinquiry.com/model.

If you are working with older students who already have considerable social and academic skills that they could share online, you might also enjoy looking at the work of Etienne Wenger's ideas about communities of practice: www.ewenger.com/theory. Another factor to consider is the need for, and benefits of, discussion around wiki creation. My experience, echoed by others (Foley and Chang, 2006; Zenios and Holmes, 2010), is that the use of a discussion forum, either synchronous or asynchronous, or some time set aside for classroom discussion, alongside the wiki, is necessary for communities of practice to develop. So, in a crowded timetable dominated by curriculum coverage, is a wiki worth your time? Investment in wikis, despite the 'quick' label, brings more benefits for teachers in the long term, for example when working with older students pursuing independent projects. Wheaton argued that:

> It made the job of supervising multiple projects enormously easier. I could track progress, make edits and suggestions and approve final documents all from a single interface. I could operate on my time schedule while the student analysts operated on theirs. I know I turned documents around to students much more quickly and lost track of where I was with certain documents much less frequently as a result of using the wiki.
>
> (Wheaton, date unknown)

For Wheaton, a wiki is not about being lost in cyberspace, but about being in a room:

At some point, remarkably early in the process, at both the individual and the group level, this shared team space has obviously proven its worth. It's where the action is. If you want the latest, you go to the room. If you want to know if someone already has the answer to a question of fact, you go to the room. If you want some help with a particularly tricky analytic method, you go to the room... Once something is put in the room, no one else has to go find it. It is all there.

(Wheaton, date unknown)

Probably the best general introduction to all these issues is Will Richardson's book *Blogs, Wikis and Podcasts and Other Powerful Web Tools*, so we will give him the last word:

Wikipedia is the poster child for the collaborative construction of knowledge... Every day thousands of people... engage in the purposeful work of negotiating and creating truth... The extent to which this happens... is truly inspiring... As we move forward toward a world where everyone has access to ideas and where collaboration is the expectation... wikis can go a long way toward teaching our students some very useful skills for the future.

(Richardson, 2010: 57–9)

References

Arnold, J. (2000) *History: A very short introduction*, Oxford: Oxford University Press.

Ashby, R. (2011) 'Understanding historical evidence: teaching and learning challenges', in I. Davies (ed.), *Debates in History Teaching*, 1st edition, Oxon: Routledge, pp. 137–47.

Ashby, R., Lee, P. and Shemilt, D. (2005) 'Putting principles into practice: teaching and planning', in S. Donovan and D. Bransford (eds) *How Students Learn: History in the classroom*, Washington DC: National Research Council, pp. 79–178.

Bain, R.B. (2000) 'Into the breach: using research and theory to shape history instruction', in P. Stearns, P.C. Seixas and S.S. Wineburg (eds) *Knowing, Teaching and Learning History*, New York and London: NYUP, pp. 331–52.

Belshaw, D. (2012) *The Essential Elements of Digital Literacy*, online at http://dougbelshaw. com/ebooks/digilit.

Black, P.J. (2003) *Assessment for Learning: Putting it into practice*, Maidenhead: Open University Press.

Brown, G. and Woodcock, J. (2009) 'Relevant, rigorous and revisited: using local history to make meaning of historical significance', *Teaching History*, 134: 4–11.

Carrington, V., Robinson, M. and United Kingdom Literacy Association (2009) *Digital Literacies: Social learning and classroom practices*, Los Angeles, CA: Sage.

Chapman, A. (2011) 'Time's arrows? Using a dartboard scaffold to understand historical action', *Teaching History*, 143: 32–8.

Chapman, A. and Facey, J. (2009) 'Documentaries, causal linking and hyper-linking for AS students', in H. Cooper and C. Arthur (eds) *Constructing History 11–19*, London: Sage, pp. 88–119.

Chapman, A. and Hibbert, B. (2009) 'Advancing history post 16: e-learning, collaboration and assessment', in H. Cooper and A. Chapman (eds) *Constructing History 11–19*, London: Sage, pp. 120–48.

Church, A. (2012) *The Digital Citizen*, online at http://edorigami.wikispaces.com/ The+Digital+Citizen.

Coffin, C. (2006) 'Learning the language of school history: the role of linguistics in mapping the writing demands of the secondary school curriculum', *Journal of Curriculum Studies*, 38 (4): 413–29.

Cohen, E.G. (1994) *Designing Groupwork: Strategies for the heterogeneous classroom*, 2nd edition, New York: Teachers College, Columbia University.

Cooper, H. and Chapman, A. (2009) *Constructing History 11–19*, Los Angeles, CA and London: Sage.

Counsell, C. (2003) 'The forgotten games kit', in T. Haydn and C. Counsell (eds) *History, ICT and Learning in the Secondary School*, London: Routledge Falmer, pp. 52–108.

Counsell, C. (2004) 'Looking through a Josephine-Butler-shaped window: focusing pupils' thinking on historical significance', *Teaching History*, 114: 30–6.

De Groot, J. (2009) *Consuming History: Historians and heritage in contemporary popular culture*, London: Routledge.

Dougherty, J. and Nawrotzki, K. (eds) (2011) *Writing History in the Digital Age*, Web-book edition, Trinity College, CT: University of Michigan Press, online at http://WritingHistory. Trincoll.Edu.

Evans, J. and Pate, G. (2007) 'Does scaffolding make them fall?', *Teaching History*, 128 pp. 18–28.

Foley, B. and Chang, T. (2006) *Wiki as a professional development tool*. Paper presented at the American Education Research Association annual meeting, April 10 2006 in session "Technology and Teacher Learning".

Foster, R. (2011) 'Using academic history in the classroom', in I. Davies (ed.) *Debates in History Teaching*, 1st edition, London: Routledge, pp. 199–211.

Garrison, D.R., Anderson, T. and Archer, W. (n.d.) *Communities of Inquiry Model*, online at http://communitiesofinquiry.com/model, accessed 20 August 2012.

Grant, L. (2006) Using Wikis in schools: A case study, Retrieved June 28, 2006, from http://futurelab.org.uk/download/pdfs/research/disc_papers/Wikis_in_Schools.pdf, accessed 28 June 2006.

Harris, R. and Haydn, T. (2008) 'Children's ideas about school history and why they matter', *Teaching History*, 132: 40–9.

Haydn, T. (2003) 'What do they do with the information? Working towards genuine interactivity with History and ICT', in T. Haydn and C. Counsell (eds) *History, ICT and Learning in the Secondary School*, London: Routledge Falmer, pp. 192–224.

Hendron, J.G. (2008) *RSS for Educators: Blogs, newsfeeds, podcasts, and wikis in the classroom*, 1st edition, Washington, DC: International Society for Technology in Education.

Howland, J.L., Jonassen, D.H. and Marra, R.M. (2012) *Meaningful Learning with Technology*, 4th edition, Boston, MA: Pearson.

Jenkins, H. (2009) *Confronting the Challenges of Participatory Culture: Media education for the 21st century*, Cambridge, MA: The MIT Press. *The John D. and Catherine T. MacArthur Foundation Reports on Digital Media and Learning*.

Laffin, D. (2009) *Better Lessons in A Level History (History in Practice)*, London: Hodder Education.

Laurillard, D. (2002) *Rethinking University Teaching: A conversational framework for the effective use of learning technologies*, 2nd edition, London: RoutledgeFalmer.

Leavitt, D. (2006) *The Man Who Knew Too Much : Alan Turing and the invention of the computer*, The Great Discoveries Series, London: Weidenfeld & Nicolson.

Lee, P. (2011) 'Historical literacy', in I. Davies (ed.), *Debates in History Teaching*, 1st edition, Oxon: Routledge, pp. 63–72.

Malaga, R.A. (ed.) (2009) *Ninth Annual IBER & TLC Conference Proceedings 2009, Choosing A Wiki Platform for Student Projects – Lessons Learned*, 1–5.

Megill, A. (2007) *Historical Knowledge, Historical Error: A Contemporary Guide to Practice*, Chicago, University of Chicago Press.

Miell, D. and Littleton, K. (2004) *Collaborative Creativity: Contemporary perspectives*, London: Free Association Books.

Moore, R. (2000) 'Using the internet to teach about interpretations in years 9 and 12', *Teaching History*, 101: 35–5.

Ofsted (2011) *History for All*, London, Ofsted, online at http://www.ofsted.gov.uk/resources/history-for-all, accessed 20 August 2012.

Richardson, W. (2010) *Blogs, Wikis, Podcasts, and Other Powerful Web Tools for Classrooms*, 3rd edition, Thousand Oaks, CA and London: Corwin; SAGE distributor.

Rosenzweig, R. (2006) 'Can history be open source? Wikipedia and the future of the past', *The Journal of American History*, 93 (1): 117–46.

Sadler, D.R. (1989) 'Formative assessment and the design of instructional systems', *Instructional Science*, 18: 119–24.

Shemilt, D. (2009) 'Drinking an ocean and pissing a cupful: how adolescents make sense of history' in L. Symcox and A. Wilschut (eds) *National History Standards: The problem of the canon and the future of teaching history*, Charlotte, NC: Information Age Publishing, pp. 141–210.

Simkin, J. (2005) Online at http://educationforum.ipbhost.com/index.php?showtopic=3249.

Tarr, R. (2011) *Using Wikis in the History Classroom*, online at www.hoddereducation.co.uk/Schools/Nests/Hodder_History_Subject_Nest/nest_blog_history/History_Blog_history/January-2011_history/Using-Wikis-in-the-History-Classroom.aspx.

Walker, S., Jameson, J. and Ryan, M. (2010) 'Skills and strategies for e-learning in a participatory culture', in R. Sharpe, H. Beetham and S. de Freitas (eds), *Rethinking Learning for a Digital Age*, New York and London: Routledge, pp. 212–24.

Wenger, E. (n.d.) *Communities of Practice*, online at www.ewenger.com/theory, accessed 28 August 2012.

Wheaton, K.J. (n.d.) *A Wiki is Like A Room... and Other Lessons Learned from 15 Wiki-Based, Open Source, Intelligence Analysis Projects*, online at www.scribd.com/kwheaton/d/2340879-A-Wiki-Is-Like-A-Room.

Wheeler, S., Yeomans, P. and Wheeler, D. (2008) 'The good, the bad and the wiki: evaluating student-generated content for collaborative learning', *British Journal of Educational Technology*, 39 (6): 987–95.

Woodcock, J. (2005) 'Does the linguistic release the conceptual? Helping Year 10 to improve their causal reasoning', *Teaching History*, 119: 5–10.

Zenios, M. and Holmes, B. (eds) (2010) *Proceedings of the 7th International Conference on Networked Learning*, edited by L. Dirckinck-Holmfeld , V. Hodgson, C. Jones, M. De Laat, D. McConnell and T. Ryberg, *Knowledge Creation in Networked Learning: Combined tools and affordances*, pp. 471–9.

Chapter 4

Using discussion forums to support historical learning

Arthur Chapman

Introduction

This chapter begins by defining and explaining discussion forums. Forms of discussion are then identified and the nature and importance of argument and of historical argument are discussed. Examples of discussion forum use in school history are explored and some general principles of effective discussion forum use are identified. The chapter draws on the author's experiences of working with discussion forums in history post-16, and on published case studies of the use of discussion boards in history across the 11–19 age range.

Discussion forums

A 'discussion forum' is a form of 'computer mediated communication' (CMC) through which participants can 'post' written messages, visible to other participants enrolled in the forum, and 'reply' to messages 'posted' by other participants in the forum (Mercer, 2000: 121–9). A discussion forum is, therefore, at least potentially, a medium for the 'exchange' of ideas.

Posts can form 'threads' or stand alone. A sequence of posts arises when an initial post is 'replied' to, this 'reply' is 'replied' to, and so on, and a 'thread' of linked posts is created, with the replies 'nested' under each other in order of posting. A series of 'unthreaded' posts arises when a number of posts are made, but when each post stands alone and is potentially the beginning of a new 'thread' but is not itself 'threaded' to any post that came before.

Messages posted to forums are, typically, archived and remain posted to the forum unless and until the forum is closed down and/or posts are deleted by the person or persons who have been empowered to 'manage' posts to the forum.[1] A discussion forum, therefore, has a 'history' and it is possible to track back through posts and threads, for a subsequent post by one participant to quote an earlier post by another participant, for a participant to refer back to and revise what they have said in an earlier post when making a new post, and so on.

CMC can be 'synchronous' (live and real time) or 'asynchronous' (Hrastinski, 2008). Discussion forums are, typically although not necessarily, 'asynchronous', which is to say that participants in discussion forum exchanges make and read posts at different times. Discussion forums are, therefore, flexible tools: students can be asked to post to them outside class at their own convenience within a particular time frame (say 'this week') and it is not uncommon to find students posting at all times of the day and night. A discussion forum can also be run synchronously at a particular time: for example, a discussion can be scheduled in a lesson or in part of a lesson or students can be asked to make their posts at a particular time outside class. Discussion forums can be run over an extended period of time (for example, three weeks) during which participants post asynchronously, they can be run in a defined window (for example, between 3pm and 4pm on a given day) during which participants post synchronously, or they can combine both approaches.

Discussion forums, of course, have to have a purpose – topics or questions to discuss. A forum as a whole can be organised in answer to a particular question or topic and individual posts and threads can be organised under sub-questions or topics. Discussions can also, and literally, have some thing or things to discuss: written texts, film and audio clips and/ or images can be embedded in the site that hosts the discussion or be hyperlinked from or attached to individual posts in the discussion.

Discussion forums are very easy to set up, technically speaking: discussion board functionality is present in most of the VLE platforms (such as Fronter or Moodle) used in schools and colleges and web-based and password protected platforms through which discussions can be set up are readily and, often, freely available online.[2] Innovative work designing bespoke educational discussion environments has also resulted in the development of 'discussion games' software that aims to scaffold the development of students' grasp of argument.[3]

Discussion forums are also easy to set up pedagogically; however, as the remainder of this chapter will show, making discussions work dialogically and as discussions, rather than disputes, monologues or exercises in mutual affirmation, requires careful pedagogic thought and preparation.

Forms of discussion: disputes, cumulative talk and exploratory argument

> The online discussion worked best where prior classwork had focused on developing argument.
>
> (Martin, 2008: 33)

Discussion forums exist, of course, to facilitate the exchange of ideas. A discussion forum and engaged participants are not, however, sufficient conditions for discussion, since participants may post monologically and simply state their individual thoughts without engaging with or responding to other participants' posts: a series of unrelated claims is not a discussion and if boards are to be dialogical rather than monological, the majority of posts must comment on other posts in the forum.[4]

Discussion forum exchanges can fruitfully be understood in terms of generic types of conversational exchange. Mercer (2000: 97–8) distinguishes between:

- 'disputational talk', in which participants assert (and re-assert) their own ideas and do not seriously engage with each other's positions;
- 'cumulative talk... in which speakers build on each other's contributions, add information... and in a mutually supportive, uncritical way construct together a body of shared knowledge and understanding'; and
- 'exploratory talk... in which partners engage critically but constructively with each other's ideas', adduce 'information' and offer clear and reasoned arguments and counter-arguments, in order to progress and develop new understandings.

Mercer's definitions resonate with both popular culture and classroom experience: in every day terms 'argument' is typically understood as verbal, and often physical, 'dispute' or as a pantomime exchange of assertion and denial ('oh yes she did'/'oh no she didn't') and students often tend towards cumulative talk when we ask them to argue, perhaps understanding it as the only alternative to dispute and/or because it is easier to affirm and support than to counter-argue and to challenge.[5] Mercer's 'exploratory talk' resonates for another reason: it involves the kind of talk – argument – that we most want to encourage as history teachers (Coffin, 2006).

Argument

Learning to argue and to understand argument are fundamental to learning history since history is constructed by reasoning about the meanings of the traces of the past that exist in the present: we know what we know about the past through the 'shaky inferential construction' of historical argument (Megill, 2007: 214). Empirical claims contained or advanced in historical texts are the result of argument, even if some of them come, over time, to be treated as givens: 'established facts' have that status precisely because they have been established as credible propositions about the past to the satisfaction of communities of historians through historical argument and debate. Complex structures of interpretation are built in analogous ways, through reasoning about the meanings of 'established' facts that result in higher order claims that characterise, explain, or evaluate those facts. Historical interpretations come to be established, again, through disciplined debate in historical communities of practice (Toulmin, 1972; Goldstein, 1976; McCullagh, 1984; Megill, 2007) and historical knowledge progresses through argument within the historical community about the claims about the past and/or the claims about how we should make sense of facts about the past that are advanced by individual historians or by groups of historians.[6]

Historians are, in Megill's striking analogy, like land reclaimers on the Zuider Zee, who stand on previously reclaimed land (established claims about the past) and aim to make more terra firma (new claims), through arguments that aim to drain and damn the sea of historical ignorance, but who perpetually face the possibility that the land on which they stand may disappear beneath the waves once again as historical research, argument and interpretation develop and change (Megill, 2007: 99).

A key aim of history education is to develop students' 'historical thinking' (Lévesque, 2008). Developing historical thinking involves helping students learn to make and sustain claims about the past through enquiry (interrogating the record of the past) and inference (reasoning about the meaning/s of the record of the past). Developing historical thinking also involves helping students learn how to evaluate and assess historical reasoning by, among other things, exploring and evaluating the claims that others have made.[7]

Discussions, in class or online, can, of course, fail and become disputes or bland mutually supporting 'cumulative talk' rather than arguments that test or develop claims. Discussion boards can, however, serve as very effective tools for scaffolding understandings of historical argument as a logical process and also as a form of interpersonal interaction focused on building or testing knowledge claims. The remainder of this chapter will explore how discussions can be organised so as to promote argument and the understanding of argument.[8]

Scaffolding argument: questions, moves and roles

To be effective, discussion requires particular types of question or topic for discussion – for an exchange of ideas to occur there must be something about which it is possible to argue in a meaningful way. Questions need, therefore, to be 'authentic questions... for which the teacher has not prespecified or implied a particular answer' (Alexander, 2008a: 15).[9] Table 4.1 contains examples of potentially 'authentic' questions, with scope for genuine debate and disagreement, deployed in successful discussion boards across the secondary age range.

Table 4.1 Examples of discussion forum questions

Year group	Conceptual focus	Question
Year 7 (11–12 years)	Causal explanation	Why was there conflict between Christians and Muslims in the Middle Ages? (Snape and Allen, 2008: 46)
Year 9 (13–14 years)	Causal explanation	The most important reason why the Nazis came to power in 1933 was that they had Hitler as a leader. Do you agree? (Martin et al., 2007: 32)
	Historical significance	Who are the most important individuals in history that we should know about? (Martin, 2008: 32)
Year 10 (14–15 years)	Causal explanation	How far was Custer responsible for the defeat of the Seventh Cavalry at the Battle of the Little Bighorn? (Martin, 2008: 32)
	Historical significance	Which period of time was the worst one in which to have a sore throat and a headache? (Moorhouse, 2006: 31)
AS and A2 (16–19 years)	Historical Interpretations	How far do you agree with Philip Morgan that Mussolini established a creeping dictatorship? (Thompson and Cole, 2003: 42)
	Evidence	Assume that you are historians beginning to research the Ranters and that you have only this collection of sources available to you at this stage. What initial conclusions is it reasonable to come to about the Ranters solely on the basis of the information you have been given? (Chapman, 2009: 22)
	Change and continuity	Does an investigation of the lyrics of Beatles' songs support the claim that dramatic changes took place in the band's thinking about love over the course of their career? (Chapman et al., 2012: 117)

Developing an understanding of argument and the ability to argue involves learning to use language – for example, the language of inference – in particular ways. Advancing an argument may involve a very broad range of types of linguistic action – participants in a discussion may need to narrate, explain, instruct, question, speculate and so on (Alexander, 2008a: 39), however, arguing entails making one of a range of 'discussion moves' (Coffin, 2007: 25). Box 4.1 identifies 'discussion moves' that are inherently argumentative and that are likely to be necessary features of any interaction that aims to establish, test and evaluate claims about the past.[10]

It is likely to be helpful to spend time clarifying and modelling what arguing is and what it means to argue before asking students to engage in argument. Arguing (stating, inferring, challenging, counter-claiming and so on) is a way of doing things with words (Austin, 1975) and to do something with words you need the relevant linguistic tools: there is good reason to think that providing students with word mats, writing frames or sentence starters linked to a range of discussion moves will also have positive impacts on the quality of discussion (Counsell, 1997; Woodcock, 2005; Ravenscroft *et al.*, 2010).

It is also likely to be helpful if discussions are accompanied by guidance about the features that contributions to discussion should have through, for example, 'discussion criteria', such as those exemplified in Box 4.2, against which posts can be assessed and peer assessed.

Box 4.1 Some discussion moves involved in arguing[a]

- Making a claim by
  - *stating* it (e.g. 'X was the case') and/or
  - *inferring* it (e.g. 'X and Y were the case, so Z must have been the case').
- Supporting a claim by adducing
  - *supporting evidence* (e.g. 'X shows that Y') and/or
  - *supporting argument* (e.g. 'Without X there could not have been Y').
- Challenging a claim or the support provided for a claim by
  - *questioning* the claim or the support provided for it (e.g. 'You say X but you don't provide any evidence' or 'Just because X was the case doesn't mean that Y had to be – Z is equally likely') and/or
  - making a *counter-claim* (e.g. 'You say it was X, however, we feel that the evidence provides more support for the claim that is was Y').
- Agreeing with all or part of a claim or challenge and or the support provided for it (e.g. 'I agree that X but Y doesn't prove it').
- Revising a claim or challenge and/or the support provided for it (e.g. 'Okay, I agree: I should have said X was likely rather than certain').

[a]   This list of 'discussion moves' has been inspired by the pioneering and systematic work of the Open University's Arguing in History project and, in particular, by Coffin, 2007: 40–2 and Martin *et al.*, 2007: 35. Other influential models of what arguing involves include Toulmin, 1969.

Box 4.2 Discussion criteria involved in an A2 discussion forum

When contributing to the discussions you should aim to:

- be *courteous* and use appropriate *academic language*
- *focus* clearly *on the issues* being debated
- *argue clearly* and in a structured way
- *support the claims that you make* with evidence and/or reasoning
- consider a number of *explanations* (when explaining why interpretations vary)
- consider a number of *criteria* (when evaluating interpretations)
- be *precise* when challenging, questioning or arguing against another person's arguments
- *respond appropriately* to questions or counter-arguments (when replying to comments from other participants on a previous post).

(Chapman *et al.*, 2012: 96)

The value of criteria in building metacognitive thinking is well understood (Black and Wiliam, 1998, 2009; Wiliam *et al.*, 2002). Discussion criteria are likely to be particularly useful in student self-assessment and in 'activating students as instructional resources for each other' (Wiliam, 2009: 12) through peer assessment. Students can be asked to make reference to criteria when posting or when replying to each other's posts, as in the following student post, from the sixth-form discussion governed by the criteria cited in Box 4.2 and in which students were asked the questions reproduced in Table 4.2.

> Would it be possible to expand upon your reasoning as to their differing perspectives? Your statement 'although coercion was a clear feature of Nazi power this was alongside support and consent from the Nazi people' is essentially the budding start of an explanation rather than a substantiated argument.
>
> And also, the second half of the question; which one would you choose as the more valid of the arguments presented and why?
>
> (History Virtual Academy, 2011)

Understanding argument and the 'moves' that are involved in making an argument can be scaffolded in a number of ways. It is plausible to suggest, for example, that turning 'moves' into 'roles' and asking individual students or groups of students to take on different roles is likely to be effective in developing understanding.[11] Student groups taking part in a discussion board could be organised, for example, such that one group or group member is tasked to advance claims in relation to a question (to be the 'claim maker/s'), another to support the claims made by the first group (to be the 'supporter/s'), another to challenge the claims made by the first and/or second group (to be the 'challenger/s'), another to ask questions and, for example, to ask any of the other groups to clarify their claims or the support for their claims, to provide further evidence or argument in support of the claims (to be the 'questioner/s'), and so on.

Teachers typically take the role of 'moderator' in discussions – the role of 'referee' or 'ring master' whose job it is to ensure that the discussion is carried out in an appropriately 'historical' manner and also to move discussion forward. The roles identified above can be distributed in a very wide range of ways – between groups and within student groups – and there is no reason why we might not, for example, ask a student or a group of students to moderate aspects of a discussion, peer assessing other students' mastery of historical argument and debate. Student understanding can be developed in many ways, for example, by modelling a post or exchanges of posts and demonstrating 'how to do it' or even 'how *not* to do it'. Moorhouse reports contributing posts to a Year 10 discussion board to 'illustrate the way in which an argument could be presented' (2006: 31) and also using student assessment of his own posts to get students thinking criterially:

> I used my initial post and asked [students]... to highlight the places where I had backed up my point with specific and relevant evidence (I had not). This allowed a revision of some of the thoughts that pupils had... It also emphasised the need for them to do what I had not done in supporting their ideas with evidence.
>
> (Moorhouse, 2006: 33)

Scaffolding discussion: structure and organisation

A successful discussion requires more than an 'authentic' question, clarity about what argument is, understanding of 'discussion moves' and, perhaps, the use of discussion criteria. Setting up successful discussions, like effective teaching and learning in general, requires attention to structure and organisation and to things such as the organisation of students into groups, timings, variety of activity, pace, and so on. Successful discussion also, of course, depends upon skilful teaching (Journell, 2008). This section deals with structure and the next section addresses the role of the teacher.

Setting up and managing a discussion, like managing a classroom, involves making a number of decisions and answering questions such as:

- 'Who will be doing what with whom?
- Why?
- How?
- When and in what order?
- For how long?

An open discussion – driven by an instruction such as 'Discuss X' – is likely to be a shapeless one. Discussions need organising and scaffolding through the allocation of roles, of tasks and so on. The Arguing in History site contains excellent guidance on this and on other aspects of discussion board design and management (Box 4.3).

Moorhouse's Year 10 discussion design integrated discussion into a scheme of work over a number of months, working up to class participation in a national online discussion competition adjudicated by an historian, and scaffolded students' understanding of argument through classroom debate and presentation, teacher modelling and peer assessment. Differentiation was achieved through the differentiated distribution of tasks – more able students being allocated more challenging research-based tasks – and through the use of student groups in which pupils were allocated different roles: researcher/s, presenter/s, writer, resource manager, timekeeper and spokesperson (Moorhouse, 2006).

> **Box 4.3 Some issues to consider when designing a discussion forum**
>
> When will the conference begin? How long will it last? Three weeks is long enough to generate activity without becoming boring. Check this against timetables. Will each class have enough face-to-face lessons within this time? Will they be able to start at roughly the same time? …
>
> Sub questions to make the task more manageable…
>
> Group sizes and composition…
>
> The minimum requirement for students' contributions and exactly what guidelines they should be given to follow, e.g. our requirement to Year 9 was as follows: Each week you will be expected to make at least two postings. Your posting should be one or two sentences long. Make sure that you back up what you write with supporting evidence. In weeks two and three at least one of your postings should be a response to someone else's posting.
>
> (Arguing in History, n.d.)

Like Moorhouse, Snape and Allen built up to discussion with a Year 7 group through a series of structured activities. Snape and Allen's activities were embedded in a virtual book tracing the itinerary of a fictional crusader (Roger) through a series of chapters that lead up to a 'discussion... directly debating the over-arching question: "Why was there conflict between Christians and Muslims in the Middle Ages?"' (Snape and Allen, 2008: 47).

> The enquiry question gave the sequence a clear focus and linked it to concepts (cause and consequence). The activities were sequenced to prepare pupils to use causal reasoning skills in argument during the summative discussion board. Throughout the sequence pupils analysed sources and answered questions that required them to make inferences from the sources about possible causes of conflict. Pupils were encouraged to synthesise their thinking about these matters in Chapter 4 through a digital diamond 9 activity that encouraged pupils to evaluate the relative importance of causes by manipulating text box diamonds in an electronic card sort and that asked them to explain the decisions they had made in written form. This process was designed to scaffold the process of formulating claims in preparation for the online conference at the end of the sequence.
>
> (Snape and Allen, 2008: 46)

A sixth-form discussion structure, developed for an inter-institutional A2 discussion involving students from a number of institutions and academic historians, is reproduced in Table 4.2. In this design students were asked to revisit a question, slightly modified in phase 2 of the discussion, in the light of peer and expert feedback over a period of four weeks. The design had a meta-cognitive intent and involved the giving and receiving of feedback and the drafting and redrafting of arguments in the light of feedback.

Table 4.2 The History Virtual Academy discussion structure 2011[a]

Phase	A. Resources	B. Questions	C. Students' tasks	D. Historian's tasks
1 (1 week)	Two contrasting interpretations of roles of coercion and consent in Nazi Germany in the form of *c.* 500-word extracts from works of scholarly history (academic papers by Richard Evans and Robert Gellately).[b]	How might you explain the fact that these historians provide different assessments of the role of coercion in Nazi Germany and if you had to choose between their assessments how might you do this?	(a) To post an answer to the question (see column B) in around 300 words and (b) to post a reply to at least one other student post.	N/A
2 (1 week)	As at week 1 and a 'third text' provided by the historian (see column D).	How might you explain the fact that historians provide different assessments of the role of coercion in Nazi Germany and if you had to choose between historians' assessments how might you do this?	(a) Post an answer to the question (see column B) in around 300 words and (b) post a reply to at least one other student post.	Make a post of around 500 words addressing the issue/topic that the two extracts provided in week 1 had focused on (see Phase 1 column A) expressing an alternative perspective on the issue/topic.
3 (2 weeks)	As at week 2	As at week 2	(a) Review their answer to the week 2 question and (b) re-post a revised answer, in around 300 words, taking account of the comments of other students and of the historian.	To respond to student posts in week 2.

Source: Adapted from Chapman *et al.* (2012: 19)

Notes
a Five discussion topics were explored through the 2011 History Virtual Academy, including the Protectorate and the American Civil War, and the same discussion structure and questions were used in all in five cases (Chapman *et al.*, 2012).
b The text extracts used in Phase 1 of the 2011 HVA Nazi Germany and American Civil War discussions and also the texts contributed in Phase 2 of these discussions by the historians who took part in them are available online in Chapman *et al.*, 2012: 108–15.

The role of the teacher

As Robin Alexander has argued, developing dialogue involves skilful teaching and, in particular, skilful questioning that, for example:

- appropriately combines invitations for close/narrow and open/discursive/speculative responses;
- uses elicitations and leading questions sparingly rather than habitually; prompts and challenges thinking and reasoning;
- balances open-endedness with guidance and structure in order to reduce the possibility of error;
- gives children time to think.

(Alexander, 2008a: 43)

What is true of facilitating dialogue in general is true of facilitating online dialogue, although the latter has peculiar features (asynchronous discussions, by definition, meet the last of Alexander's desiderata above, for example). There are two extremes to navigate between: a closed or tightly structured approach will, very probably, become a straightjacket and disable discussion of even the most 'authentic' of questions; a totally open or unstructured approach, on the other hand, is likely to lead to shapelessness and, given students' predilection for cumulative talk, to a lack of challenge, claim and counter-claim (Journell, 2008) and, perhaps, to erroneous or unhelpful ideas remaining unchallenged and, therefore, apparently legitimised (Thompson and Cole, 2003: 40).

Too definitive a tone – on the part of students or teachers – can kill discussion dead. As Dave Martin has observed, in a comparative analysis of three inter-institutional discussions:

Posts that were more closed were more likely to close down the discussion. The following example, whose emboldened first word implies certainty, received no replies: '*Obviously* he should have taken the better guns & men because who knows that might of been enough to win the battle.'

(Martin, 2008: 35, emphasis in original)

Keeping discussion going, on the other hand, makes demands on teachers, for example: 'teachers needed to write clear and interesting argument prompts as students could simply ignore them' (Martin, 2008: 36). The following exemplify approaches to questioning that are likely to engage students, the first is from one of Martin's Year 10 discussions and the second from an historian engaged in a Year 13 discussion.

You're right about the US losing the battle but winning the war – why couldn't the Plains Indians follow up their victory with further successes?

(Martin, 2008: 37)

We're generally agreed that historians' political views influence what they write, but how does this work? Is it like cheering for Arsenal or creationism, where supporters defend a fixed conclusion against every challenge? Or is it more about viewpoint, where (for example) being black or female or royalist makes one aware of issues that have been overlooked without necessarily leading one to fixed conclusions?

(Cited in Chapman, 2011: 12)

The role of the teacher in keeping the discussion going through 'moderation' has already been alluded to in preceding sections and is critical – students need to be reminded of what is expected of them, through reference to criteria, reminders about timing, and so on. Students also need time to get used to the medium and a discussion that is scaffolded through a series of tasks – as in the Moorhouse and Snape and Allen designs already discussed – is likely to work better than one that is not. The role of the teacher in checking that students are on task, are posting appropriately, and so on, is also, obviously, a critical aspect of discussion moderation, and discussions need to be regularly checked and supervised in order to achieve this (Arguing in History, n.d.).

Engaging learners: competition and collaboration

Asynchronous computer-mediated communication (ACMC) has a number of obvious advantages over face-to-face communication in breaking down barriers of time and space – I can conduct an asynchronous online discussion with somebody on the other side of the world and not have to worry, for example, about the fact that I am sending them a message at 3 o'clock in my afternoon when they are (one hopes) soundly asleep and in the middle of their night.[12]

These facts about ACMC give discussion forums a number of potential advantages over normal classroom exercises in engaging student motivation. Discussions can readily be set up between institutions, or between classes or age groups in the same institution, despite the barriers to communication that physical distance or differences in timetable usually present. It is possible, in other words, for students to interact *through* history with people with whom they cannot, as a rule, readily interact *in* history.[13]

Interaction and competition can engage and motivate students. A number of case studies exist in which students in different institutions were enabled to argue and debate with each other (Moorhouse, 2006; Martin, 2008) and argue with academic historians (Thompson and Cole, 2003; Chapman, 2009; Chapman and Hibbert, 2009; Chapman *et al.*, 2012) through discussion forums. In a number of these cases, in addition, a competitive format was adopted in which it was possible to 'win' the discussion. These case studies suggest that, when managed and moderated carefully, such interactions can be engaging and motivating for students and add value in ways that it would be hard to achieve easily face to face.[14]

Conclusions

This chapter set out to draw attention to the value of discussion forums as tools for developing historical learning and to identify a range of aspects of discussion forum design and operation that are likely to be important to the successful realisation of the potential of this learning tool.

The only way to learn how to use discussion forums, however, is to try them out and to think through the implications of the decisions that immediately arise. Should you set a word limit for posts? If you do not, students may write posts of highly variable length which may, or may not, be desirable depending upon your students and what you are trying to achieve. Should students be empowered to start new threads or should this be something that only the teacher can do? Starting new threads promotes student autonomy – students can start a whole new discussion topic – on the other hand it increases complexity and the greater the number of threads there are, the harder it is to follow a discussion, the easier it is to 'lose the thread' and the greater the probability, perhaps, that student posts may not receive replies. Here, as elsewhere, there are judgement calls.

The examples discussed in this chapter argue that discussion forums can be powerful tools for developing students' understanding of history as an interpersonal practice (discussion/debate) and also as a rigorous practice (argument). Too many of the assessment tools that we depend upon in history are monological: whether we ask students to set out an argument in response to a question, to review the range of arguments that exist on a particular question or to critique an existing argument (Coffin, 2006: 76–87), we typically ask them to do so as individuals and to compose 'a special type of monologue, a rhetorical presentation of evidence by one speaker or writer... which considers the pros and cons and offers a considered conclusion' (Mercer, 2000: 96). Monologues have their uses, of course: all historians engage in them in their writing, and television history, from A.J.P. Taylor to Schama and Ferguson, has tended to be dominated by one voice.[15] History, however, is not an individual affair and historical knowledge progresses through dialogue in disciplined communities of practice rather than through bravura performance (Megill, 2007).

Discussion forums have the potential to help pupils understand how knowledge is constructed and tested collectively and, thus, the potential to develop key disciplinary understandings. They also have the potential to help students exercise and develop their powers of historical argument and thus to help prepare them to slay the exam question bugbears whose long shadows so often cramp our style and theirs (Historical Association, 2005b).

Notes

1 Usually the power to delete posts is exercised by the forum 'moderator' or the forum 'administrator': the former is the person who acts as forum referee and rule-setter, whose interventions aim to keep discussion moving forward by intervening formatively and normatively; the latter is the person who is responsible for practical aspects of running the discussion (e.g. setting it up and issuing passwords). Both roles can, of course, be taken by the same person. Participants can be permitted, or not permitted, to delete and/or edit their own posts and this is one of the many administrative decisions that need to be made when a forum is set up.

2 Free sites are available to primary and secondary ('K-12') teachers through Wikispaces (www.wikispaces.com).

3 InterLoc enables synchronous 'dialogue games' (www.interloc.org.uk) and is discussed in Ravenscroft, 2007 and Ravenscroft *et al.*, 2010.

4 For extended discussions of dialogue in pedagogic contexts, see Alexander, 2008a and 2008b.

5 As Ravenscroft observes, 'critical behaviour... breaks usual social norms' and can seem 'socially impolite' (2007: 462). Comic explorations of dispute include Monty Python's 'argument clinic' sketch (Monty Python, 1972), which also contains a very effective definition of argument, and Newman and Baddiel's 'History Today' sketches in which history is modelled as abuse (Newman and Baddiel, 1993).

6 Examples of the range of issues that the historical community argues about can be found in many places, for example, in reviews of historical works. To take three examples: Hobsbawm's (2009) review of a work by Overy turns on questioning of the kind of question that Overy asks; Duffy's (2009) review of a work by Thomas turns on objections to the conceptualisation of religion organising the book's claims; and Siegelbaum's review of a work by Figes turns on objections to Figes' substantive and methodological presuppositions (Siegelbaum, 2008).

7 There are well-developed traditions of practice focused on helping students construct historical claims – see, for example Riley, 1999; Wiltshire, 2000; Cooper, 2007. Work on evaluating claims is, arguably, less well developed. Chapman, 2010 and 2011 outline two approaches to these issues.

8 This chapter focuses on using discussion forums as tools for understanding historical argument. There are other uses to which discussion forums could be put, of course, including historical simulation. Wilson and Scott (2003) exemplify a CMC simulation using email.

9 A good deal of thought has been given to the construction of enquiry questions in history education. See, for example Riley, 2000 and the discussion at The Historical Association, 2005a: 2–6.

10 Mastering these 'moves' is also likely to make a valuable contribution to students' performance in public examinations since they are forms of expression that are likely to evince approbation and credit from examiners.

11 An analogous approach, in a different context, is the 'thinking hats' approach that applies Edward de Bono's work to teaching decision making (Pugh, 2009). Engaging pupil interest and engagement by 'jigsawing' activities is often a highly effective strategy: controversies can be enacted in discussion forums by asking different groups of students to argue for and against particular stances associated with positions that have arisen in controversies. The teacher can also 'feed in' new discussion components while a discussion is in process, for example, by introducing new or revisionist arguments, such as Fritz Fischer's arguments about the causes of World War One, into a discussion in order to shake up debate (see Phase 2 of the discussion structure in Table 4.2 for a further example of this kind of approach).

12 Chapman and Hibbert (2009) report a discussion forum in which 18–19-year-old students in Cornwall and Surrey engaged in a discussion that was assessed by an historian in New Zealand.

13 Some complex issues arise, of course, when setting up discussions between institutions or between age groups (for example, e-security issues, issues of access to pass-word protected VLEs, firewalls in one institution that block out users from another institution, and so on): the technical issues are readily addressed through effective site administration and the e-security issues underline the importance of the close supervision of discussion forums noted above (the moderation of discussions and the scrutiny of posts).

14 Engaged and motivated students, of course, tend to be willing students. Drawing on ICT functionality – in discussion forums, in wikis, and so on – can be a way of increasing the time and the energy that students devote to history, a subject that tends not to be as generously timetabled in actual classrooms as one might hope.

15 Alternatives to the 'tellydon' narrative monologue are possible, of course, as a 13-part 1985 series on the history of Wales co-written and co-presented by two historians with markedly different perspectives demonstrates (Vaughan-Thomas and Williams, 1985). I am grateful to Terry Haydn for drawing my attention to this series.

References

Alexander, R. (2008a) *Towards Dialogic Teaching: Rethinking classroom talk*, York: Dialogos.

Alexander, R. (2008b) *Essays on Pedagogy*, London and New York: Routledge.

Arguing in History (n.d.) *Guidelines for setting up an asynchronous text based computer conference*, Milton Keynes: The Open University, online at http://arguinginhistory.open.ac.uk/conferencing.cfm, accessed 19 January 2012.

Austin, J.L. (1975) *How to do Things with Words*, edited by J.O.Urmson and M.Sbisà, Oxford: Oxford University Press.

Black, P.J. and Wiliam, D. (1998) *Inside the Black Box*, London: King's College London, School of Education.

Chapman, A. (2009) *Supporting High Achievement and Transition to Higher Education Through History Virtual Academies*, Liverpool: Higher Education Academy for History Classics and Archaeology, online at www2.warwick.ac.uk/fac/cross_fac/heahistory/elibrary/internal/cs_chapman_highachievement_20091001, accessed 17 October 2010.

Chapman, A. (2010) 'Taking the perspective of the other seriously? The importance of historical argument', *Euroclio Bulletin*, 28: 13–18.

Chapman, A. (2011) 'Times arrows: Using a dartboard scaffold to understand historical action, *Teaching History*, 143: 32–8.

Chapman, A. (2012) 'Beyond "bias" and subjectivity? Developing 16–19 year old students' understandings of historical interpretations through online inter-institutional discussion', in R. Ghusayni, R. Karami and B. Akar (eds) *Learning and Teaching History: Lessons from and for Lebanon: Proceedings of the Third Conference on Education organized by the Lebanese Association for Educational Studies held in Beirut, Lebanon, 25–26 March 2011*, Beirut: Arab Cultural Center.

Chapman, A. and Hibbert, B. (2009) 'Advancing History post-16: using e-learning, collaboration and assessment to develop AS and A2 students' understanding of the discipline of history', in H. Cooper and A. Chapman (eds) *Constructing History 11–19*, Los Angeles, London, New Delhi, Singapore and Washington: Sage, pp.120–48.

Chapman, A., Elliott, G. and Poole, R. (2012) *The History Virtual Academy Project: Facilitating inter and intra-sector dialogue and knowledge transfer through online collaboration*. Warwick: History Subject Centre, online at www2.warwick.ac.uk/fac/cross_fac/heahistory/elibrary/internal/br_chapman_hva_20120117, accessed 17 January 2012.

Coffin, C. (2006) *Historical Discourse: The language of time, cause and evaluation*, London and New York: Continuum.

Coffin, C. (2007) *The language and discourse of argumentation in computer conferencing and essays: Full Research Report*, ESRC End of Award Report, RES-000–22–1453, Swindon: ESRC, online at www.esrcsocietytoday.ac.uk, accessed 25 May 2009.

Cooper, H. (2007) *History 3–13: A Guide for Teachers*, Abingdon: David Fulton Publishers.

Counsell, C. (1997) *Analytical and Discursive Writing and Key Stage 3*, London: The Historical Association.

Duffy, E. (2009) 'Common thoughts', *London Review of Books*, 31 (14): 18–19.

Goldstein, L.J. (1976) *Historical Knowing*, Austin and London: The University of Texas Press.

Historical Association (2005a) *Final Report – Historical Association's Key Stage 2–3 History Transition Project*, London: The Historical Association, online at http://czv.e2bn.net/e2bn/leas/c99/schools/czv/web/website_files/final%20report.pdf, accessed 15 January 2012.

Historical Association (2005b) *History 14–19: Report and recommendations to the Secretary of State*, London: The Historical Association.

History Virtual Academy (2011) *History Virtual Academy 2011 Project Data Sets*, Unpublished Research Data, Ormskirk: Edge Hill University.

Hobsbawm, E. (2009) 'C (for crisis)', *London Review of Books*, 31 (15): 12–13.

Hrastinski, S. (2008) 'Asynchronous and synchronous e-learning', *Educause Quarterly*, 31 (4): 51–5, online at http://net.educause.edu/ir/library/pdf/EQM0848.pdf, accessed 1 January 2012.

Journell, W. (2008) 'Facilitating historical discussions using asynchronous communication: The role of the teacher', *Theory and Research in Social Education*, 36 (4): 317–55.

Lévesque, S. (2008) *Thinking Historically: Educating students for the twenty-first century*, Toronto: University of Toronto Press.

McCullagh, C.B. (1984) *Justifying Historical Descriptions*, Cambridge: Cambridge University Press.

Martin, D. (2008) 'What do you think? Using online forums to improve students' historical knowledge and understanding', *Teaching History*, 133: 31–8.

Martin, D., Coffin, C. and North, S. (2007) 'What's your claim? Developing pupils' historical argument skills using asynchronous text based computer conferencing', *Teaching History*, 126: 32–7.

Megill, A. (2007) *Historical Knowledge/Historical Error: A contemporary guide to practice*, Chicago: University of Chicago Press.

Mercer, N. (2000) *Words and Minds: How we use language to think together*, London and New York: Routledge.

Monty Python (1972) 'Argument Clinic', *Monty Python's Flying Circus, Episode 29*, London: BBC, online at http://pythonline.com, accessed 2 January 2012.

Moorhouse, D. (2006) 'When computers don't give you a headache: the most able lead a debate on medicine through time', *Teaching History*, 124: 30–6.

Newman, R. and Baddiel, D. (1993) 'History Today', *Newman and Baddiel in Pieces, Episode 2*, London: British Broadcasting Corporation, online at www.youtube.com/watch?v=VrMBHZWe2S8, accessed 21 December 2011.

Pugh, R. (2009) 'Put your thinking hat on: How Edward de Bono's ideas are transforming schools', *The Independent*, 29 January 2009, online at www.independent.co.uk/news/education/schools/put-your-thinking-hat-on-how-edward-de-bonos-ideas-are-transforming-schools-1518507.html, accessed 17 January 2012.

Ravenscroft, A. (2007) 'Promoting thinking and conceptual change with digital dialogue games', *Journal of Computer Assisted Learning*, 23: 453–65.

Ravenscroft, A., McAlister, S. and Sagar, M. (2010) 'Digital dialogue games and interloc: A deep leaning design for collaborative argumentation on the web', in N. Pinkwart (ed.) *Educational Technologies for Teaching Argumentation Skills*, Sharjah: Bentham Science E-Books, online at http://staffweb.londonmet.ac.uk/~ravensca/Interloc_arg_bk(d).pdf, accessed 15 January 2012.

Riley, C. (1999) 'Evidential understanding, period knowledge and the development of literacy: a practical approach to "layers of inference" for Key Stage 3', *Teaching History*, 97: 6–12.

Riley, M. (2000) 'Into the Key Stage 3 history garden: choosing and planting your enquiry questions', *Teaching History*, 99: 8–13.

Siegelbaum, L. (2008) 'Witness protection', *London Review of Books*, 30 (7): 13–14.

Snape, D. and Allen, K. (2008) 'Challenging not balancing: developing Year 7's grasp of historical argument through online discussion and a virtual book', *Teaching History*, 134: 45–51.

Thompson, D. and Cole, N. (2003) '"Keeping the kids on message …" one school's attempt at helping sixth form students to engage in historical debate using ICT', *Teaching History*, 113: 38–42.

Toulmin, S. (1969) *The Uses of Argument*, Cambridge: Cambridge University Press.

Toulmin, S. (1972) *Human Understanding: Volume 1, General introduction and part 1*, Oxford: Clarendon Press.

Vaughan-Thomas, W. and Williams, G. (1985) *The Dragon has Two Tongues: A history of the Welsh*, London and Cardiff: Channel 4 Television/Harlech Television.

Wiliam, D. (2009) *Assessment for Learning: Why, what and how?* London: Institute of Education.

Wiliam, D., Black, P.J., Harrison, C., Lee, C. and Marshall, B. (2002) *Working Inside the Black Box: Assessment for learning in the classroom*, London: King's College London, Department of Education and Professional Studies.

Wiltshire, T. (2000) 'Telling and suggesting in the Conwy Valley', *Teaching History*, 100: 32–5.

Wilson, M. and Scott, H. (2003) '"You be Britain and I'll be Germany…" Inter-school emailing in Year 9', *Teaching History*, 110: 32–5.

Woodcock, J. (2005) 'Does the linguistic release the conceptual? Helping Year 10 to improve their causal reasoning', *Teaching History*, 119: 5–14.

Chapter 5

Using blogs and podcasts in the history classroom

Dan Lyndon

The emergence of Web 2.0 in the early twenty-first century, which encouraged participation, collaboration and interaction on the internet, has had a profound influence on the way in which the World Wide Web has steadily become part of everyday life. The consequence for educators has been equally significant, with the need for teachers to explore how these developments, with the opportunities provided for learners to contribute, share and debate, might help them to improve teaching and learning in their subject. Inside the history classroom there has been a proliferation of inspiring and engaging ways that teachers and their students have been participating, collaborating and interacting with the emergence of blogging and podcasting tools that are easily accessible and user friendly. This chapter will explain what blogging and podcasting means and how they can be used to support the teaching of history. It will also look at a series of case studies based on the work that I have produced in my extended history classroom.

Blogs

In its simplest form a blog, or as it was originally known, a weblog, is a form of online diary. A blog is essentially a website that allows the author to easily and regularly update the content. Most blogs allow the reader to contribute in the form of a (usually written) response and this is why blogs form part of the development known as Web 2.0. There are a growing number of blogging websites that are extremely user friendly even for those with limited ICT experience. The most popular is Blogger (www.blogger.com) and another particularly popular site for teachers is Edublogs (http://edublogs.org). Each site has detailed tutorials that walk through the process of setting up a blog which can be achieved in about 30 minutes.

Will Richardson, in his seminal text *Blogs, Wikis, Podcasts and Other Powerful Web Tools for Classrooms*, lists a range of ways in which blogging can be used by teachers and students, including:

- posting homework assignments
- providing reading/stimulus material
- providing examples of student work
- creating class newspapers, online book clubs, poetry and creative writing.

(Richardson, 2009: 39)

He goes on to explain that there are a number of reasons why blogs are so useful for improving student learning:

> [They] truly expand the walls of the classroom … archive the learning that teachers and students do, facilitating all sorts of reflection and metacognitive analysis that was previously much more cumbersome … [are] a democratic tool that supports different learning styles … and can enhance the development of expertise in a particular subject.
> (Richardson, 2009: 27–8)

It is in that spirit that many history educators have set up their own blogs or used them in their (extended) classroom. It is possible to categorise blogs used in the history classroom in a variety ways; those that are student driven – these encourage students to participate fully in interacting with the blog using a range of different techniques including peer and self-assessment, collaborating on project work and responding to stimulus material. Examples of student-driven blogs will be explored in the case studies that follow. There are also blogs that are teacher driven – these encourage the sharing of good practice and often represent a chance for the author and participants to reflect on their own practice. An excellent example of this would be www.onedamnthing.org.uk produced by Ed Podesta, the Head of History at Little Heath School and PGCE Tutor at the University of Oxford. This blog is best summed up by the following words on the introductory page:

> This site is for history teachers, to help them to think about and plan their history teaching, as it seems to me that the best history lessons or series of lessons are often those that have been thought about very carefully.
> (www.onedamnthing.org.uk/?page_id=207, accessed 27 October 2011)

A similar example comes from the publisher Hodder (www.hoddereducation.co.uk/Schools/Nests/Hodder_History_Subject_Nest/nest_blog_history.aspx) which has postings from a varied collection of history educators, each being asked to contribute over a series of blogs on a theme of their choice ranging from active learning to multicultural British history. There are also blogs that are content driven – these can be used by teachers and students as a way of informing their understanding of key individuals and events. An excellent and innovative example of this is wwar1.blogspot.com which is 'made up of transcripts of Harry Lamin's letters from the First World War. The letters will be posted exactly 90 years after they were written'. This blog can be used to give a fascinating insight into the experiences of a soldier from the fields of Flanders to the Italian front. Another delightful example is www.howtobearetronaut.com which has an enormous catalogue of weird and wonderful images and web links that can be used to liven up any lesson.

Case study 1 – The Equiano blue plaque campaign blog

The Equiano blue plaque campaign blog (http://ridingspirates.edublogs.org) was a collaborative project that I worked on with another history teacher, Donald Cummings, who was working as an Advanced Skills Teacher at the Ridings School, a mixed 11–18 comprehensive in Halifax. I was working in the same role at Henry Compton School in Fulham, a boys 11–16 inner-city comprehensive and had been producing teaching material about the anti-slavery campaigner Olaudah Equiano for an exhibition at the Birmingham Museums and Galleries in 2007. The blog was written as part of a project that encouraged Year 8 students from both schools to collaborate on a campaign to get a blue plaque from English Heritage to recognise the contribution that Equiano made to the abolition of slavery. In the lessons leading up to the use of the blog the students were taught about Equiano using resources from the teaching pack that I had produced which included a large number of sources from his autobiography *The Interesting Narrative of Gustavus Vassa, or Olaudah Equiano, the African*. Once the prior knowledge had been established the students were given time in an ICT room and later at home to contribute to the blog. They were asked to respond to the following postings put up by the teachers: 'What was the most significant moment in Equiano's life?' and 'Why should we study Equiano today?'

The pupil response was fascinating, particularly as this was the first time that they had experienced using a blog. The insightful and thoughtful reflections, perhaps aided by the fact that they were publishing for a wider audience are shown by the following examples:

> JS Year 8 says (19 June 2008) I think that in a way Olaudah Equiano was a lucky man because not many slaves were allowed to buy their own freedom. The reason for that is because he learnt himself [sic] to read, write and also to do maths. I think that the happiest part of his life is when he got married and had children but also when bought his freedom. So I think Olaudah Equiano deserves a blue plaque placed outside his house in London.
>
> (http://ridingspirates.edublogs.org/2008/06/13/
> olaudah-equiano-an-interesting-story/comment-page-1/#comments)

> EA Year 8 says (17 June 2008) Olaudah Equiano was a slave once in his life and then bought his own freedom and then lived in London with his family and wrote his own book. It was published on Grove Street in Halifax and we want a plaque in London and where he published his book, Grove Street in Halifax.
>
> (http://ridingspirates.edublogs.org/2008/06/13/
> olaudah-equiano-an-interesting-story/comment-page-1/#comments)

These examples demonstrate the students' understanding of the events associated with Equiano, and they also start to justify their support for the campaign for a blue plaque. This, however, is not particularly different from a piece of written work carried out in the classroom. Where the blog played a distinguishing role was the opportunities for the participants to reflect on the other contributions that had been made and respond to them:

> LC Year 8 says (19 June 2008) BW I disagree with you because after Olaudah Equiano bought his own freedom, he went to england [sic]. He was born in Nigeria but his kids were born in England. I think this was the most significant part because his family had a chance to live a free life.
>
> (http://ridingspirates.edublogs.org/2008/06/13/
> olaudah-equiano-an-interesting-story/comment-page-1/#comments)

> BW Says (20 June 2008) I also disagree with LC because if he wasn't freed he wouldn't have been able to have children in the first place and we are trying to get him a blue plaque not his children!
>
> (http://ridingspirates.edublogs.org/2008/06/13/
> olaudah-equiano-an-interesting-story/comment-page-1/#comments)

The chance for the students to reflect on the contributions made by their peers was a significant factor in improving their understanding not only of the content but also as a way of sharpening up their analytical skills. This was demonstrated by the examples of the letters that were written to English Heritage that were also posted on the blog. The opportunity to respond to feedback about their postings was taken up by participants and this engaged them further in the project. One student in particular responded a number of times and even cited further research ('I've just found out that he has a green plaque but thats [sic] nothing compared to a blue plaque') that had been independently taken to support their argument.

The blog entries also allowed the teachers to respond to the student responses and extend their thinking; for example, when KS wrote 'I think Equiano's significant event was when he was freed too' was followed by an intervention asking 'Can you explain why it was so important? What reason could you give?' Unfortunately, in this case there was no follow-up from the student, but clearly the blog provides an opportunity for an extended discussion between student and teacher allowing time for reflection and response, counter-response.

Overall, the blog was a very exciting and stimulating opportunity for the students from different locations, backgrounds and contexts to collaborate effectively to support each other's learning. Once the initial work on the blog had been completed, the follow-up activities included the students writing letters to English Heritage and posting them to each other so that they could be peer marked. The following posting which was written on the blog a few weeks later sums up why the activity was such a positive experience for all involved:

> Ridings to Henry Compton says (11 July 2008) To everyone at Henry Compton, we all enjoyed reading your letters, they were the same quality as ours. It seems really weird talking to people from another school but it's kind of fun.
> (http://ridingspirates.edublogs.org/2008/06/13/
> olaudah-equiano-an-interesting-story/comment-page-1/#comments)

Case study 2 – Peter the Great revision blog

The second example of how students can use blogs can be illustrated through the Peter the Great revision blog (http://peterthegreatrevision.blogspot.com) which was set up in 2011 for a group of Year 12 AS History students at Fortismere School, an 11–18 mixed comprehensive in Muswell Hill, London. There were two aspects of the AS course that the blog reflected: an essay based on their own knowledge and an essay based on sources. The activity was completed as part of a revision programme shortly before their summer exam, with teaching time allocated to the work as well as time at home. The following lesson the students completed a timed answer to the question they had been working on. The students also completed a short questionnaire about their reflections on the use of the blog.

The following question was posed on the blog: 'Russia's success in the Great Northern War of 1700–1721 was due mainly to Peter the Great's reform of the army and navy.' Explain why you agree or disagree with this view', and this was followed by a series of instructions:

- Your task is to post up what you consider to be your most important argument first of all and justify why you have made that choice.
- You can also respond to other posts and argue either in support or against them. You must use evidence to back up the points that you make.
- Once the discussion has ended you should use the posts as the basis for your revision for this question which you will complete next lesson.

The initial responses from the students showed a good understanding of the question that was posed and it was apparent quite quickly that the students were responding to the entries that their peers had posted. This is a possible indicator of the greater influence of social media and Web 2.0 compared with the previous case study, with students being much more familiar with the interactivity of blogging. Some correspondents took the opportunity to support previous points, using new evidence to back up their points, whilst others were prepared to challenge, in one case raising questions for their peers:

> Are you saying that a fully functioning Swedish army would have lost to Russia's measly 'reformed' force? The Swedes had dominated the Baltic for half a century and were a military force to be reckoned with … are you telling me the trained killing machine that was the Swedish army still wouldn't have been able to beat the measly Russian force if there had been no winter.
>
> (http://peterthegreatrevision.blogspot.com/2011/04/
> delay-is-like-death.html#comments)

The most interesting and powerful responses came from one student who was prepared to challenge four of the postings. In class she was a very quiet, conscientious student who was willing to contribute only when prompted. The class tended to be dominated by a small group of confident boys who could be intimidating in their mannerisms and egocentric behaviour. The opportunity provided by the blog meant that she was able to put forward her opinions in a way that was safe and secure and meant that her response was validated. The following example demonstrates her confidence and her insight into some of the weaknesses of her fellow posters:

> [Your] answers to why Charles didn't attack straight away have been mentioned in the posts a bit above you, just to let you know! I don't think 'luck', as you say has anything to do with this. Also, are you implying that Peter's eagerness is a bad thing? I disagree that 'History was written by the victors' how could that be, when millions of sources exist that show the hardships of the ordinary man?
>
> (http://peterthegreatrevision.blogspot.com/2011/04/
> delay-is-like-death.html#comments)

The second activity that the students completed was using the blog to respond to a source-based essay question:

> Use sources A, B, C and your own knowledge. How far were Peter's Westernisation policies driven by the needs of war? (24 marks).

And the instructions that were provided asked the students to 'Find the best quote from each source to back up your argument (either in support or against the question). For each quote you need to provide a sentence to explain why you chose it.' Again students were expected to respond to the postings made by their peers. This time the response was not so strong in terms of the interactivity, with most students only completing the initial task, albeit very successfully. However there was one good example of reflection with the student able to bring in additional material to support the initial statement:

I agree with X's comments on source A. Her argument is supported by the Peter's setting up an Admiralty College in 1718. In addition, by the end of Peter's reign, the number of iron foundries has increased from 20 to 200, and the College of Manufacture had been set up.

(http://peterthegreatrevision.blogspot.com/2011/05/
this-time-we-are-going-to-try-and.html#comments)

In terms of the interactivity that using the blog provided, the students clearly responded better to the initial essay-based activity compared to the source-based activity. There could be a number of reasons for this: the latter activity involved a comparison between sources that could have been more challenging to complete online, as they did not have the function to highlight key parts of the text; although both tasks required students to reflect on the postings made by their peers, the latter was more focused on identifying key aspects of the text that were effective in supporting an argument. This may have narrowed the response from the students rather than engaging them in a debate over the key arguments, reflecting the challenge that the teacher blogger faces when thinking about maximising the most effective uses of the blog in the classroom.

After the students had participated in the activities they were asked to reflect on their experiences and complete a short questionnaire. Although this was a comparatively small sample, the responses were illuminating in a variety of ways:

- 70 per cent of the students believed that the process of contributing to the blog was Very or Quite Useful;
- 100 per cent of the students that responded to the question 'Did you use the blog to help you prepare for the timed question?' felt that the blog was Very or Quite Useful.

When asked how the process of blogging could be useful for revision purposes the following responses were particularly insightful:

[I was] interacting in a question and answer session which helped me to better understand my points.

The blog [was helpful] because you could write it and read over it instead of talking and listening.

You can think about the information you've learnt and argue for and against other people's points.

However it was not all positive:

Blogs require that everyone is willing to back up what they say, otherwise is can become a stream of simple statements.

[It is] too limiting, hard to have enough time to do this process for every question.

It is too different from the revision compared to every other subject.

Using a blog to support student understanding of exam style questions clearly had a mixed response from the students, however from the teaching perspective there were many benefits, particularly as one respondent commented that blogging 'allows you to see strong opposing arguments that can be used in your own essays', which is clearly significant for the development of key historical and analytical skills.

Podcasting

A podcast is an audio (or less commonly, a video) file that is hosted online on a website or blog that can be downloaded and played through a computer or handheld mobile device such as an MP3 player. There are a range of audio recording software packages that can be used to create podcasts, the most popular being Audacity (http://audacity.sourceforge. net). Once the recording has been made, the output (usually an MP3 or WAV file) is uploaded onto a website and distributed through channels such as iTunes, where users can subscribe to a multiplicity of different podcasts. An excellent user guide to podcasting can be found in Will Richardson's book *Blogs, Wikis, Podcasts and Other Powerful Web Tools for Classrooms* (Richardson, 2009).

In pedagogic terms podcasts can be categorised as Digital Audio Learning Objects (DALO) which often have the following key features; they are simple to produce, they are immediate, they are educationally focused, they are reusable and engaging (Lee *et al.*, 2008: 504–5). As a consequence, the use of podcasts is a valuable tool to enhance the learning experience of students in the history classroom. According to research produced by Lee *et al.*:

> Podcasting also holds great potential for allowing students to articulate their under-standing of ideas and concepts, and to share the outcome with an audience they value ... Second, students may not always realise that the actual processes of interactive dia-logue and collective problem solving are essential to knowledge creation ... Students need to become increasingly aware that knowledge is not constituted simply by indi-vidual effort, but collectively.
>
> (Lee *et al.*, 2008: 518)

Podcasting represents a great opportunity to capture the creativity and imagination of the students in a format that can be kept permanently and referred to over a longer period of time. Banks of podcasts can be built up to support revision in particular or to extend pupil understanding in greater depth.

As with blogs, podcasts can be categorised in a variety of ways: those that are produced by students and/or teachers to enhance the learning experience. Examples of these will be shown in the case studies below; and those that are mainly informative and content driven. Some of the best examples of the latter style of podcasts that can be used in the history classroom include www.bbc.co.uk/schools/gcsebitesize/audio/history which covers the key aspects of the GCSE History courses in a style that is entertaining as well as instruc-tive. Similarly, www.mrallsophistory.com/revision.html has a number of revision podcasts produced by a history teacher for his GCSE and IGCSE classes, which includes content as well as exam skills; www.historyextra.com/podcast-page is the podcast directory of the *BBC History magazine* which covers a vast range of historical figures and events, and http:// historyofengland.typepad.com is an excellent example of specialist podcasts, in this case focusing on Medieval Britain. There is also a new forum http://historicalpodcasts.freefo-rums.org/index.php designed for people to respond to the historical podcasts that have been produced, which also has a blog http://historicalpodcasts.blogspot.com that features the different podcasts available. It is possible to find podcasts that cover virtually every aspect of the history that is studied in schools; however, you may wish to be more creative and get your students to produce their own podcasts. A link to other examples of podcasts can be found at www.uea.ac.uk/~m242/historypgce/ict/welcome.htm, including links to the Historical Association's series of podcasts, and ranking sites of particularly popular history podcasts.

Case study I – GCSE Germany podcasts

As part of the GCSE Modern World or SHP course on Germany 1918–39 the students have to study the problems in Germany after the First World War; 1923 was a particularly challenging year for Germany with the invasion of the Ruhr, the Hyperinflation Crisis and the Munich Putsch. Once my students had completed the lessons that covered the content they were set a task of producing a podcast in the form of a radio broadcast from Germany reflecting on the 'year of crisis'. The instructions for the task and a writing frame can be found on the comptonhistory.com website (http://comptonhistory.com/gcse/1923%20 year%20of%20crisis.pdf). The students were given an hour to produce their broadcast and then asked to record their work using Audacity. One podcast in particular stuck out as it demonstrated why activities such as podcasting can really tap into students' creativity and extend their thinking and application of knowledge. A small group of Year 10 students decided that they wanted to create their podcast in the style of Star Wars! The podcast was recorded using a laptop video camera rather than Audacity, so the end result was posted on YouTube (www.youtube.com/watch?v=mWKQ7JaUyuo).

Another podcast activity that was produced on the same unit was the 'Democracy to Dictatorship' podcast (http://comptonhistory.com/gcse/democ2dictatpodcast. pdf) which asked the students to create a series of interviews with people reflecting on the Reichstag Fire, Enabling Act and the Night of the Long Knives. Again students used Audacity to record the podcasts, with some experimenting with adding additional music to add dramatic tension (http://comptonhistory.com/audio/lukas.mp3 and http://comptonhistory.com/audio/aaron.mp3). Both of these examples demonstrate how podcasting can be an extremely effective way for students to reflect on a unit of work in a way that is engaging and creative. However, the significant advantage of podcasting is that the work is kept as a permanent record and can be accessed at any time which makes it extremely valuable over the long term rather than as a static one-off activity.

Case study 2 – Revision podcasts for AS History

One of the most effective forms of revision can be the creation and use of podcasts. In addition to the work that my students completed on the Peter the Great blog, each class also spent some time producing a series of revision podcasts to answer two 12-mark questions – one from their own knowledge and one based on sources. The students worked in pairs to collectively produce an answer to the question and then made a recording of their work using Audacity. Once that had been completed and marked it was posted up on to the school VLE (Virtual Learning Environment) and the Peter the Great revision blog (http://peterthegreatrevision.blogspot.com) which meant that it could be accessed by the students at any time. Alternatively, the file could be downloaded and used on an MP3 player or on their mobile devices.

The students were asked to reflect on their experiences of producing a podcast for revision purposes. The baseline questionnaire that was carried out before the activities revealed that only three per cent of the students had actually created a podcast before (this compared to 30 per cent of the cohort that had used a blog); 75 per cent of the respondents found the process of creating a podcast Extremely, Very or Quite Useful, and of those who used the podcasts for revision before the timed question that was set the following lesson, 100 per cent found that the process was Very or Quite Useful. The following written responses were very positive:

> It is more interacting and engaging than simply reading a textbook.

> Podcasts are useful for revising as they take a lot of the strain away that is done through writing. They are easily accessible through MP3 players and iPods and give a different approach to learning which in many cases is highly appreciated by students.

> They are useful for auditory learners because by hearing the information in small amounts often the information is likely to stay in your mind.

> [It was a] more interesting way to revise and [I am] more likely to remember hearing it rather than just reading it.

> I could listen to them while doing other things.

However, other responses were less positive (perhaps revealing the student's awareness of their preferred learning styles):

> I'm not used to using other forms of revision, other than reading and writing and so I don't think about using podcasts. Also I am not a good auditory learner.

> I remember things better from writing them down.

> I prefer reading information than listening to it.

Overall, the response to the activity was fairly mixed with a significant number of students enjoying the novelty of revising in a different way, although it is clear that there was a preference among others for more traditional methods. The potential for combining podcasts with a range of alternative strategies could therefore have a positive impact in supporting and deepening student understanding.

Conclusion

The emergence of Web 2.0 has seen the explosion of tools that allow users to participate, collaborate and interact online and this has been matched by some educators in the classroom who have seized the opportunity to use formats such as blogs and podcasts to inspire and engage their students. There are many excellent examples of both blogs and podcasts that can be used to instruct students and expand their knowledge. There is a place for simply using blogs and podcasts which have been produced by academic historians and accomplished and expert history teachers. High-quality podcasts can be excellent revision aids given the ubiquity of pupils' use of MP3 players. They can also be used to 'model' to pupils what is involved in producing a high-quality podcast as opposed to a dreary and unhelpful one.

Listening to a podcast is not necessarily a thrilling and powerful learning experience. Pupils need inducting into the skills needed to discern what makes podcasts useful and appropriate for purpose. Sometimes pupils can learn from listening to professionally produced podcasts that are flawed or that are not fit for their needs. However, the most powerful way in which podcasts can be used is by the students themselves. The potential for students and teachers to create online portfolios, keeping a permanent record of their material is very exciting and with the emergence of cloud technology (whereby users can access everything that they need virtually without being tied down to a particular host computer) the limitations faced by past users are slowly being eroded. Both formats also provide an opportunity for students to take greater ownership of their learning, particularly as the likelihood of their work being used by a wider audience enhances the motivation and can lead to spectacular and creative outcomes. History teachers should seize the chance to extend their classroom and by using blogs and podcasts allow their students to become knowledge creators, engaged debaters, reflective learners and critical thinkers. For those interested in exploring these developments further, in addition to the Richardson (2009) text, Churchill (2009) and Green *et al.* (2008) also provide useful information.

References

Churchill, D. (2009) 'Educational applications of Web 2.0: using blogs to support teaching and learning', *British Journal of Educational Technology*, 40 (1): 179–83.

Green, T., Brown, A. and Robinson, L. (2008) *Making the Most of the Web in Your Classroom*, Thousand Oaks, CA: Corwin.

Lee, M., McLoughlin, C. and Chan, A. (2008) 'Talk the talk: learner-generated podcasts as catalysts for knowledge creation', *British Journal of Educational Technology*, 39 (3): 501–21.

Richardson, W. (2009) *Blogs, Wikis, Podcasts and Other Powerful Web Tools for Classrooms*, Thousand Oaks, CA: Corwin.

Chapter 6

Documentary film making in the history classroom

Richard Jones-Nerzic

This chapter is in two sections. In the first part, I outline some ideas about why history teachers might consider making documentary films with their pupils. Informing this section is a polemic suggesting that the traditional 'apprentice' model of history teaching, in which the history pupil is treated as a trainee historian, needs to be overhauled. In my view, pupils need to become informed, critical users of the range of ways in which the past is interpreted and presented, both academic and popular. The documentary history film is perhaps the most important example of popular presentation of the past and is now extensively used in the classroom and yet rarely used critically. Providing opportunities for the history pupil to make 'historical' film, will not only broaden their awareness of how the past is used (and abused) but also enhance their appreciation of the importance of history as an academic discipline.

The second section of this chapter is more practical. If the reader is in no need of being persuaded about the value of making pupil documentary films, then they might jump straight ahead to this second section which deals more practically with how documentary film making might be incorporated into the history classroom.

PART 1: WHY HISTORY TEACHERS SHOULD BE MAKING DOCUMENTARY FILMS WITH THEIR STUDENTS

> I am convinced that the combination of words and music, colour and movement can extend human experience in a way that words alone cannot do. For this reason I believe in television as a medium, and was prepared to give up two years' writing to see what could be done with it.
>
> (Clark, 1969: 10)

The story of how Lord Clark was persuaded by David Attenborough into writing and presenting the genre-defining documentary series *Civilisation*, is highly pertinent to the history teacher toying with the idea of making films. Produced in 1968, *Civilisation* was an attempt to effectively exploit the new technology of the era, colour television. My first argument for making documentary films is the same: we should because we can now. Clark's second point is more profound: that the multimedia quality of documentary television provides a more powerful means of communication than is possible with written words alone. This reflects my second argument. In my view, pupils making historical documentaries can not only, in

Clark's words, 'extend human experience' but also extend pedagogically their experience of 'doing history' in the twenty-first century. In brief, we should not only be making films because we can, but also because we should.

Because we can

We haven't made films with students before, simply because it was not technically possible to do so. When I started teaching history 20 years ago, it was not realistic to propose that pupils make their own documentary films. It was hard enough to get regular access to a TV and video and even harder to get hold of a cassette worth showing. I can clearly remember only a decade earlier, as a secondary school pupil, the excitement of being shepherded into a purpose built 'audio visual theatre' to watch a film of Macbeth on the only VHS player in a school of 2,000 pupils. Needless to say, I never saw a history documentary in my whole time in school. I think sometimes we forget just how much has changed in the history classroom.

Just ten years ago there were very few classrooms with data projectors and interactive whiteboards. Microsoft Windows had just followed Apple and incorporated video editing software into the operating system, but most users had no idea that they had it, let alone what to do with it. In any case most computers were too slow to process video files and dial-up internet lacked the bandwidth to enable effective file sharing. Most people still used floppy discs to carry data; cameras took photos that we picked up from the chemists, and mobile phones only made phone calls. Ten years ago we would have to spend a number of lessons teaching pupils how to edit video and work through the frustrations of unreliable equipment and software. Digital video cameras were prohibitively expensive and never loaned to pupils. And even if you managed to finish a film, how could it be shared? Computers didn't come with DVD burners and YouTube didn't exist until 2005.

And now? Most of our pupils have probably already made films before they came to secondary school. They may well have their own YouTube channel or video albums on their Facebook account and under the desks in your classroom there are probably 20 or so mobile phones that can shoot high-quality video with sound. So why not see what they can do with it?

Because we should

As with all ICT applications in the classroom, digital film making must provide a value-added benefit to learning that could not be provided or provided as effectively if it were not used. There are good reasons why we should be making history documentaries with history pupils that might be summarised under three headings: motivation, skills and depth.

Motivation – beyond the 'artificial constraints of the exercise book'

The first reason for making documentary films is that it can help engage and motivate a wider range of pupils in the study of the past, than might otherwise be possible with traditional – pencil and paper – classroom activities.

Ten years ago I wrote an article about how the internet was going to transform history teaching. I suggested that doing 'well' in history, whether in 1950 or in the year 2000, was 'still largely calculated by how well the student performs within the artificial constraints of the lines of the traditional exercise book' (Jones-Nerzic, 2001). Reading my observations now makes me wonder how much the internet revolution has changed history teaching in the last decade. To what extent have we been able to exploit the ten years of ICT revolution to provide opportunities for students to be assessed outside the 'traditional exercise book'?

If the study of school history is to be of value it must help the student makes sense of the world in which they live today. The carefully selected content of the history curriculum can obviously do this, but the narrow largely literary skills we rely on to convey this content is very out of step with the multimedia world we now inhabit. In the words of the BFI's *Film: 21st Century Literacy Strategy* (nd):

> We live in a world of moving images. To participate fully in our society and its culture means to be as confident in the use and understanding of moving images as of the printed word. Both are essential aspects of literacy in the twenty-first century.

More than two-thirds of pupils in England and Wales decide to drop the study of history at the first opportunity. There are many reasons for this (Haydn, 2011: 31) but perhaps school history's tendency to ape the priorities and methods of academic history is partly to blame. I am sure we agree that historians, like dentists, play a vitally important role in society, but what academic historians (or dentists) actually do for a living would be for most of us, and especially our pupils, extraordinarily dull. As Historian Brian Brivati wrote in an A Level 'document analysis' primer, 'Anyone who does not feel excited by the prospect of sitting in an archive waiting for invariably brown folders, contained in box files and tied up by irritating pieces of ribbon, should not consider becoming an historian' (Brivati, 1994: 19). Indeed. This somewhat explains my vocation as a history teacher rather than as a historian. But more importantly it illustrates the fact that historians try to study the past on 'its own terms' and get excited by the prospect of an engagement with the past as a 'foreign country' (Lowenthal, 1985). By contrast, we history teachers are engaged in a constant battle to make our subject relevant, we draw comparisons between past and present to make school history 'meaningful, useful and engaging' (Haydn, 2011: 38). But also much of what has evolved as the dominant skills and assessment activities of the history classroom is still based on the narrow, largely linguistic domain of the professional historian. Biology teachers do not treat their pupils like budding dentists and doctors, so why do history teachers valorise the narrow methodology of the historian?

The research evidence (QCA, 2005) suggests that pupils continue to find history 'hard' because of our over reliance on traditional, linguistic skills (Haydn, 2011: 238). Film making is one of a number of approaches through which pupils can broaden their engagement with the past. Film making requires the deployment of a range of 'intelligences' (Gardner, 1983) and an extraordinarily wide range of skills: performing to camera, film editing, image and music research, script writing, camera operation, as well as historical research and writing. Film also involves almost endless creative choices about how the narrative is to be constructed and presented. History through film making ceases to be just learning about the past and starts to be about how meaning is created in the present. This is not just about active learning but also learning with ownership of the narrative. There can be significant pride in the product because film is a public, shared experience not a closed, restrictive dialogue between pupil and teacher. A sense of audience throughout the productive process, whether imagined or real can be a powerful motivator. And in terms of assessment for learning, previously published films provide models of good practice to inform and inspire learning outcomes.

Skills – becoming '*bricoleurs*, sophisticated multimedia rag-pickers'

The second reason for making documentary films is that, through the practical experience of making films, pupils begin to acquire a more critical appreciation of how film works. These skills are important because film is now probably the most influential means through which an understanding of the past is acquired. As media professor Patricia Aufderheide argues, documentaries 'are often the first door through which people walk to understand the past' (Aufderheide, 2007: 132).

One of the potential dangers of the ICT revolution is that most school investment has gone into hardware that helps to reinforce traditional didactic pedagogic methodologies. The ubiquitous IWB is a wonderfully powerful presentational tool, but despite creative teachers engaging their students and getting them 'up and involved', it remains essentially a presentational tool for a largely passive audience. A walk through school corridors equipped with data projectors, suggests that one of the dominant uses is for the projection of video. This has perhaps been the biggest change in history teaching over the last 20 years. Looking back over my teacher planner from 20 years ago, some of my classes would not have seen a video at any point during the year. Today, it would be unusual if the same class didn't see at least some video, at least once a week.

History on television today is, in the words of John Tosh, the 'new gardening' (Tosh, 2008: 6). As early as 2003, it was calculated that dedicated history documentary channels in the UK were broadcasting as much as ten hours of history programmes per day (MacCallum-Stewart, 2011: 1). In the US 'Presence of the Past' project, 81 per cent of those interviewed said they had watched films or television programmes about the past in the previous 12 months, compared to only 53 per cent who had read about the past (Hughes-Warrington, 2007: 1). The celebrated documentary film maker Ken Burns blames the lack of interest in traditional history on its 'murder … by an academic academy dedicated to communicating only with itself' (Curthoys, 2011: 9). For their part, historians dismiss popular history as not quite the real thing; they question unsubstantial narratives and are happy to point out errors in factual detail. Sean Wilentz in his essay 'America Made Easy' have gone further, attacking documentarian Burns' *Civil War* as 'crushingly sentimental and vacuous' and savaging the TV historian Simon Schama as a sad 'scholarly defection to the universe of entertainment' (Wilentz, 2001: 3).

There is an alternative approach. Some historians such as David Harlan, Dipesh Chakraberty and Ann Rigney (Jenkins *et al.*, 2007) attempt an accommodation with popular histories such as film documentary or digital gaming rather than simply dismissing them as imposters. (Donnelly and Norton, 2011: 155). Whether they make a persuasive case for the professional historian, only the historian can judge; but for the history teacher whose task it is to equip pupils with the critical tools to engage with the past in all its representations, David Harlan's conclusion has an obvious resonance:

> If our students are to become thoughtful and resourceful readers of the past in a culture as dispersed and eclectic as this one, they will have to become adept at finding their way between competing but equally valid truth claims made in distinct and often divergent modes of historical representation. They will have to become *bricoleurs*, sophisticated multimedia rag-pickers … cutting and pasting, weaving and reweaving interpretive webs of their own devising.
>
> (Harlan, 2007: 122–3)

Unfortunately, film has too often been used as a class management, reward-driven tool. Film is an alternative to work – 'can we watch a video?' – reinforcing the uncritical, passive use of film as 'entertainment' or 'the great escape'. We would not give pupils even ten minutes of silent reading without expecting them to evaluate the content of what they have read. Nor should we allow them to be so uncritical about what they watch. We have to work against all the hypnotic cultural baggage that says 'these are moving pictures let yourself be entertained'. So if we want to make pupils critical users of film, they must first become producers themselves. If we do not, we are like English teachers who refuse to allow students to write their own stories and poems.

But here again we face the problem of the 'apprentice' model of history teaching. Exam questions that ask 'how might this source be useful to a historian' reinforce the assumption that only historians properly use the past. History in school ought to do more than replicate the Rankean tradition of empirical historiography. Although pupils should come to appreciate the unique value of the professional historical method, there should also be opportunities to examine other ways – which are increasingly powerful – through which the past is used and abused. The history classroom skills of critical analysis and objective evaluation are of inestimable value, but they tend to be learned in an almost purely literary context. Via the internet, the multimedia explosion of the last 20 years has undermined the authority of published print and the non-terrestrial broadcast revolution has undermined the authority of independently regulated quality public broadcasting. Traditional history teaching designed for industrial age pencil and paper classroom is of declining relevance in a post-modern world increasingly presented by a deregulated media.

Depth – beneath the 'transparent revelation of truth'

The third reason for making documentary films is that it helps make some of the hardest intellectual challenges of the history classroom just a little bit easier. This is not about dumbing-down a subject that is struggling to compete in a crowded post-14 humanities curriculum. On the contrary, this is about making history's most exciting philosophical discussions intelligible to as wide a range of pupils as possible. Through making documentary films, students are made explicitly aware of the epistemological challenge of getting the story of the past straight. Film offers a multimedia range of very practical tools – music, narrative, drama, text and image – through which multiple alternative narratives can be created. As tools they are infinitely more flexible, familiar and intelligible to our pupils than the subtleties of words alone can allow. Film can open the door to interpretation that words alone keep firmly shut.

When epistemological and interpretative questions arise in the history classroom, they tend in practice to demand either very little from students or altogether too much. In its most simplistic form, students are invited to explain why non-historical (popular history) accounts about the past are unsatisfactory or unreliable. Again, the history 'apprentice' model is at work here, as it 'boundarises' (de Groot, 2009: 249) what is and is not a 'proper' way to interpret the past. In the trainee historian 'apprentice model', analysis of purpose and reliability is conducted almost exclusively at the level of 'primary' sources, still reflecting what E.H. Carr characterised as 'the fetishism of documents' (Carr, 1961: 10). Rather than engage with and recognise the values of non-historical interpretations of the past, releasing a middle ground of accessible interpretative formats for the pupils to evaluate, only the purist, tribally defended form of history is valued (Samuel, 1994: 4) and the opportunity is missed.

In its most challenging form, students are expected to explain how and why professional historians disagree with each other. But historiographical analysis at school can rarely go beyond 'name dropping historians' into appropriate schools of thought. A detailed textual reading of an historian, an appreciation of method or political motivation, is beyond all but the most gifted history pupils. Even for Margaret MacMillan's university undergraduates, historical method is 'no more demanding than digging a stone out of the ground' (MacMillan, 2010: 9). History is popularly perceived as just a cumulative process of gradually uncovering the past; that once the past is known then that particular chapter can be closed. For most school pupils the idea of evolving historiographical debate must be even more perplexing; historians may as well be magicians who somehow conjure up meaning through a mystical communion with the 'documents'.

This is where documentary film can help provide a more accessible example method of how interpretation is created. Documentary film makers and historians are both engaged in a remarkably similar process of representing reality through what Levi-Strauss described as 'retrospective reconstruction' (Lowenthal, 1985: 215). In neither process of 'reconstruction' – historical or documentarian – is there an absolute narrative reality to check the account against. All we have are the structure-less facts which by themselves have no 'order of meaning' (White, 1990: 5). So, as Aufderheide argues, documentarians who tell history with film encounter and share all the same challenges facing the historian (Aufderheide, 2007: 91). And they also share a presentational product, film or text, which sustains an illusion that what is revealed, is a 'transparent revelation of truth' (Aufderheide, 2007: 132).

When we begin to work with pupils on interpretation and historiographical issues, we are faced with the difficulty of explaining that the past and history are very different things; that history is as much made as it is uncovered; that it is alright and normal that historians disagree and they may disagree without one being right and the other 'biased' (Chapman, 2011: 97–8). However, unlike history, the 'illusion' of documentary film as non-interpretive, naïve realist reporting of what actually happened is far easier for pupils to deconstruct. Film offers a concrete illustration of how almost limitless meaning can be created from the same material. But, more importantly, film also enables pupils to move beyond deconstruction to the active construction of their own interpretations. The manipulation of images in particular; the juxtaposition and separation of words from pictures and sounds provides a highly accessible means of illustrating the arbitrary artifice of narrative. In addition, we might usually feel uncomfortable asking pupils to construct one-dimensional interpretations that eschew the norms of historical balance and objectivity, but this is exactly what historical documentaries tend to do (see the 'bad history' case study example below).

Finally, documentary – through its contrast with academic history – can really help the pupil appreciate what a historian does. Documentary provides something concrete and enough like history to make the comparison workable, but different enough to demonstrate what is distinctive. Making the comparison between history and documentary enables the student to appreciate the historian's role of studying the past 'in and for itself' rather than 'tailored to present day purposes' (Lowenthal, 1998: x). So, by examining the full variety of ways in which the past is represented from the academic to the popular, it gives students a better understanding of what history is and isn't. And as Rigney argues: 'precisely because of this variety, it is all the more important to focus on the specific contribution of historians to the circulation of knowledge...' (Rigney, 2007: 158).

PART 2: HOW HISTORY TEACHERS MIGHT MAKE DOCUMENTARY FILMS WITH THEIR STUDENTS

Getting started – 'What if I have never made a film before?'

Before making films with students it is probably sensible to familiarise yourself with the basics of the technique. As with all ICT applications the most effective acquisition of necessary skills comes with 'just-in-time' learning that resolves an existing problem (Riel, 1998). Many history teachers will show historical film in class that are a little too long or occasionally irrelevant to precise needs of the lesson. A good way into video editing is to take a longish clip and cut it down to a relevant size and shape, perhaps adding questions in natural pauses in the film. Most history departments now have a bank of digital resources, of old VHS cassettes that have been digitised or DVDs that have been ripped into single files, all of which will provide an ideal raw unedited film for your project. Alternatively, you could download a video from a source such as YouTube or the BBC using a website such as mediaconverter (www.mediaconverter.org) or the latest version of RealPlayer (www.real.com), both of which allow the user to download and convert the video into a format compatible with whatever video editing software you use.

The best software to begin learning film making is probably Windows Moviemaker. As with most video editing software it is easy to use, but also has the advantage of being built into the Windows operating system. This means the PC classrooms in school will have it, as will the student's PC at home. This is important in allowing your students' classroom experiences to be continued seamlessly at home.

It takes just a few moments to get to grips with the basics of video editing. There are three simple stages in the film-making process: importing the unedited film, editing it and rendering it. The first and third stages are done by the computer with a click of a button, editing is the interesting and creative part. In this stage you will be able to clip or cut sections from the film, import and edit music and stills, add text and effects and an audio narration. (A tutorial providing step by step directions for editing using Windows Moviemaker can be found in Ahrenfelt and Watkin (2008: 69–72) and at www.eatsleepteach.com/ict-and-e-learning/using-movie-maker-with-your-students.)

The best way to learn is to experiment; perhaps ask a film-savvy student to give up a break time to get you started. As with most ICT packages there are always students who know more and know better than the teacher. Part of effective teaching is to recognise this and use it to your advantage. It can be a good opportunity to encourage these student experts to do some of the technical teaching for you and you must be prepared to let the experienced film makers do some practical mentoring for the less experienced during the course of the lesson.

Three case study examples

The following three examples offer a gradual increase not in the sophistication of the historical learning involved but rather in the level of technical expertise and extent of curricula time commitment.

1 Digital storytelling

A digital story is a short, first-person video narrative created by combining recorded voice, still and moving images, and music or other sounds (Tollmar, 2006). The concept of digital storytelling was first developed in Berkeley, California in the early 1990s when a group of writers, artists and computer technicians collaborated to find a way to incorporate new computer technology with storytelling (www.storycenter.org).

In the history classroom today, the concept of digital storytelling provides a technically unchallenging introduction to film making that can yield very rich history learning rewards. A useful starting point might be the documentation of a school history trip. Requiring the students to produce a film of the day encourages them to focus; to listen and look closely without the burden of filling out a standardised worksheet. A few key questions, a notebook and a digital camera are all that are needed to produce a challenging activity. The completed films become themselves 'histories' of the fieldwork day and each unique documentary is a personal interpretation of the day's events. Each account can be contrasted with the next, thereby providing a concrete case study for discussion about the subjective, contrived nature of historical narrative: In what ways are the films different? Why are they different? Is the difference explained by the personality of the author or the author's experience? What does it mean to produce an 'accurate' film? What does it mean to produce good history?

Family and local history also lend themselves particularly well to digital storytelling. By combining carefully selected images with a short, focused narrative, a short film can be made in next to no time. A few scanned family images or a selection of stills snapped at a local histor- ical site of interest, can provide the basis of a piece of work that can really engage the student as a presenter about the past. The next step is to encourage the student to use video to record the testimony of the historical actors as they recall the events captured by the photographs. The process of making such a film can provide a powerful 'oral history' experience for all those involved (see http://storycenter.org/cs_education.html for a range of school case studies).

2 Bad history

This activity is designed to familiarise students with the principle techniques of documentary film making and how and why those techniques are used. First, the aim is to demonstrate to students how meaning can be arbitrarily created, irrespective of the images of 'reality' shown. For this we need to deconstruct documentary, recognising and naming the various, already familiar, techniques used. The second aim is to demonstrate the difference between academic history and documentary film history. The most important of these differences is the reluctance of documentary to evaluate competing interpretations of past events in favour of a singular plotted – exposition/resolution – structure. As Patricia Aufderheide (2007: 92) explains:

> [U]nlike print historians who can digress, comment, and footnote, documentarians work in a form where images and sounds create an imitation of reality that is itself an implicit assertion of truth. This makes it harder for them to introduce alternative inter- pretations of events or even the notion that we do in fact interpret events.

To achieve this, students consciously set out to produce one-sided, 'bad histories' that reinforce a one-dimensional perspective on the past. By having different groups of students produce films that reinforce different established interpretations, we can conclude as a group by viewing and analysing how interpretations are created and which documentary techniques are effective and why. Choose a historical topic that has relatively accessible, contrasting interpretations. Ideally this might be something with distinct historiographical schools of thought. Modern history where stock archive video footage is available works better, but the visuals can also be done though contemporary art. I first developed this activity with the debate over responsibility for the start of the Cold War, but it works just as well with other history debates.

Assuming the students have been taught the main aspects of the historiography, the first stage involves familiarising the students with documentary technique. Over the years I have collected and edited short clips that exemplify the techniques I am looking for – narration types, ambient music, stock archive footage, expert 'talking heads', graphics, etc. – but pretty much any short extracts will do as long as they allow the teacher to ask the following sorts of questions:

- Why are actors employed to do anonymous unseen 'voice of god' narration but not talking to camera in 'on-screen dialogue'?
- When, how and why is archive footage used?
- What role does music have in establishing mood?
- What is the message of the extract?
- What are the strengths and weaknesses of using dramatic re-enactments?
- How and where are academic historians filmed?
- Why is more than one historian used?
- Why is there no debate between them?
- What are the commercial implications of documentaries that have high production values?

The point of this introductory analysis is to begin to transform the students from passive consumers to active producers of film. Through asking questions about why historians are invariably filmed in 'academic' contexts, for example, students begin to look beyond the obvious linguistic message to the background 'signifiers', where rows of academic books communicate the unspoken authority of the foreground expert.

The second stage of the process involves the students making their films. This requires careful planning with clearly communicated requirements and stages/deadlines in the production process. For example, I provide the students with short pieces of stock archive footage that must feature in the film. This is to reinforce the idea that the meaning of an image is not fixed. They all have to use stock footage of Secretary of State, George Marshall but whether the Marshall Plan was the most 'unselfish act in history' or evidence of US economic imperialism depends on the narrative the students produce. To make sure this is fully a group project I also insist that all members of the group appear in the film either as narrators, historical experts, oral history witnesses or dramatic re-enactors.

Having made these films for more than ten years now, it has gone from massively time-consuming, computer lab activity for a film studies enthusiast with a high tolerance for technical frustrations (me), to something that can be done by any teacher who is willing to give it a go. Unlike ten years ago, many students already know how to make film, have their own video cameras, can find, download and convert their own archive stock footage or music and can upload their completed work for the world to see. Whether a model example to inspire future students, a virtual extension of the classroom display board or something for proud relatives to share on Facebook, the prospect of 'publication' can be a significant source of motivation. When a student's work has been viewed over 50,000 times and inspired dozens of positive feedback comments from around the world, the concept of assessment takes on a radically new perspective.

3 Students as documentarians

The final example builds naturally on the critical and practical skills developed in the first two activities. It can be the most demanding and ambitious sort of project, but the rewards can also be significant. In this activity students are encouraged to produce unique historical documentaries that are based on their own documented, original research. In documentary terms this means that the key footage in the film is not 'stock footage' but rather 'actuality footage', that is, film that the students shoot themselves.

The sort of footage the students might be expected to shoot clearly depends on the nature of the historical project. But certain standard documentary formats suggest themselves. Oral history interviews are relatively straightforward to organise and shoot. Location filming at a local historical or heritage site can provide rich visual, contextual material and an opportunity for the student presenter to provide 'on screen dialogue'. Short interviews with academic historians at the local university can be arranged via the school liaison officer. Even feature-style dramatic reconstructions can be achieved with a little imagination, a few props and an appropriate set and camera in close-up. There is no limit and the pupils can amaze you.

The most ambitious project I have been involved with in this respect exploited the one-off opportunity of the first state visit of Queen Elizabeth II to Slovakia in 2008. At the time I was teaching history and film at the British School in Bratislava and I was able to work closely with the British Embassy, British Council and an Emmy award-winning Slovak film director to produce an oral history project about the Czechoslovak kinder transport organised by the 'British Schindler', Sir Nicholas Winton (www.internationalschoolhistory.net/BHP/index.htm). The project required a three-week suspension of the history curriculum, not insignificant time off school for me and the students, and a whole weekend of filming. The obvious benefits of such a project are incalculable. The students met and worked with historically significant figures, diplomats, authors, presidents, award winning journalists, film makers and even the Queen.

But there were less obvious benefits that will be common to any similar, even if less ambitious, documentary projects. The transferable skills involved in participating in such a project are rarely required in a classroom situation: the logistics of arranging the shoot, getting permissions, borrowing equipment and managing a time budget, and being part of a team of people responsible for the script, lighting, sound, camera and editing. But, most importantly, through their interviews they documented an historical event through the eyes of participants who had often never been interviewed before. They added to the historical record. There is something of unquantifiable importance that comes from the immediacy of being in the presence of the past. As the veteran speaks, eyes focused on the distance recounting from their 'mind's eye', we get a glimpse of the 'aura' that Walter Benjamin attributed to the non-reproducible moment of the experience itself. And it is all captured for the world to see.

I should stress that not all film making needs to be a 'major production': it can also entail students doing smaller individual projects. Some examples can be found on the *International School History* website (see 'Useful websites and software' below).

In conclusion, it doesn't take much to start making film. All it need take is a suggestion from the teacher: to 'why not make a film' rather than another PowerPoint or desktop published document. The benefits can be enormous in terms of motivation, media literacy and higher order historical thinking. The *Film: 21st Century Literacy Strategy* concludes that 'the significance of audio-visual media is changing profoundly; it has grown from being a vehicle for art and entertainment to become a core part of how we communicate and do business'. Nobody is suggesting that documentary film making need become a core part of history lessons any more than that historians 'should themselves write novels, design computer games, or experiment with graphic novels' (Rigney, 2007: 156). But neither should school history fail to adapt to a world that is now saturated by representations of the past that historians didn't write and that 'apprentice historians' cannot read.

Useful websites and software

International School History – www.internationalschoolhistory.net/documentary/index.htm – An extended hypertext version of this chapter with examples of the video case studies and practical advice for film making.

The National Archive, Focus on Film – www.nationalarchives.gov.uk/education/focuson/film – An excellent classroom-focused site that among other things allows students to access and edit archive film materials. Film footage can be downloaded for free.

Film Education – www.filmeducation.org – An outstanding resource for anyone interested in analysing and making film in the classroom. Excellent practical activities about popular films often used in the history classroom.

British Pathé – www.britishpathe.com – One of the biggest film and newsreel archives in the world, containing over 90,000 individual film items and 12 million stills. The archive covers an enormous range of subjects including modern British and world history, news, fashion, sport, entertainment, travel, warfare and twentieth-century social history.

Library of Congress, Digital Collections – www.loc.gov/library/libarch-digital.html – The Library of Congress has made digitised versions of collection materials available online since 1994. It includes digitised photographs, manuscripts, maps, sound recordings, motion pictures and books.

Audacity – http://audacity.sourceforge.net – Free, open source software for recording and editing sounds.

RealPlayer – http://uk.real.com/realplayer – Latest versions allow the user to download videos from most popular video sites in one click for free. The site also enables the conversion of video files into formats compatible with most video editing software including Windows MovieMaker.

References

Ahrenfelt, J. and Watkin, N. (2008) *Innovate with ICT*, London: Continuum.

Aufderheide, P. (2007) *Documentary Film*, Oxford: Oxford University Press.

Brivati, B. (1994) 'Private papers', in P. Catterall and H. Jones (eds) *Understanding Documents and Sources*, Oxford: Heinemann, pp. 19–24.

Carr, E.H. (1961) *What is history?* Basingstoke: Palgrave Macmillan, 2001.

Centre for Digital Storytelling, www.storycenter.org, Berkeley, CA.

Chapman, A. (2011) 'Historical interpretations', in Ian Davies (ed.) *Debates in History Teaching*, London: Routledge, pp. 96–108.

Clark, K. (1969) *Civilisation: A Personal View by Lord Clark*. DVD viewing notes accompanying the documentary series, BBC2 Entertain Video, 2005.

Curthoys, A. (2011) 'Crossing over: academic and popular history', *Australasian Journal of Popular Culture*, 1 (1): 7–1, online at www.intellectbooks.co.uk/File:download,aid=10825/ ajpc.1.1.7.pdf.

de Groot, J. (2009) *Consuming History: History and historians in contemporary popular culture*, London: Routledge.

Donnelly, M. and Norton, C. (2011) *Doing History*, London: Routledge.

Film: 21st Century Literacy 'A strategy for film education across the UK', online at www.21stcenturyliteracy.org.uk, accessed 28 November 2011.

Gardner, H. (1983) *Frames of Mind: The theory of multiple intelligences*. New York: Basic Books.

Hughes-Warrington, M. (2007) *History Goes to the Movies*, London: Routledge.

Harlan, D. (2007) 'Historical fiction and the future of academic history', in K. Jenkins, S. Morgan and A. Munslow (eds) *Manifestos for History*, London: Routledge, pp. 108–30.

Haydn, T. (2011) 'History teaching and ICT', in Ian Davies (ed.), *Debates in History Teaching*, London: Routledge, pp. 236–48.

Jenkins, K., Morgan, S. and Munslow, A. (2007) *Manifestos for History*, London: Routledge.

Jones-Nerzic, R. (2001) 'The laptop revolution', *Teaching History Online* 4. www.spartacus. schoolnet.co.uk/history4a.htm, accessed 28 November 2011.

Lowenthal, D. (1985) *The Past is a Foreign Country*, Cambridge: Cambridge University Press.

Lowenthal, D. (1998) *The Heritage Crusade and Spoils of History*, Cambridge: Cambridge University Press.

MacCallum-Stewart, E. (2011) *Television Docu-Drama and The First World War*, online at www. inter-disciplinary.net/ptb/www/War2/stewart%20paper.pdf, accessed 28 November 2011.

MacMillan, M. (2010) *The Uses and Abuses of History*, London: Profile Books.

QCA (2005) *Pupil Perceptions of History at Key Stage 3: Final Report*, London: QCA.

Riel, M. (1998) 'Education in the twenty-first century: just in time learning or learning communities', paper presented at *Challenges of the Next Millennium: Education & Development of Human Resources*: Fourth Annual Conference of the Emirates Center for Strategic Studies and Research, Abu Dhabi, 24–26 May, 1998, online at http://faculty. pepperdine.edu/mriel/office/papers/jit-learning, accessed 15 January 2012.

Rigney, A. (2007) 'Being an improper historian', in Keith Jenkins *et al.* (eds) *Manifestos for History*, London: Routledge, pp. 149–59.

Samuel, R. (1994) *Theatres of Memory*, London: Verso.

Tollmar, P. (2006) 'Digital storytelling', *e-help Seminar 22*, Gothenburg 9–10 September 2006, online at www.e-help.eu/seminars/tollmar.htm, accessed 28 November 2011.

Tosh, J. (2008) *Why History Matters*, Basingstoke: Palgrave Macmillan.

White, H. V. (1990) *The Content of the Form*, London: John Hopkins University Press.

Wilentz, S. (2001) 'America made easy: McCullough, Adams, and the decline of popular history', *The New Republic*, 1 July, online at www.tnr.com/article/books-and-arts/90636/ david-mccullough-john-adams-book-revie, accessed 10 December 2011.

Chapter 7

We need to talk about PowerPoint

Terry Haydn

Introduction

Why is this an important issue for history teachers? In part, because of the increasingly influential role that PowerPoint (or other presentation software) has played in history teaching over the past decade, particularly since the widespread availability of data projectors within 'ordinary' classrooms (OECD, 2010). In some schools, the combination of data projector and PowerPoint presentation has become one of the most prevalent modes of pedagogy, superseding the 'textbook' paradigm which had previously been dominant in history teaching in the UK (Beswick, 2011; Haydn, 2011). A recent OECD study of the use of new technology in UK classrooms suggested that, in some schools, pupils were being given a 'staple diet' of PowerPoint (or interactive whiteboard) presentations as they moved from lesson to lesson (OECD, 2010). One of my colleagues recently told me that large numbers of pupils at his school had sent a petition to the head teacher to protest about the excessive use of PowerPoint, and a number of the mentors in our initial teacher education partnership have told me that they sometimes forbid student teachers to use PowerPoint for a period of time, as they are concerned about student dependence on this mode of teaching. At the time of writing, it seems reasonable to claim that PowerPoint (or equivalent) is a routinely used tool for teaching history in the UK.

It is not just a problem of the pervasiveness of PowerPoint and the possibility that history teachers and student teachers may be over-reliant on it as a teaching approach. The use of PowerPoint is also problematic because it is sometimes used maladroitly, in a way that fails to sustain learners' attention. When I give talks about the use of ICT, I routinely ask students if they have ever been severely bored by a PowerPoint presentation: usually, every hand goes up. There cannot be many people reading this who have not shared this experience. As far as I am aware, it is the only ICT application internationally recognised as a cause of death. A Google search on 'Death by PowerPoint' brought up 2.2 million hits; an image search of the same phrase, 2.8 million hits.

So what is it about PowerPoint that evinces such responses and outcomes? How can history teachers respond intelligently to the issues arising out of the easy access to such presentation software?[1]

One approach would be to think about 'how to make PowerPoint less boring'. It is probably helpful to give some thought to what PowerPoint does well, and what it is less well suited to. However, there is a real danger that if reflections are limited to analysing the affordances and limitations of the software, we fall into the trap of what Mishra (2012) terms 'technocentism'; that is to say, considering the use of the technology as if it was the only influence on engagement and effective learning, rather than being just part of the 'equation', alongside the subject knowledge of the teacher and the general pedagogic skills of the teacher.

Another possible question would be 'How good are your presentation skills?' or 'How good are you at using PowerPoint?' These approaches would also risk going down a path that might provide only partial solutions. Is that what we are doing in lessons, 'giving a presentation'? The vast augmentation in the power or armoury of the teacher in terms of presentation tools over the past decade has in some cases led to the temptation for teachers to *increase* the proportion of the lesson that is teacher led, at the expense of dialogue between teacher and pupils and pupil-to-pupil dialogue (Heppell, 2011; Walsh, 2006). This is not to say that teacher-led components of lessons are per se a bad thing, but that the balance between teacher presentation, and the opportunity for dialogue, 'active' learning and 'knowledge construction' (Alexander, 2004; Mercer, 2000) by pupils may be adversely affected. There is the danger of the teacher lapsing into 'Look what I can do with a whiteboard' mode, rather than thinking of how to ensure an appropriate degree of active pupil participation in the lesson. The idea that it is about the teacher's 'performance skills' goes against most recent research and inspection findings that stress the importance of active pupil involvement in learning (see, for example, Alexander, 2004; Ofsted, 2011; Wiliam, 2011). Whiteboard and PowerPoint 'wizards' may be tempted to overdo presentation-style teaching (because they are good at it), leading to what has been termed 'passive engagement' on the part of learners (see Figure 7.1). If you are primarily concerned about becoming expert at using the advanced or more esoteric features of PowerPoint, this chapter has little to say, but there are over 17 million results for a Google search on 'Advanced PowerPoint', so there is help 'out there' on this.

Figure 7.1 The dangers of technocentrism ('Look what I can do with a whiteboard')

So what are we trying to do in lessons? Northedge (1992) suggests that we generally hope to do at least some of the following in our teaching sessions:

- capture and maintain the attention of learners;
- make the topic meaningful to learners;
- interpret/present the content of the lesson in a way that is clear and comprehensible for learners;
- encourage the learners to relate the content of the session to contingent/related problems or issues associated with the content being covered (to make links to other learning);
- encourage learners to question their assumptions and preconceptions;
- get some key points across in a way that the learners will remember and understand;
- encourage learners to be prepared to contribute actively to the session, to *participate* in the lesson;
- leave learners motivated to think and learn more about the topic;
- draw on the prior knowledge/experience/opinions/beliefs and feelings of the learners.

Wiliam (2011: 46) would add to this list 'activating learners as instructional resources for one another'; that is to say, teaching in such a way that the amount of learning overall is increased by getting learners to talk, discuss, argue and develop their thinking – to learn from each other as well as from the teacher. The implications of this are that PowerPoint presentations should generally provide some opportunities for 'socially constructed learning'.

This list may not be comprehensive, but it gives us some things to think about in terms of what we are trying to achieve in lessons, and in terms of how useful PowerPoint might be in trying to achieve these things. As most experienced teachers are aware, there is much more to effective learning than just 'giving a good presentation' (see Chapter 1 for further elucidation of this point). It is worth keeping in mind that in recent research about what pupils like and dislike about being in history classrooms, the teacher talking for too long ('He's like a Duracell battery, he just goes on and on…' in the words of one pupil) was one of the top three complaints (QCA, 2005). In the words of Punya Mishra, 'a lecture is just a lecture' (http://punya.educ.msu.edu/2009/05/05/is-a-lecture-just-a-lecture). This is not to suggest that presentation skills are unimportant if you are a teacher (or a pupil), but I would argue that the issues and challenges around using PowerPoint are much broader than the development of 'presentation skills'. Given recent evidence about the importance of collaborative, dialogic and enquiry based learning (see for instance, Alexander, 2004; Ofsted, 2011; Wiliam, 2011), there are dangers in starting to think about lessons as 'presentations'. For readers who are particularly interested in presentation and design issues, Reynolds (2005, 2008) offers a number of suggestions related to the use of PowerPoint.

So, the questions I would like to pose are, 'How good is PowerPoint at helping teachers to achieve the aims listed above?' and 'How can teachers make the most effective use of presentation software to enhance learning in their lessons?'

What's wrong with PowerPoint?

There have been several critiques of the educational use of PowerPoint, with several of them pointing out that the software was originally designed for commercial and 'pitching purposes', with the result that many design features of PowerPoint sit uneasily in an educational environment (see, for example, Adams, 2006; Tufte, 2006).

As early as 1999, Norvig parodied the use of PowerPoint with a slide show based around the idea of what Lincoln's Gettysburg Address would have been like had Lincoln had access to PowerPoint (http://norvig.com/Gettysburg). Mycue and Martini (2000) found that the replacement of overhead projectors with PowerPoint as the standard method of 'delivery' in their educational institution had a detrimental effect on student test scores, leading to a (helpful) enquiry as to why this was the case. In a systematic review of the use of PowerPoint, Levasseur and Sawyer (2007) found little convincing evidence from any study to suggest that using PowerPoint improved learning outcomes, but nor was there clear evidence of deficits in learning outcomes caused by the use of PowerPoint. Using cognitive load theory, Sweller (2007) suggested that using PowerPoint was actually harmful for learning as student attention was unhelpfully split between listening to the teacher and trying to read what was on the slides.

Perhaps the most damning dissection of the intrinsic flaws of PowerPoint comes from Tufte (2006: 4), and the points he makes may be worth reflecting on when you consider them in relation to your own experience with PowerPoint, both as perpetrator and victim:

> Foreshortening of evidence and thought, low spatial resolution, an intensely hierarchical single-path structure as the model for organising every type of content, breaking up narratives and data into slides and minimal fragments, rapid temporal sequencing of thin information rather than focused spatial analysis, conspicuous chartjunk and PP Phluff, branding of slides with logotypes, a preoccupation with format not content, incompetent designs for data graphics and tables and a smirky commercialism that turns information into a sales pitch and presenters into marketers ... With little information per slide, many, many slides are needed. Audiences endure a relentless sequentiality, one damn slide after anothe ... Impoverished space encourages imprecise statements, slogans, abrupt and thinly-argued claims.
>
> (Tufte, 2006: 4–5)

A particularly important point made by Tufte is that PowerPoint is not good for working with dense and extended text, and he suggests that within the use of PowerPoint, teachers should use handouts that allow users to move into 'text mode', which will enable learners 'to contextualise, compare, narrate and recast evidence', adding that, 'in contrast, data-thin, forgetful displays tend to make audiences ignorant and passive' (Tufte, 2006: 15).

He goes on to argue that the core ideas of teaching: 'explanation, reasoning, finding things out, questioning, content, evidence, credible authority – not patronising authoritarianism – are contrary to the cognitive style of PowerPoint (Tufte, 2006: 7).

It should be noted that Tufte's criticisms relate to 'the standard default PP presentation' (2006: 4). There is nothing to stop teachers eschewing the default paths that can seduce them into accepting the pathways and formats that the software designers suggest.

What's good about PowerPoint?

I suspect that many of those who are so dismissive of PowerPoint did not spend years in the classroom when a blackboard and chalk were the main form of presentation technology. Those of you who are old enough to remember the rigmarole of setting up reel to reel film in the classroom ('It was great as you always knew you were going to get a free lesson', as one former pupil remarked), or laboriously slotting slides into the carousel projector, or holding up a picture for the class to look at or pass round, will be aware that PowerPoint has made some things easier for the teacher. In combination with the facility of the internet to get hold of powerful 'impact' resources (see Chapter 1 for a more developed explanation of this term), PowerPoint makes it easy to show images, sounds, animations and moving image clips to pupils. In the words of Adams (2006: 408), PowerPoint 'allows teachers to gather and organise an astonishing array of digitised materials … into a single file'.

Steve Beswick (Microsoft Director for Education in the UK) argues that:

> In the right hands it is an exciting tool that engages the students through multimedia and teachers are doing amazing things with it … When we talk to teachers and students about PowerPoint, we always show them the 'Death by PowerPoint' video [www.youtube.com/watch?v=lpvgfmEU2Ck]. We show them the different features they could use and they tell us 'I never knew PowerPoint could do that'.
>
> (Beswick, 2011: 4)

There is the suggestion here that it is about technological sophistication: that knowledge of the advanced technical features of PowerPoint will enable the teacher to deliver a more powerful and effective presentation. However, I would argue that PowerPoint presentations that are stultifyingly boring are dull not because they fail to use the advanced and sophisticated technical features of the application, but because the authors have lost sight of how to engage the audience with the ideas and content of the presentation. In the words of an Advanced Skills Teacher, 'If you haven't got a good idea in the first place, just shoving up a PowerPoint isn't going to do the job' (OECD, 2010). When you think about the outstanding practitioners who do sessions at major history education conferences in the UK, what proportion of them use the advanced features of interactive whiteboards and PowerPoint? This brings us back to Mishra and Koehler's TPACK Framework and the point that ideas, content and subject knowledge matter just as much, if not more than technological expertise (Mishra and Koehler, 2006). I would quite like to become expert at using the advanced features of PowerPoint and the interactive whiteboard, but every time I have to do a teaching session, my first priories are to try to think about what are the most important ideas and points I want to make relating to the topic, how to get those points across in a way which will engage learners and hold their attention, and how to acquire 'impact' resources that will help me to do those things.

What mistakes do some teachers make with PowerPoint?

This list is compiled from feedback from student teachers, reporting on their own experiences of being on the 'receiving end' of PowerPoint, both at school and university, and recent research findings about the use of PowerPoint in educational contexts. Many readers will already be aware of some of the points made, but the feedback gleaned from recent cohorts of PGCE students suggests that in spite of this, the phenomenon of 'the boring PowerPoint' has not yet been eliminated.

Text too small to read

This seems to be so obvious that it is hardly worth mentioning, but I still attend lectures and presentations where the teacher, in many cases an otherwise highly intelligent person, breezily asks if those at the back of a 500-seat lecture theatre can read the 12-point font presented. Some tutorials suggest a minimum size of 20-point font, but (obviously?) it depends on the size of the room. A simple solution is to stand at the back of the room and check, and take a couple of minutes to adjust font size if you have got it wrong.

Too much text on slides and just reading through what is on the slide

Suggestions for the maximum amount of text to put on a slide commonly vary between 40 and 70 words. There is also the question of whether, if you are not going to lapse into reading through a slide that learners are quite capable of reading for themselves, you stop talking in order to allow time for the audience to read through the text, avoiding the danger of 'cognitive overload' that Sweller (2007) refers to. There is a danger here of slowing down the pace of the session. The answer perhaps is that 'it depends': there is a judgement call here, occasionally a piece of prose is so powerful that you want them to read every word and have a moment to think about it. On other occasions it might be more appropriate to talk through and comment on a slide as they are looking at it. It is probably not a good idea to lapse into always doing one or the other.

Loss of eye contact with learners: looking at the screen rather than the learners

Ward (2003: 5), describing his own 'routine, dull and anodyne' experiences of learning through PowerPoint, points to lack of eye contact between teacher and learners as one of the most alienating characteristics of PowerPoint use:

> Once the computer came into play, it invariably became a process of tutor with remote handset talking to the screen and flicking through the sequence of pages. Not talking to us, not making eye contact and engaging with the electronically illuminated faces staring screenwards. Just talking to the screen, pressing the button and talking until all the slides were complete.

The use of an annotated 'handout' mode print-off of the slides can partly obviate this problem; at least the teacher is not obliged to face away from learners, and can think ahead for a few slides whilst the pupils are looking at an embedded moving image clip or doing a task arising out of the presentation. But it is also about having a reasonably secure knowledge of what is on the slides, and having the composure to intersperse glancing at the screen or notes with making eye contact with the audience. Although I have taught for over 30 years, whenever I have to do 'a talk', I still ink in an 'R!' on the back of my hand (to remind myself to at least pretend to appear relaxed and at ease whilst talking), and a picture of an eye, to remind myself to make intermittent eye contact with the learners (see Figure 7.2). Composure is another 'non-technical' facet of using PowerPoint. Sometimes, my students lapse into talking in a mannered, artificial and over-loud way when using PowerPoint, rather than just talking 'normally'. Adroit 'delivery' is part of using PowerPoint effectively, but it is less about being declamatory, rhetorical and loud, and more about being calm, relaxed and natural in tone and manner.

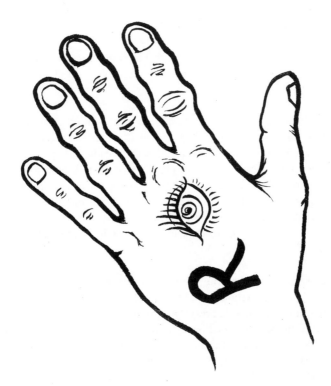

Figure 7.2 The Haydn Composure Wizard

Persistent 'salami slicing' of slides

What Tufte (2006: 6) terms 'the dreaded slow reveal', where the teacher reveals just one line (or bullet point) of a slide, then reveals a second line, and so on. There are some occasions when there is a particular point to 'phasing' a slide, for example, where some sort of paradox or surprise is revealed which surprises the learners and disturbs their preconceptions. But doing it routinely deadens the pace of what the teacher is saying: in the words of one PGCE student 'You start thinking, Oh God, how long is this going to last? It also smacks of a sort of Stalinist control-freakery' (as if to say, 'I am only going to let you think about one thing, and then if you are good/don't protest, I will give you another morsel of my thoughts. You are subject to my will; you will only think about what I tell you to – one line at a time').

Unthinkingly reverting to PowerPoint and its default settings

Lodge (2009) makes the point that PowerPoint is 'easy technology'; once you get used to it, it is easy to 'knock up a few slides, put in a few images, insert a couple of moving image clips...'. It is easy to lapse into using a PowerPoint in lessons almost in an unthinking way, as a sort of default first step. PGCE Students who are asked to 'shadow' a pupil for a day report that PowerPoint often dominates the pupil's day; in some cases it has become 'a first port of call' in putting together a lesson. I can recall attending a one-day conference and being the fifteenth speaker. The previous 14 speakers had all used PowerPoint (and I used it): the end of a perfect or complete 'PowerPoint Day'?

Just to make things worse, some users unthinkingly use the default settings that PowerPoint provides, which prompt the use of bullet points on all slides. Adams (2006: 395) reminds us that,

> For educational use in particular, it must be borne in mind that the default settings have been chosen for business and sales audiences ... It is not that PowerPoint necessarily precludes other ways of presenting ideas in a wide variety of knowledge forms, but rather, these other forms are less frequently represented, simply because it may not be immediately apparent to a teacher ... how to step away from the default settings and explore other possibilities. To do so requires thoughtful initiative, that is, wakefulness to the habituating trends embedded in PowerPoint's user interface and a willingness to flex it in other directions, or to choose not to use it when it is inappropriate to the teaching task.

The excessive use of bullet points is one of the most criticised traits in PowerPoint use (see, for example, Tufte, 2006; Macmillan, 2011). As Macmillan points out, as well as 'pace' issues, if you bullet point just about everything, particularly important 'key' messages will not stand out (it was this attribute of PowerPoint that led to the application being blamed for the Columbia Space Shuttle disaster – see www.washingtonpost.com/wp-dyn/content/article/2005/08/29/AR2005082901444.html).

This doesn't mean that bullet points are definitively 'a bad thing': there may be room for a final slide that lists the three or four most important points you want pupils to remember, but overuse can lead to disengagement and 'diminishing returns' in terms of impact.

Cluttered slides

Madian's research (1995) suggested that the 'bells and whistles' of multimedia effects often distracted pupils from the essence of the learning that was required and Tufte (2006) is scathing about PowerPoint 'phluff': the logos, branding, transition effects and background motifs that meretriciously adorn many presentations and that often have nothing to do with the knowledge or content that the slides cover. Most teachers are aware that pupils can waste a lot of time deliberating over fonts, colours, multimedia effects and backgrounds when they are asked to use PowerPoint, but it is not just pupils who waste time over such details. I can remember a phase when I used to spend time producing presentations that had white text on a black background. I still think this looks OK, but as long as the pupils can clearly and easily see what is on the screen, I don't think the colour and the 'phluff' matter anything like as much as the quality of the ideas and resources that go on the screen. One of the distinctive features of Google was the simplicity of the screen compared to other search engines. Having gone through a phase of 'trying to make the slides look pretty', I now try to avoid putting anything on slides that might distract learners from the ideas and content of the presentation.

Trying to do everything through PowerPoint

PowerPoint is good for some things; for instance, showing an image, or playing an embedded digitised moving image clip, or showing an animation of a map showing change over time. However, it is less effective if the teacher wants to work with quite long texts, such as documents, newspaper articles or other forms of dense text. Sometimes, teachers are tempted to stay within PowerPoint to work with text, segmenting or simplifying text in order to fit it within the constraints of the software, instead of using a handout and 'toggling' in and out of the use of PowerPoint. Sometimes, even images are better given out to learners rather than being just shown on screen, especially if they are to be discussed and annotated. This also can help to 'break up' or 'chunk' the lesson into more 'components' and avoid 'PowerPoint fatigue' and lapse of concentration, by varying modes and inputs. I have found that some card sort exercises work better if the cards are given out to pupils and organised by hand rather than the often more time-consuming method of on-screen manipulation. It also seems to encourage discussion between pupils, and the dialogic learning that is thought to be so valuable (Alexander, 2004; Hogden and Webb, 2008), if they have the materials in their hands, and can discuss things with each other rather than having to speak up in front of the class as a whole.

Excessive use of PowerPoint that is exclusively led and controlled by the teacher

Several students reported that PowerPoint was often used, or at least 'kept on' right through whole lessons, and that whiteboard and PowerPoint lessons often tended to be quite 'teacher-led', with pupils spending large proportions of lessons watching, listening and absorbing, rather than 'talking and doing'. One of the paradoxes of increasing use of ICT in history classrooms in recent years (Ofsted, 2011), is that in spite of the claims by politicians and those selling ICT to schools that ICT promotes 'interactive learning' (Haydn, 2003), the combination of interactive whiteboards and PowerPoint use has led to an increase in 'teacher-led' learning, and a reduction in pupil talk (see, for example, Heppell, 2011; Walsh, 2006).

The ease of use and convenience of PowerPoint, and the fact that it is very useful for several of the things we often want to do in lessons has (in some cases) disturbed the balance between teacher-led forms of teaching, and the time given to teacher–pupil dialogue and pupil to pupil dialogue.

Failure to involve learners whilst using PowerPoint

Heppell characterises some use of PowerPoint as a 'stand and deliver' mode of teaching, where the teacher stands, talks and transmits large quantities of information to learners who, other than listening, and perhaps taking notes, play no active part in the lesson (Heppell, 2011). This can be a way of 'spoon-feeding' pupils, and it can be a way of covering content very quickly. There is nothing wrong with lessons containing *some* teacher-led components. Often, high-quality teacher exposition is an essential part of the lesson, a way of getting pupils interested in the topic, a way of getting across key knowledge and ideas. I have real worries about students who eschew the challenge of 'leading the learning', from the front of the class, and who dive into groupwork and 'discovery learning' without scaffolding it so that these activities are worthwhile. However, there is an art to interspersing PowerPoint-led components of lessons with elements that force learners to participate more actively in the learning process (see next section), and there is a judgement call involved in terms of when to switch PowerPoint off and move into a less teacher-directed phase of the lesson. Wiliam (2011) argues that the best learning takes place when the learners have had to work harder than the teacher. It can be salutary to reflect on how hard pupils have had to work (and think) in your PowerPoint sessions compared to you.

Too many slides and/or too slow a pace through slides

I hesitate to mention this, having recently sat through a presentation that was really interesting and that (I found out afterwards) used over 200 slides (Punya Mishra, Keynote address at the TIES Conference, University of Barcelona, 1 February). At the time of writing, this presentation was available online at http://ties2012.eu/en/pg-videos.html: should it disappear, a summary can be found at www.uea.ac.uk/~m242/historypgce/ict/welcome.htm.

However, for most mortals, anything over 50 slides (and perhaps fewer than this), risks diminishing returns in terms of learner attention, especially if they are run all in one go, without any interspersed activities. Much depends on the 'density' of slides. If each slide is trying to make several points, this impacts on the pace and 'load' of the session. I can remember one National Strategy PowerPoint which on slide a hundred and something had the cheerful banner 'Ready for more!' without any obvious sense of irony. Another way of thinking about slide construction is the principle of 'one idea per slide', or what Lodge (2009: 190) calls a 'billboard' approach to slide construction, and I think there is something to be said for this approach (see the Mishra presentation for an example of this approach). Of course, much depends on the quality of the ideas and resources that are 'billboarded'.

How can we improve our use of PowerPoint?

A few technical things

Although I am trying to argue that levels of technical proficiency in PowerPoint are not the only or even most influential determinants of how well it is used, it is clearly helpful to have a sound grasp of some of the most useful affordances of the software.[2]

One of the most important and useful facets of PowerPoint is the 'Insert' menu at the top of the screen. At the click of a button, it is possible to insert an image, a graph, a map, an audio file, a moving image clip, or (if you have internet access in the room), anything from the World Wide Web, perhaps the richest source of 'impact' materials in the history of education.[3] If internet access is not available in the classroom, web-based resources can be saved and used in the classroom by saving them to portable hard drives and memory sticks, and sites such as keepvid.com can be used to save moving image clips to hard drives. Given the abundance of 'impact' resources on the internet, it surprises me that student teachers do not make more use of this facility when using PowerPoint.

Other useful functions within PowerPoint are the facility to 'zoom' into images (i.e. to enlarge and frame particular elements within an image). Some images lend themselves to this more than others: Breughel's *Triumph of Death*, and *Sir Henry Unton* (artist unknown) are obvious examples of images that lend themselves to this technique. The ability to 'crop' images so that you just get the bits that you want, or you demonstrate the power of image editing to pupils is also useful, as are the functions that allow the author to highlight text, use a 'mouse trail' to move objects around on a slide, or to insert blank shapes and text boxes into a slide. This last feature allows pupils to insert 'speech' shapes and 'thought' bubbles into a slide, to contrast 'text and sub-text'. This can be useful when trying to get pupils to understand the difference between the public declarations of politicians and their ulterior motives (I am thinking of topics such as the Munich Conference of 1938, or images of Churchill, Stalin and Roosevelt at Yalta). Tutorials explaining how to do all these things can be found on Johannes Ahrenfelt and Neal Watkin's Website *Eat, Sleep, Teach*, at www.eatsleepteach.com/ict-and-e-learning/ how-to-make-powerpoint-less-boring (or in their book, Ahrenfelt and Watkin, 2008). Another technique, designed to get pupils to think about particular questions as they are watching a moving image clip embedded into PowerPoint, is to insert text boxes with the questions you want the pupils to think about, around the outside of the area of the screen which is playing the media clip.

There are also some keyboard shortcuts that are useful; pressing the 'Alt' and 'Tab' keys at the same time enables users to toggle quickly and easily between their PowerPoint presentation and the DVD drive, or 'pre-loaded' internet pages or Word files. Pressing the 'w' or 'b' key will blank the screen (to either white or black) so that the screen is not a distraction when you are moving to a phase when you want them to focus on what you are saying rather than the screen.

There are also a number of 'web interactivities' and Web 2.0 applications that can be worked into PowerPoint presentations, which add 'learner agency' to the presentation, rather than them being simply passive recipients of 'the show'. One example of the former, for older pupils, is *The World's Shortest Political Quiz* (www.theadvocates.org/quiz), which can be useful when trying to develop learners' understanding of the terms 'left wing' and 'right wing'. The quiz asks learners to express their opinions on ten political questions (five related to government intervention in the economy and five related to issues of personal liberty).[4] After taking the quiz (which takes about three minutes), either individually, or with the teacher simply entering the majority decision from a 'show of hands', the program assigns learners to a point on the political spectrum, making the point that it is not just as simple as a 'Left wing–Right wing' continuum. It also gives more information about the political terms involved, and allows them to compare their position with the views of over 13 million other people who have done the quiz. Finally, the exercise can be used to make a point about internet or information literacy. The results indicate that a large proportion of the respondents are 'libertarian' in their political attitudes and position (whether they are consciously aware of this, or even understand what the word means or not). The site is run by the Libertarian Society, and therefore 'has a position' on the political spectrum, which may not be apparent to learners, even after they have done the quiz and looked through the follow-up materials. This is just one example of the thousands of web interactivities that are available on the internet.

Web 2.0 applications that can be worked into PowerPoint presentations include *Googlefight* and *Google ngram*, which can be particularly useful when dealing with 'significance' issues, and *Voicethread* and *Wallwisher* (see Chapter 1 for an explanation of what these applications do). All these applications provide the opportunity for learners to be actively involved in the presentation.

Response systems, such as *Turning Point*, *ActivExpression* and *Qwizdom* (sometimes termed 'Voting technology/software') also offer the opportunity for learners to make active contributions in the course of a PowerPoint presentation. Such systems have been criticised as 'expensive toys' ('Why can't they just put their hands up?' 'Why can't they just show red/yellow/green flash cards?'), but in my experience, learners do seem to enjoy using these tools, and if the school possesses such equipment, it does not eat into departmental capitation. As Walsh (2006) has noted, much depends on how sparingly and discerningly the technology is used. Classroom response systems can be used for batteries of dreary multiple-choice factual retention tests, or for the provocative and thoughtful promotion of argument and debate, problematising the issues involved and getting learners to question their assumptions about historical issues. Cheaper alternatives to 'clicker' technology are the *Poll Everywhere* application (see Chapter 9), or pupil use of the wireless mouse, which allows pupils to vote, draw freehand or otherwise make changes to slides from their desks (see www.microsoft.com/multipoint/mouse-mischief for further development of this option). Free 'Add ons' such as *Plex* (http://tinyurl.com/7euetku), which enables learners to 'sub-contract'/collectively construct a presentation and move round it non-sequentially, and STAMP (http://tinyurl.com/5wx4w9g), which allows learners to insert their own captions and subtitles onto moving image clips, also offer the opportunity for *pupil* activity and agency in the use of PowerPoint.

On the borderline of 'technical' and 'creative' ideas relating to PowerPoint is the issue of design. How well designed are your PowerPoint slides, how skilfully do you use images? This is another differential in teachers' use of PowerPoint. In an interview, a history AST (Advanced Skills Teacher) who is very accomplished in his use of PowerPoint argued that some teachers pay more attention to design than others:

> PowerPoint should get teachers to think about good designs for presenting ideas and communicating concepts. There is a big difference between a low resolution picture which has been slapped onto a slide with lots of text, compared to a higher resolution picture which has been positioned from a designed point of view with relevant text (if any). I know this sounds a bit techie but it really isn't, it's simply about how you present messages – young adults are all about good design, so why should we not learn from for example Nancy Duarte's *Resonate – presenting visual stories that transform audiences* (2010) or Garr Reynolds *Presentation Zen* (2009) – about designing coherent and visually stunning PowerPoint slides to engage learners to want to find out more?

Other, 'non-technical' things

The following points are more about general pedagogy whilst using PowerPoint rather than familiarity and expertise in using the full breadth of the technical features of the program.

The suggestions and examples can be grouped under four overarching principles. First, the quality of the lesson will be partly influenced by the quality of the resources that have been gathered together (this applies to 'supplementary materials', as well as the content of the slides); this is related to Ben Walsh's idea about the importance of 'Building learning packages', and the ways in which ICT makes it much easier to do this (Walsh, 2003). I have argued elsewhere (Haydn *et al.*, 2008) that initiative with resources is one of the important differentials between 'competent' and 'inspirational' teachers. Some teachers are content to go with 'what is in the departmental stockpile', while others go to inordinate lengths to hunt down *anything* that might help them to make a point in a powerful and effective way.

(There is perhaps also a degree of creativity and imagination involved in thinking about what resources might enable a point to be made in a memorable way).

A second principle is to make every effort to ensure that learners *participate* during PowerPoint-based sessions, so that learners are not 'playing truant in mind'. This is important because there is evidence that 'high-engagement' classrooms have better learning outcomes than those where pupils do not make any active contribution to the lesson (Mercer *et al.*, 2004).

A corollary of this is that pupils must be *made to think* during the course of PowerPoint presentations. 'Thinking' is perhaps one of the most important forms of activity in a lesson. And the thinking should preferably be about the intellectual content of the lesson, rather than focusing on how clever the teacher's use of PowerPoint was. Adams cites the example of the student who forgot she was watching a PowerPoint slide:

> I remember one day watching a lecture and realising that I had forgotten it was PowerPoint. I mean, I had forgotten about the particular slide I was looking at and was focusing on the content. It was partly I think because what was being covered required some thought and concentration on my part.
>
> (Adams, 2006: 403)

Schick argues that the real 'interactivity' arising out of ICT use is the changes that technology use effects in the mind of the learner, or the seeds of new ideas planted into their minds (Schick, 2000).

Adding to the importance of trying to ensure that PowerPoint is used in a way that forces students to think about the content of the presentation is Willingham's claim that it is only when students are made to think about things that they remember them:

> Your memory is not a product of what you remember or what you try to remember; it's a product of what you think about ... Whatever students think about is what they will remember ... memory is the residue of thought ... The obvious implication for teachers is that they must design lessons that will ensure that students are thinking about the meaning of the material.
>
> (Willingham, 2009: 53–4, 63)

The fourth general point is that the effectiveness of the presentation will depend as much on the quality of the teacher's accompanying questioning and exposition as on what is on the slides. Even most really strong 'impact' resources will only work well when complemented by skilful teacher exposition and questioning.

Some examples

In terms of incorporating some form of 'activity' for learners and trying to 'make them think', to avoid them being entirely in 'reception' mode throughout the presentation:

- At some points, ask pupils to put their hand up to express a view or position ('Can you put your hand up if you agree...?/if you think...?/if you understand...?'). A variation on this is to say 'Can you put your hand up if you are listening to what I am saying?' and just carry on talking, rather than stopping to draw their attention to the question, to see how many pupils have lapsed into 'truanting in mind'.

- Ask questions at intervals instead of staying constantly in 'telling' mode. 'Why…?' and 'How…?' questions are often better than knowledge recall and comprehension questions in that it gets learners to think about meaning for a longer period. It can also be interesting to ask pupils to predict or guess 'what happened next…?' or to think of captions to fill in speech and thought bubbles on a slide (Walsh, 2006). A variation on this is to give pupils a two minute pairwork task to answer a question posed on a slide (for instance, 'Which of these three statements most accurately describes the policy of appeasement?'). Obviously, much depends on your skill in asking intriguing questions (Wiliam, 2011): when you do this, is there an animated buzz for the two minutes before feedback, or does it result in desultory compliance?

- At intervals, get pupils looking at and working with an annotated handout; ask pupils to explain particular numbered points within the text, or give them tasks that oblige them to shorten or select from the information they have been given so they are obliged to think about the problem (postcard or post-it exercises, 'in not more than 50 words', 'in one sentence…'). Alternatively, lead pupils through the annotated text, explaining key sections, à la John Fines.[5]

- It is also possible to build a degree of 'choice' into the presentation, asking pupils to decide which aspects of a topic they wish to pursue, and using hyperlinks to provide alternative pathways through the material. My colleague, Andy Mee does this when he does a session about Web 2.0 applications for my students, using voting technology to ask them which applications are of most interest to them, and then clicking on the hyperlink that leads to the slides on the top few applications they have chosen. This again provides a degree of 'agency' for learners.

- Mycue and Martini suggest the insertion of blank or 'puzzle' slides, where the learners have to decide what should be inserted into the blank slide, given the question or problem posed. They argue that 'learners remember best what they have to some extent had to work out for themselves', and that instead of aiming for instant clarity, learners should sometimes be 'made to work' to get the answer to the question (Mycue and Martini, 1999). An example of this is Figure 7.3, a Bolshevik slogan from the First World War, which takes a moment to work out in terms of meaning, and which can be used in conjunction with the 'Blue eyes, brown eyes' clip on YouTube (www.youtube.com/watch?v=9yWxAND5qB4&feature=related), and the Wikipedia entry on Fritz Fischer and the causes of the First World War (http://en.wikipedia.org/wiki/Fritz_Fischer), to try to get across the theory that wars are sometimes started to divert attention from internal problems. A variation on this is to use Battersby's idea of 'The golden nugget', and ask pupils to suggest what should go in the blank slide that represents the single most important idea they should try to remember from the session (Battersby, 1997).

- Collis (2012) argues that learners who have understood what has been taught during the session should be asked to construct some form of learning artefact or text, which can be posted to a VLE to help other or subsequent learners ('What helped me to understand it was…', 'A good way of remembering it is …', 'The most difficult bit is …'.

- In terms of initiative with resources, this is only partly about scouring the internet for 'impact' resources. Most history teachers read newspapers and magazines, watch television, and use social media. It is partly about always being on the lookout for an image, a quote, a moving image clip, a map that might help to make a particular point in a powerful and effective way, or 'open up' a topic to make links across time and to the present. Social bookmarking sites such as Delicious (http://delicious.com) and Evernote (www.evernote.com), scanners, DVD recorders and memory sticks have made it easier to build up 'collections' of impact resources that can be incorporated into PowerPoint.

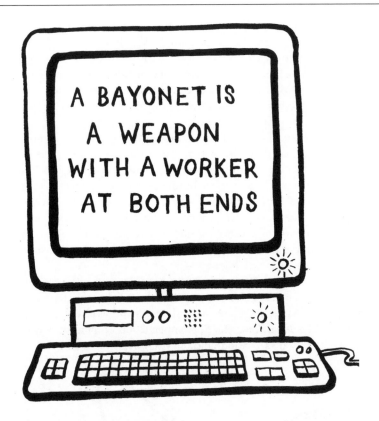

Figure 7.3 Bolshevik slogan in the First World War

- 'Top ten incredibly offensive vintage ads' has a number of images that quickly and powerfully make the point that social attitudes to race and gender have (to at least some extent) changed over time (http://totallytop10.com/current-affairs/odd-news/top-10-incredibly-offensive-vintage-ads).
- It does not take long, using Google Images, Mary Evans Picture Library, Flickr and other image sites, to build up collections of pictures and cartoons around particular historical themes, topics and people. If you are teaching a topic that involves the concept of revolt or protest (The Peasants' Revolt, The Chartists, The Suffragettes…), a collection of images showing the many ways in which people have protested against monarchs and governments can lead to an interesting discussion about the continuum between 'Writing to your MP', and more militant forms of action, the pros and cons of the various strategies for resistance or change, and provide an overview of the 'Big Picture' and change over time relating to the concept of protest.
- Sometimes an image or collection of images can make a particular point quickly and effectively. At the time of writing, it was possible to get a sequence of images featuring David and Victoria Beckham at a basketball match by doing a Google search. The images can be put in sequence on PowerPoint to tell a story, which most viewers can put together using 'inference'; an important concept in history, and one that is sometimes difficult to explain or exemplify. Viewers of the slides were not present at the time, and did not hear what was said, and yet most of them

will have made inferential judgements about what happened. For further development of this point, see the third page of Ahrenfelt and Watkin's 'Learn 2.0' section on their 'Eat, sleep, teach' website (www.eatsleepteach.com/category/learn-2-0). Another instance of using a short sequence of slides to make a particular point – in this case about the difference between causes and correlations – can be found in a PowerPoint presentation about Alan Turing at www.uea.ac.uk/~m242/history-pgce/ict/powerpoint/welcome.htm.

- It is not a question of how extensive these collections are, it is more about selecting images that promote thought, or that might disturb learner preconceptions. As well as using newspaper articles in the classroom, and interleaved into PowerPoint presentations (see Chapter 1), newspaper headlines can be scanned in to make links to the present, and to get learners to think differently about a topic. There are many learners who think that domestic service ended after the Edwardian Era, and that Slavery was abolished in the early nineteenth century. It does not take long to collect a number of sources – newspaper headlines, posters, cartoons – that argue that slavery is still around, it just changed its form (see Figure 7.4):
  - 'Upstairs, downstairs 2012-style: there are now more domestic workers in Britain than in Victorian Times' (*The Independent,* 12 February 2010: 26).
  - 'Children in chains: there are more slaves in the world today than at any time in history' (*The Guardian,* 28 September 2000, online at www.guardian.co.uk/media/2000/sep/28/tvandradio.television3).

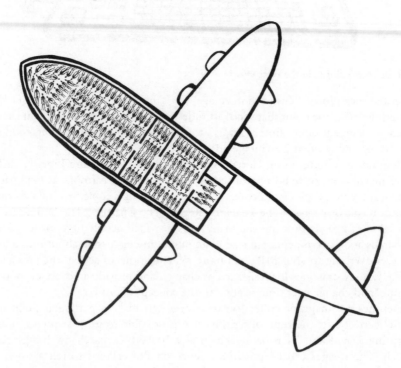

Figure 7.4 Slave transport

It is worth noting that, even if you have got hold of some good resources for your PowerPoint, the teacher's skills of exposition and questioning make an important difference to how effectively the resources will be deployed. There is still a need to think about what you have to say about the visual prompts, and what questions you are going to ask of them. Two examples of resources that need skilful exposition to get the most out of them are given below.

- It does not take long to build up a collection of pictures and cartoons of Queen Elizabeth II which present her in very different ways as her reign has progressed (with 'informal' and less 'respectful' images becoming more prevalent in more recent years). I usually select around a dozen, chosen to suggest a decline in deference to the royal family over the past 60 years. I give them out as a card sort and ask learners (in groups), to put them in what they think is chronological order, to think about in what ways the images are different, and finally, why the images are 'different over time', before playing them as a slide show, and complementing the pictures with information about film audiences standing and singing the National Anthem at the end of films in the 1960s, the decline in 'status' of the Queen's Christmas message, and other manifestations of 'the wind of change' in cultural and social attitudes. This also helps to make the point that history is not just about events and Acts of Parliament, but gradual change over time. Ian Mortimer's article (*Telegraph Weekend*, 31 March 2012) 'The great queen: parts 1 and 2', then provides a useful resource/task, for getting pupils to compare the reigns and situations faced by Queen Elizabeth I and Queen Elizabeth II (www.telegraph.co.uk/history/9176453/The-Great-Queen-parts-1-and-2.html).
- The graph on the National Archives Website showing the effect of the introduction of school dinners on the weight of the children receiving them has been described by Ben Walsh (2012) as a particularly useful and powerful source (see Figure 7.5). The graph does show quite clearly that the children's weight goes up in term time, and comes down in the school holidays. However, without some teacher exposition to draw out the wider significance of this innovation, and the changes over time in the availability of food to children, the full potential of the source may not be realised. Before showing the source, students could be asked whether they have ever eaten school meals, and what they think of them, whether they think school meals are 'big deal'/'a good idea'/'an important development in history'? After the graph has been shown, the emaciated state of British soldiers in the Boer War could be mentioned, and Walsh asks learners what many of these schoolchildren would be doing several years after the graph was produced; why were so many young people attracted to going into the army, was it just patriotism? What are the main health problems facing children in relation to food today?

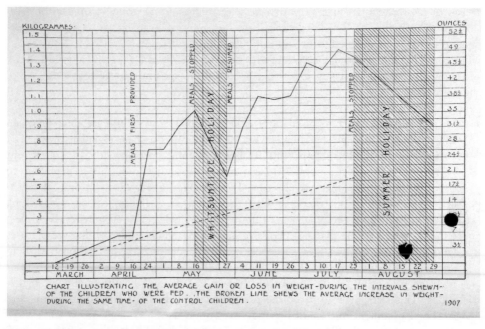

Figure 7.5 The introduction of school dinners

Pecha Kucha

I would not want to finish the chapter without mentioning the 'Pecha Kucha' phenomenon. The idea was developed by two Australian architects working in Tokyo in 2003. Their idea of architects coming together for an evening to share ideas was being spoiled by overlong PowerPoint presentations, so they brought in a rule that there could only be 20 slides maximum, and only 20 seconds to talk on each slide (with slides put on automatic timing). Only having a limited number of slides, and time per slide does of course concentrate the mind in terms of what are the core essentials of your message. The idea (not dissimilar from 'Teachmeets' in its aim) can of course be pared down to less than 20 slides and 20 seconds per slide, and it does inject a degree of pace and urgency (and fun) into PowerPoint sessions. It can be useful to experiment with Pecha Kucha, with or without pupils, whether or not you adhere to 'the rules'. (There are several examples of Pecha Kucha presentations, tutorials and guidance on YouTube.)

Conclusions

It goes without saying that we should try to educate pupils, as well as ourselves, in the effective use of PowerPoint, and into the art and craft of explaining ideas well.

In spite of the limitations of PowerPoint, and the misjudgements that teachers sometimes make in using presentation software, it is a useful tool. The effective use of PowerPoint depends only to a small degree on advanced technical expertise, and to a much greater degree on good subject knowledge, resourcefulness in collecting and deploying high-quality 'impact' resources, creativity and imagination in terms of *pedagogic* subject knowledge ('How can I get these ideas across in an engaging and meaningful way?'), and accomplished exposition and questioning. If your ideas, resources and interaction with pupils are poor, then your PowerPoint presentations will probably be poor also.

Notes

1 Although I have chosen to focus on the use of PowerPoint, as it is currently the most commonly used form of presentation software in UK classrooms, I am aware that there are a range of other options available, whether in the form of interactive whiteboard software, or alternatives to PowerPoint such as *Keynote, Prezi, Slide Rocket, Zoho* and *Google Docs Presentation.* Most of the points I attempt to make in the chapter apply to all these options.

2 I am aware as I write this section that many readers will already be familiar with most, or perhaps all of these points, and if you already have a good grasp of PowerPoint's features, you may wish to skip this section. However, there may well be some readers who are not familiar with all the points made in this section.

3 I am aware that school filtering systems often severely limit the proportion of resources from the World Wide Web that can be used in classrooms, but there is still quite a wide range of resources that are accessible. Harrison (2003: 39) noted that the internet provided 'an extraordinary supplement to the resources normally available to the history teacher', and the 'Insert' button within PowerPoint makes it possible to use this 'extraordinary supplement', whether through the insertion of a hyperlink to the web page required, or by linking to a file that has been saved to a hard drive or memory stick. The facility to bring the treasures and gems of the web into the classroom still strikes me as an underexploited facet of PowerPoint use.

4 A longer and more sophisticated version of the quiz can be found at www.politicalcompass.org.

5 Fines argued that even younger pupils could 'cope' with quite challenging texts if the teacher 'led them through it'.

References

Adams, C. (2006) 'PowerPoint: habits of mind and classroom culture', *Journal of Curriculum Studies,* 38 (4): 389–411.

Ahrenfelt, J. and Watkin, N. (2008) *Innovate with ICT,* London: Continuum.

Alexander, R. (2004) *Towards Dialogic Teaching: Rethinking classroom talk,* York: Diagolos.

Battersby, J. (1997) 'Differentiation', unpublished lecture, University of East Anglia, October.

Beswick, S. (2011) Quoted in L. Lightfoot, 'Are your pupils bored by the whiteboard?' *Times Educational Supplement,* propedagogy section, 16 December: 4.

Collis, B. (2012) 'Digital learners: will they surprise us?', Keynote address at the Technology in Education and Society Conference (TIES), University of Barcelona, 1 February.

Duarte, N. (2010) *Resonate: Presenting visual stories that transform audiences,* Hoboken, NJ: John Wiley & Sons.

Harrison, S. (2003) 'The use of ICT for teaching history: slow growth, some green shoots. Findings of HMI inspection 1999–2001', in T . Haydn and C. Counsell (eds) *History, ICT and Learning,* London: Routledge, pp. 38–51.

Haydn, T. (2003) 'What do they do with the information? Working towards genuine interactivity with history and ICT', in T. Haydn and C. Counsell (eds) *History, ICT and Learning,* London: Routledge, pp. 192–224.

Haydn, T. (2011) 'The changing form and use of textbooks in the history classroom in the 21st century: a view from the UK', in S. Popp (ed.) *Analysing History Textbooks: Methodological issues, yearbook of the International Society of History Didactics,* Schwalbach: Wochenschau Verlag, pp. 67–88.

Haydn, T., Arthur, J., Hunt, M. and Stephen, A. (2008) *Learning to Teach History in the Secondary School,* London: Routledge.

Heppell, S. (2011) 'Letter to Queensland', online at http://heppell.mobi, accessed 4 April 2012.

Hogden, J. and Webb, M. (2008) 'Questioning and dialogue', in S. Swaffield (ed.) *Unlocking Assessment,* London: David Fulton, pp. 73–89.

Levasseur, D. and Sawyer, J. (2007) 'Pedagogy meets PowerPoint: a research review of the effects of computer generated slides in the classroom', *Review of Communication,* 6 (1), 101–23.

Lodge, J. (2009) 'Travels with PowerPoint: reflections on using slideware in teaching', in A. Jackson (ed.) *Innovations and Development in Initial Teacher Education*, Bristol: ESCalate, pp. 187–95.

Macmillan, D. (2011) Quoted in L. Lightfoot, 'Are your pupils bored by the whiteboard?' *Times Educational Supplement*, propedagogy section, 16 December: 4.

Madian, J. (1995) 'Multimedia – why and why not?' *The Computing Teacher*, April: 16–18.

Mercer, N. (2000) *Words and Minds: How we use language to think together*, London: Routledge.

Mercer, N., Dawes, L., Wegerif, R. and Sams, C. (2004) 'Reasoning as a scientist: ways of helping children to use language to learn science', *British Educational Research Journal*, 30 (3): 359–77.

Mishra, P. (2012) 'Creative teaching with technology: introducing the TPACK framework', Keynote address at the TIES Conference, University of Barcelona, 1 February, online at http://ties2012.eu/en/pg-videos.html, accessed 19 February 2012.

Mishra, P. and Koehler, M. (2006) 'Technological pedagogical content knowledge: a framework for teacher knowledge', *Teachers College Record*, 106 (6): 1017–54, online at http://punya.educ.msu.edu/publications/journal_articles/mishra-koehler-tcr2006.pdf, accessed 18 November 2011.

Mycue, A. and Martini, F. (1999) 'Using presentation software to get students to think', paper presented at the CHC Conference, Saratoga, July.

Northedge, A. (1992) *Induction Course for New Lecturers*, London: University of London, Institute of Education, September.

OECD (2010) 'Case studies of the ways in which initial teacher education providers in England prepare student teachers to use ICT effectively in their subject teaching', Paris: OECD, online at www.oecd.org/dataoecd/42/39/45046837.pdf.

Ofsted (2011) *History for All*, London: Ofsted.

QCA (2005) *Pupil Perceptions of History at Key Stage 3: Final Report*, London: QCA, online at www.uea.ac.uk/~m242/historypgce/qcafinalreport.pdf, accessed 14 November 2011.

Reynolds, G. (2005) 'What is good PowerPoint design?' online at http://presentationzen.blogs.com/presentationzen/2005/09/whats_good_powe.html, accessed 11 October 2011.

Reynolds, G. (2008) *Presentation Zen*, Berkeley, CA: New Rider.

Schick, J. (2000) 'Taxonomy of interactivity', *History Computer Review*, 16 (1): 9–25.

Sweller, J. (2007) 'PowerPoint should be ditched', online at www.presentationzen.com/presentationzen/2007/04/is_it_finally_t.html, accessed 15 November 2011.

Tufte, E. (2006) *The Cognitive Style of PowerPoint: Pitching out corrupts within*, Cheshire, CT: Graphics Press.

Walsh, B. (2003) 'Building learning packages: integrating virtual resources with the real world of teaching and learning', in T. Haydn and C. Counsell (eds) *History, ICT and Learning*, London: Routledge, pp. 109–33.

Walsh, B. (2006) 'Beyond multiple choice', presentation given at the e-help seminar, Stockholm, 6–7 October, online at www.e-help.eu/seminars/walsh2.htm, accessed 11 November 2011.

Walsh, B. (2012) 'Using ICT to teach history', seminar University of East Anglia, 16 January.

Ward, T. (2003) 'I watched in dumb horror', *Guardian Education*, 20 May: 7.

Wiliam, D. (2011) *Embedded Formative Assessment*, Bloomington, IN: Solution Tree Press.

Willingham, D. (2009) *Why Don't Students Like School?* San Francisco, CA: Jossey-Bass.

Chapter 8

'I am Spartacus'

Making the most of the Spartacus website

John Simkin

In early 1997 I was invited to my daughter's house to see a demonstration of the internet. It was not the first time that I had encountered this new technological development. The previous year my brother-in-law had attempted to show me the web. However, after a couple of hours searching all we were able to find was a series of university home pages with very little content. It was very much like that in 1996.

The first website Steve showed me was 'Nine Planets' (http://nineplanets.org). After looking at a couple of pages I turned round to him and said: 'I want a website of my own'. He replied, 'No problem, I can do you one.' As it turned out, he couldn't, but I will be eternally grateful to him for opening the door to this new form of communication.

As the title of the website suggests, it contained nine main pages. What excited me were the links to other pages. For example, on the 'Sun' page, the first sentence read: 'The Sun is by far the largest object in the solar system.' Clicking the word 'largest' takes you to another page that includes several photographs showing the relative sizes of the different planets. This process mirrored the way my mind worked when I was reading a history book. Certain words or phrases in the text triggered off questions. Occasionally they can be answered by using the index or the author's notes. Sometimes I would put the book down and go to my bookshelves for the answer. Usually, the question goes unanswered and I return to reading the narrative. This website showed me that I could now write a very different type of history book.

Even more important than this, this new form of communication would solve a problem that I had been grappling with since I first started producing teaching materials. I had done this ever since my PGCE year in 1976–77. The books that I was given to use were little better than those employed by my history teachers in my secondary school in Dagenham during the 1950s.

When I was at school I had not developed the idea of deferred gratification. I judged everything as it related to my life at the time. All my friends were the same. We were in a school where it was not possible to take external exams. School was just a holding base for people waiting to work in the local factories. Therefore, our teachers were judged on their ability to make the lessons interesting. To me, history lessons were made up of teachers telling fairly uninteresting stories about the past who then forced you to copy out chunks of text from books. Those who taught me history failed dismally in this and I left school at 15 without an interest, let alone a love, of the subject.

Soon after I started work I was befriended by a man who was 15 years older than me. Bob Clarke's son had died at birth and I did not have a father, so in a way he sort of adopted me. During lunch-breaks he used to tell me interesting stories about being a child in London during the Blitz. But like all good teachers he not only told interesting stories, he also asked good questions.

Bob was a supporter of the Labour Party and when I was 18 he suggested I joined the Harold Hill Young Socialists. Although we lived on a council estate, some of the members had received a decent education at the local grammar school. We even had one member who had dropped out of university. The members of the group often referred to history in the discussions that we had. Most of these seemed to be about the Russian Revolution. The problem was that they seemed to be reading different history books as they were constantly disagreeing about what had happened in the past. They tended to spend a lot of time arguing about the roles of people I had never heard of such as Leon Trotsky, who seemed to be a messiah to some members. However, there were others, who pointed out his many deficiencies with references to things such as the Krondstat Uprising.

I found this very confusing as we never had debates in history at school. I was given the impression that there was only one version of the past and there was nothing to debate. In fact, as I loved talking, I might have enjoyed those history lessons if we had been encouraged to express our own opinions about these matters. However, I was fully aware that I could not really take part in these heated debates because I had no real knowledge of the subject. I therefore joined the local library and after reading several books I joined the anti-Trotsky camp in discussion. Over the next few years I developed informed opinions about a whole range of topics. I realised that my history teachers had given me the wrong impression of the subject. It was not about stories that you had to memorise. It was about constructing your own stories by studying primary and secondary sources.

This was reinforced when I studied for my degree at the Open University. Naturally, I wanted to continue with this approach in my own teaching. During my PGCE year at Sussex University I was assigned to a school that had a fairly traditional approach to teaching history. However, they were very understanding about my unwillingness to use the textbooks available and I was given permission to produce my own teaching materials.

I was also lucky with my first appointment. Although most of the teaching was fairly conventional, we did have a short course in Year 9 (13–14-year-old pupils) using Schools Council materials, called: 'What is History?' This course introduced the student to the use of primary and secondary sources and the issue of interpreting the past.

In 1980 a small group of teachers and academics in the Brighton area came together to discuss teaching materials. While we approved the move towards school-based curriculum development we felt that the Schools Council had not done enough to turn the theory into practice. One problem was that not enough money had been made available for school-based curriculum development. Even if these funds were increased we were only too aware that this gave considerable power to those who supplied these funds and that any decision to withdraw support would bring an end to the project (see Young, 1976).

We therefore decided to form a curriculum development group that was self-financing. This meant that we would have to sell the materials that we developed. We eventually decided to form a publishing company. In this way we hoped we would be able to overcome some of the problems encountered by the Schools Council Project teams when they reached the publishing stage of their work (see Stenhouse, 1980 for further development of this point).

The Tressell Teachers' Cooperative was established later that year. The group met once a week. Our early discussions provided us with some important guiding principles. The group decided that hopefully their materials would help to encourage: the development of pupils' analytical and critical faculties; group work to improve pupils' verbal skills and decision-taking; the fostering of creative skills and development of skills that enable young people to deal more adequately with the changes that are taking place in society.

I wrote the first two books we published: *The Mysterious Case of the Mary Celeste* and *Contemporary Accounts of the First World War*. This immediately raised a problem that I felt in 1997 could be solved by internet publishing. The issue concerns the size of the publication. The teacher doing the buying is looking for value – they will always consider the time they spend on any particular topic. I always wanted to produce materials on topics that history departments would be willing to spend at least half a term on. In reality, it would be just a couple of lessons, so I always had a serious editing problem.

In the 1980s teaching materials were printed in black and white. Therefore it was possible to have print-runs as low as 1,000. By the 1990s, development in printing technology meant that it was possible to publish books in full colour. The problem with this was that to make a profit on these books, you now had to have print-runs of 20,000. Once full-colour books arrived in the classroom, students lost interest in black and white books. At the time I was running Spartacus Educational, and like all the other educational publishers I had to abandon the idea of publishing black and white topic books.

After looking at the 'Nine Planets' website I realised that I could once again publish material that looked at subjects in more detail. At the time I was working on a book on the women's suffrage movement. I knew that the vast majority of history teachers would only spend a couple of weeks on the subject. However, I knew that if I produced material for just a couple of lessons, I would be guilty of distorting what actually happened during the struggle for the vote.

If you look at any school textbook on the subject, they concentrate on a few major figures. The authors would argue that is because of the space available. However, this distorts the past. For example, most textbooks concentrate on the activities of Emmeline Pankhurst and her daughter Christabel Pankhurst. This is because both women led dramatic lives being arrested, imprisoned and going on hunger strikes. They are also remembered for their campaigns to get young men to join the armed forces at the beginning of the First World War and therefore textbook authors conveniently link together two important issues – the war and the granting of women the vote.

The Pankhursts were head of an organisation, the Women's Social and Political Union (WSPU), that had at its peak only a membership of 2,000 people. It also virtually ceased to exist by 1914. All the leading members of the WSPU were in prison, in very poor health or were living in exile, and membership was down to a handful of active members. It was virtually a defunct organisation, whereas the National Union of Women's Suffrage Societies (NUWSS) had over 600 groups and an estimated 100,000 members.

The Women's Freedom League and the United Suffragists, were also far more important than the WSPU was in 1914. Yet how many textbooks mention those organisations? The reason for this is that the political activities of these three groups, organising petitions, letter writing campaigns, political lobbying, public meetings in towns and cities, etc. are considered to be boring by textbook authors who tend to concentrate on what they consider to be the exciting and dramatic acts of the WSPU.

It is forgotten that the NUWSS was campaigning for the vote for women and working-class males, whereas the objective of the WSPU was votes for middle-class women. That is why the NUWSS had the support of the Labour and Liberal parties and why the leaders of the WSPU ended up in the Conservative Party and the National Union of Fascists.

The question I faced was how I could produce a textbook on women's suffrage that portrayed the reality of the situation at a size and price that would be purchased by schools. The answer was that I couldn't. But what I could do was to provide it free of charge via the web.

A website like this enables you to spend time on the leaders of the NUWSS and other groups such as the Women's Freedom League. Both these groups, unlike the WSPU, opposed the First World War and refused to become involved in the recruitment campaign. A website is not restricted by space in the same way that a textbook is, and allows the teacher to explore with the students the complex nature of history and different interpretations of events.

Creating the Spartacus Educational turned out to be more difficult than I was led to believe. I was told I could have a website by September for the very reasonable price of £200. I then took the very bold step of ordering 7,000 Spartacus Educational mouse mats. These were then sent out to all the heads of history departments with news that they would soon be getting access to free educational resources.

The problem was that the man I employed to do this for me never kept to his deadlines and eventually admitted that he was not able technically to do what I had asked him to do. He had previously only created home pages for small businesses. I then had to give the job to a man who worked for my internet provider. Anyway, the few history teachers who did have the internet in September 1997 did have access to the biographies of 20 women involved in the suffrage campaign. But the cost of this had been so expensive it would have been impossible to expand the project.

Although I had a website it seemed that it would not be developed. Then I read an article in a computer magazine that claimed that a new piece of software enabled you to create your own website. The review said the software, called WebMaster, was very easy to use. This was good news as my skills in this area were very limited. I got a copy of this software and within hours I was creating my own web pages.

This new development changed the way I taught. At the time I was teaching a Year 10 local history GCSE unit on the subject of women's suffrage. I decided to use the website to explore the debate that took place in East Grinstead between 1906 and 1914 on the subject of votes for women. To resource this unit I spent a lot of time looking at back copies of the *East Grinstead Observer*. Most of the information came from the letters page and reports on meetings of the NUWSS in East Grinstead. There were also a couple of local women who were supporters of the WSPU.

There was tremendous opposition to women's suffrage from the local Conservative Party (one of its leading figures, Wallace Hills, was editor of the *East Grinstead Observer*). The Liberal Party tended to support the NUWSS (but they were very hostile to the WSPU). Their local parliamentary candidate, Charles Corbett, was a member of the Men's League for Women's Suffrage and his wife (Marie Corbett) and his two daughters (Margery and Cicely) were very active in the NUWSS.

There was a serious riot in East Grinstead in 1913 when a group of youths began throwing stones at speakers at a public meeting of the NUWSS. It was later discovered that these youths had been paid by local members of the Conservative Party. They were upset that the NUWSS had joined forces with the Salvation Army to demand the vote and legislation to control the selling of alcohol in the town (there were very close links in the town between the Conservative Party and the Brewing Industry).

I was able to trace the relatives of several people included in this campaign. This included the sons of two of the campaigners, Margery Corbett and Edward Steer, the daughter of Cicely Corbett, and the granddaughter of Marie and Charles Corbett. They were able to give me photographs, letters, membership cards, newspaper clippings, etc.

East Grinstead also had a branch of the Anti-Suffrage Society. It was led by Lady Jeannie Musgrave, who had a road named after her that was very close to the school. I also discovered that Kitty Marion, a leading figure in the WSPU arson campaign, lived in Hartfield, a small village close to East Grinstead. Marion actually endured 200 force-feedings in prison during her hunger strikes. This is more than any other member of the WSPU. Not too far away, Dr Octavia Wilberforce, the great grand-daughter of William Wilberforce, and Elizabeth Robins, a leading figure in the Actress Franchise League, were running a retreat for suffragettes recovering from hunger strike, at their fifteenth-century farmhouse at Backsettown.

I decided to produce biographies of these local people and put them on my website. Each student then was given one of these characters to study. As we only had one computer in the school with an internet connection I had to print out the pages for the student to use in the classroom. The website now has biographies of over 200 women involved in the struggle for the vote, at www.spartacus.schoolnet.co.uk/women.htm.

The students had to be these characters in several debates we had on women's suffrage and related subjects. For example, these characters were deeply divided over topics such as the rules governing the local workhouse, the establishment of a park in the town for children (some did not want to increase the rates to pay maintenance costs) and the First World War.

This was a great success and got me thinking about how I could use the internet with my other classes. During my research I discovered some great newspaper reports on the First World War in East Grinstead. We taught the subject in Year 9. I therefore photocopied these articles and letters and put them into different topics. In the early days of the war the newspaper published a large number of letters sent by men on the Western Front to their parents and wives back home. I soon had a collection of articles/letters for each person in the class. The task was to create an encyclopaedia of East Grinstead and the First World War. They had to write up their own entry for the encyclopaedia. This was provided on disc and I was then able to upload it to the school website. In this way we created a teaching resource for schools in the town. We also turned some of the work into pamphlets that we sold on parents' evenings.

One boy asked me if he could do a piece on Iran and the First World War. Although his mother was from East Grinstead, his father came from Iran. The marriage had broken up and his father had returned to his country of birth. I of course said yes and he was able to email his father with the URL of his homework after it had been uploaded. I still remember the expression on his face when he told me what his dad had said about his homework. The pleasure this one boy received from this exercise justified all the time it took to organise this activity.

I did a similar thing when I studied the Second World War. Once again we placed the focus on events in East Grinstead. This included a case study of the bombing of the Whitehall Cinema. On 9 July 1943, a lone German aircraft that had lost the rest of its party on the way to London decided to drop its bombs on East Grinstead instead. One of these bombs hit the Whitehall Cinema, which at the time was showing the film *Hopalong Cassidy*. It was full of school kids. The raid killed 108 people and another 235 were seriously injured. It was the largest loss of life in any air raid in Sussex. However, as the kids discovered, it was not reported in the newspapers at the time. It was only after Germany had been defeated that details were published in the national and local newspapers. A detailed account of the Whitehall Cinema bombing can be found at www.spartacus.schoolnet. co.uk/2WWwhitehall.htm.

A lot of the children had grandparents who experienced this raid. They were able to interview them and report back to the rest of the class. Unfortunately I left the school around this time and this material was never added to the school website. Nor did anyone get appointed to maintain the website I had created for the students. Their material is therefore no longer available online.

During this period I discovered that a website is also a great place to organise historical simulations. In their book *Simulation in the Classroom*, John Taylor and Rex Walford (1972: 17) argued that an educational simulation has three main components:

1   Students take roles which are representative of the real world and involve them making decisions in response to their assessment of the situation that they have been placed in.
2   Students experience simulated consequences which relate to their decisions and their general performance in the simulation.
3   Students monitor the results of their actions and are encouraged to reflect upon the relationship between their own decisions and the resulting consequences of their actions.

An essential part of a simulation involves the student playing a role of a character in the past. One of the major objectives of the creator of the simulation is to help the student understand the situation of that person.

In his book, *The Process of Education* Jerome Bruner argues that simulations encourage active learning. However, Bruner prefers some simulations to others. He argues that the value of any piece of learning over and above the enjoyment it gives is that it should be relevant to us in the future. That is something I always take seriously when I am constructing a simulation (Bruner, 1960).

Other arguments in favour of simulations include:

1   They are usually problem based and are therefore helpful in the development of long-term learning.
2   They normally involve the use of social skills that are directly relevant to the world outside the classroom.
3   Simulations deal with situations that change and therefore demand flexibility in thinking.

This was the background to the creation of the Yalding Project. My main objective was to help the students to understand life in a medieval village (Yalding) and a medieval town (East Grinstead).

The simulation lasts for six months in real time. The complete simulation plus teachers' notes can be found at www.spartacus.schoolnet.co.uk/Yalding.htm. The activity begins with a look at Richard FitzGilbert, a Norman knight who took part in the Battle of Hastings. After the battle he became the Earl of Clare and one of England's largest landowners. For the next few weeks the students follow the history of the Clare family between 1066 and 1330. This involves looking at issues such as castle building, feudalism, the Domesday Book, religion, Thomas Becket, the Magna Carta, Origins of Parliament, the Clares in Ireland, the Clares in Wales and the Battle of Bannockburn, where the last of the Clare male line was killed. The Clare Estates (only the king owned more land than the Clares) were then divided up between Gilbert, 10th Earl of Clare's three sisters.

The simulation looks at just one village under the control of the Clare family. The village is Yalding in Kent. I chose Yalding because a lot of its manor records have survived. It also has the same church and stone bridge that existed in the fourteenth century. It is still farmed and the common land still exists and they still hold the village fair there today as they did in the fourteenth century. The land is fertile but the village continues to suffer from the flooding that plagued the medieval residents of Yalding.

The simulation starts in 1336. Each student is given a character that was resident in Yalding at that time. They are all given a house in the village and details of their family, animals, land, farming equipment, etc. Some are serfs and some are free. Each student is a head of a family with children. In 1375 they will become the son or daughter of their first character.

Every week the students receive via the website an update of their changing circumstances. For example, increasing revenues means they can buy more animals or if they are serfs, their freedom. During the simulation the students experience events such as harvesting, meetings of the Manor Court, a Village Fair, the Hundred Years War, the Black Death, Statute of Labourers Act, the Poll Tax, a visit from John Ball, and finally the events of 1381.

The highlights of the simulation include when the village is hit by the plague and when they have to decide whether to join the Peasants Revolt (a slight majority usually decide to take part).

All the material in the simulation is differentiated. So also are the characters. Therefore it is possible for the teacher to allocate the students roles that are applicable to the abilities of the individual. All this is explained in the teachers' notes available online.

Schools that use the simulation are recommended to arrange a visit to Yalding. Several features are the same as in the fourteenth century. The students get a particular thrill when they visit the churchyard and they see the names of the relatives they have been playing on the tombstones. Inside the church are the names of past vicars and of the men who were killed in both world wars. Using these sources of information, they will discover that unusual names such as Singyard and Brickenden have survived in the village for over 700 years.

During this period of teaching at Sackville Comprehensive I was able to create several historical simulations on my website. One involves the issue of child labour at the beginning of the nineteenth century (www.spartacus.schoolnet.co.uk/Twork.htm).

Each student is given the name of an individual who was involved in the debate that was taking place at this time. This included factory owners, factory reformers, child workers, parents, journalists, religious leaders and doctors. The student is then given an instruction sheet with details of what they need to do. This includes writing an account of their character and a speech on the subject of child labour.

Each character had an entry in the Spartacus Encyclopaedia. This provided them with a biography and sources that enable the student to discover his or her views on the issue. The website also includes information under headings such as factory pollution, parish apprentices, factory food, punishments, working hours, accidents and physical deformities. There are also entries in the encyclopaedia on the machines the children used and the type of work they did in the factory.

It is interesting the way they react when they discover who their character is. Initially, they are much happier about playing the role of a factory owner. They quickly develop the idea that they are in some way responsible for the wealth that the character has obtained. Those who are given the role of a child worker are less happy at first but the more they investigate their situation, the more involved they become in the need to find ways of overcoming the problems that they face.

The exercise helps to explain the complexity of child labour in the nineteenth century. The students discover that some factory owners, such as John Fielden and John Wood, were actually leaders of the pressure group trying to bring an end to child labour. At the same time, social reforming journalists such as Edward Baines were totally opposed to any attempt by Parliament to regulate the use of labour. Even doctors did not agree that it would damage a child's health to be standing for 12 hours a day in a factory where windows were kept closed and the air was thick with the dust from the cotton. What the children discover from their in-depth studies is why the individuals felt the way that they did. In the debate that follows, this is revealed to the rest of the class.

Richard Nerzic-Jones, who taught this simulation in his international school in Toulouse, has made a very good film on using the simulation. This is also available online (www.uea.ac.uk/~m242/historypgce/drama/childlabour.htm).

Another example concerns the Cuban Missile Crisis. The simulation comes at the end of a detailed study of the relationship between Cuba and the United States in the twentieth century. This involves a study of the three main characters in these events, John F. Kennedy, Fidel Castro and Nikita Khrushchev.

During the Cuban Missile Crisis Kennedy established the Executive Committee of the National Security Council to advise him what to do. The students have to imagine they are members of this committee. They are given six possible strategies for dealing with the crisis. They have to work out the possible consequences of these strategies before advising Kennedy what to do (www.spartacus.schoolnet.co.uk/COLDcubamissileA.htm).

A final example concerns Russia in 1914. The students are given information about the character they are playing. This includes their beliefs and objectives. The students are then placed in four discussion groups: Group A (supporters of Nicholas II and the autocracy); Group B (liberals and moderate socialists); Group C (Mensheviks and Socialist Revolutionaries) and Group D (Bolsheviks). Each group has to decide how to respond to different events that took place between 1914 and 1917. The students are warned that there could be spies in their groups. During the simulation they have the freedom to move to another group. In fact, if they keep to their beliefs and objectives, some will actually do this. For example, Trotsky is likely to move from Group C to Group D during the simulation. If they do not go of their own accord the teacher plays God and tells certain characters to move. Playing the simulation students should get an idea of why the Bolsheviks gained power in 1917 (www.spartacus.schoolnet.co.uk/LRUSsimulation.htm).

At the end of the simulation the students go to the Russian Revolution section of the website and discover what happened to their character during 1917. They then write a brief summary of what happened, comparing their decisions with those of their character. The final task is for the students to write about what happened to their character after the Russian Revolution. A session could then be organised where the students tell the rest of the class about their fate.

Having your own website enables you to turn the student from a consumer into a producer. In 2003 research was carried out at the United States National Learning Lab in Maine to assess the most effective way that young people can learn (United States National Learning Lab, 2003). The researchers employed a variety of different teaching methods and then tested the students to find out how much they had learned. From this the researchers were able to calculate what they called the Average Retention Rate. The results were as follows:

- teacher talking to a class (5%);
- student reading a book (10%);
- student watching an audio visual presentation (20%);
- student watching a teacher demonstration (30%);
- students taking part in a discussion group (50%);

- students involved in an activity that is related to what the teacher wants them to learn (75%);
- students teaching others (90%).

Although we must obviously be careful about the amount of weight we place on a single piece of research, these findings accord with other pieces of research cited in this volume which suggest that if learners are at least to some extent actively involved in the process of learning, they are more likely to be able to remember what they have learned, and to integrate it into their existing understandings in a way that may make the knowledge and understanding gained more 'usable' and intelligible.

A student in a traditional teaching environment can be very passive or docile but when he or she has to take on the role of teacher, the student is empowered. Anybody who has read the novel *A Kestrel for a Knave* (by Barry Hines) or seen the film *Kes* (directed by Ken Loach) will remember the scene where Billy Casper teaches the rest of the class about kestrels. Billy Casper undergoes a transformation in this scene because probably for the first time in his life he has been given the opportunity to share his knowledge and expertise.

How can we as teachers create similar situation to the 'Billy Casper effect' in the classroom? One example concerns the subject of the Home Front. During the war the British government was constantly monitoring the success of its various policies concerning the Home Front. The government was also aware of the possibility that it might be necessary to introduce legislation to deal with any emerging problems (www.spartacus.schoolnet.co.uk/2WWhomeAC.htm).

The students have to imagine they are living in Britain in December 1941. The students are asked to write a report on one aspect of government policy (evacuation, rationing, refugees, etc.). The web page provides work on a total of 36 different topics, so it should be possible for each student to have a different topic.

The student has to report back to the class about the topic he or she has investigated: (1) Each student has to provide a report on what has been happening in their assigned area since the outbreak of the war; (2) The student then has to make proposals about the changes they would like to see in government policy. (These proposals are then discussed and voted on by the rest of the class.)

The next stage could be for them to carry out a local study on this aspect of the war. This could then be uploaded as a website that could be used by future generations of students.

One way of introducing a new topic is to look at a couple of sources that encourage the student to think deeply about the period of history they are studying. For example, the following sources could be given to a class who are just about to start a course on the First World War.

1   Graham Greene was born in Berkhamsted in 1904 and published his autobiography, *A Sort of Life* in 1971.

> There were dramatic incidents even in Berkhamsted. A German master was denounced to my father as a spy because he had been seen under the railway bridge without a hat, a dachshund was stoned in the High Street, and once my uncle Eppy was summoned at night to the police station and asked to lend his motor car to help block the Great North Road down which a German armored car was said to be advancing towards London.

> (Greene, 1971: 49)

2   *The Morning Post* (14 March 1916)

> At Southampton yesterday Robert Andrew Smith was fined for treating his wife to a glass of wine in a local public-house. He said his wife gave him sixpence to pay for her drink. Mrs Smith was also fined £1 for consuming, and Dorothy Brown, the barmaid, £5 for selling the intoxicant, contrary to the regulations of the Liquor Control Board.

3   Commander Alfred Rawlinson employed blind men in 1915 to sit on the top of high buildings with a pole attached to their heads (Rawlinson, 1924).

4   *The New York Times* (14 November 1914)

> There has occurred at one of the concentration camps in which … German and Austrian subjects of military age are interned an incident which is calculated to evoke some caustic comment when the details become known in Germany.

> One night toward midnight the British guard on duty at one of the concentration camps near London was alarmed by unwanted sounds from the camp. Evidences of a struggle in which a fairly large body of men was taking part were audible, and very soon, when the lights were brought to bear on the scene, became visible.

> A number of men were seen rushing toward one of the exits. The soldier on guard at this particular point fired as the men approached him, and another near by also discharged his rifle. Eventually order was restored and an investigation begun.

> It appeared that the trouble had arisen out of a bawl among some of the inmates of the camp. Instead of being an attempt to escape by rushing the guard, as the soldiers who fired had thought, the disturbance had been nothing more than a free fight among a number of the prisoners.

> Unfortunately the sentries' shots had taken effect. One German had been killed and another wounded. The matter is now under further investigation.

The students are told to write an explanation of these four passages. The class is then given the opportunity to discuss their views about these sources. It is important that at this stage the teacher does not indicate the accuracy of any comment made and does not provide any further information on these matters.

For homework, the students are allowed to use the internet to explain these four sources. This is a test of their ability to use search engines. If they can do this, they will arrive on my website and they will discover the following explanations.

1   Graham Greene was describing the anti-German feeling that existed in the United Kingdom in 1914. Anyone who could speak in German was suspected of being a spy. Greene was not the only one to report dachshund dogs being attacked. James Hayward has argued: 'Famously, dachshund dogs (although not apparently Alsatians) were put to sleep or attacked in the streets, a persecution which endured so long that in the years following the war the bloodline had to be replenished with foreign stock' (Hayward, 2002: 7). The reason for the hostility towards dachshunds was that at the beginning of the war they were seen as a symbol of Germany. Political cartoonists commonly used the image of the dog to ridicule Germany. This continued during the Second World War when Hitler's face was put on the body of a dachshund. This caused a stir when in 1943 the United States government used such a cartoon to advertise

war bonds. Hans Morgenthau, the Secretary of the Treasury, was forced to issue an apology where he denied there was any intention of questioning the patriotism of the owners of dachshunds (*The New York Times* (5 April 1943). A full account of these anti-German incidents can be found on my website: www.spartacus.schoolnet.co.uk/FWWantigerman.htm.

2   During the First World War, David Lloyd George, the Chancellor of the Exchequer, led the campaign against alcohol. He had been told by shipbuilders and heads of war factories that men's wages had gone up so much that they could earn in two or three days what would keep them in drink for a week. A Newcastle shipbuilder complained that double overtime on Sunday meant no attendance on Monday. In January 1915, Lloyd George told the Shipbuilding Employers Federation that Britain was 'fighting Germans, Austrians and Drink, and as far as I can see the greatest of these foes is Drink'.

The government was particularly concerned about the amount of alcohol being consumed by female munitions workers. A survey of four pubs in London revealed that in one hour on a Saturday night alcohol was consumed by 1,483 men and 1,946 women. Newspapers claimed that soldiers' wives were 'drinking away their over-generous allowances'. *The Times* reported that 'we do not all realise the increase in drinking there has been among the mothers of the coming race, though we may yet find it a circumstance darkly menacing to our civilisation' (*The Times*, 7 February 1916).

In October 1915 the British government announced several measures they believed would reduce alcohol consumption. A 'No Treating Order' stated that any drink ordered was to be paid for by the person supplied. The maximum penalty for defying the Government order was six months' imprisonment. *The Spectator* gave its support to the legislation. It argued that it was the custom of the working-classes to buy drinks for 'chance-met acquaintances, each of whom then had to stand a drink to everyone else' and believed that this measure would 'free hundreds of thousands of men from an expensive and senseless social tyranny' (*The Spectator*, 16 November 1915). A detailed account of legislation can be found on my website: www.spartacus.schoolnet.co.uk/FWWalcohol.htm.

3   In January 1915, two Zeppelin navel airships 190 metres long, flew over the east coast of England and bombed great Yarmouth and King's Lynn. The first Zeppelin raid on London took place on 31 May 1915. The raid killed 28 people and injured 60 more (www.spartacus.schoolnet.co.uk/FWWzeppelinraids.htm).

Soon after this raid, the government appointed Alfred Rawlinson to take charge of early anti-aircraft defences. In his book, *The Defence of London, 1915–1918* (1924), he explains how he placed naval guns in Regents Park and Tower Bridge and a number of Hotchkiss six-pounders scattered about the city (Rawlinson, 1924).

Ernest Sackville Turner explains in *Dear Old Blighty* (1980) that Rawlinson also developed an early warning system against the Zeppelins:

> An early inspiration in the war against Zeppelins was to recruit the blind, whose ability to hear the throb of distant engines was deemed to be greater than that of the sighted. In south-east England they manned a binaural listening service which fed information of range and altitude to the defences. Commander Alfred

Rawlinson, who claims some credit for this innovation, has explained that the system was based on the natural instinct which urges a person, on hearing a distant sound, to turn his head towards it, so that it is heard equally in both ears. In the early experiments the blind man was fitted with a stethoscope to intensify his hearing and a pole was attached to his head, which would turn in the direction of the raider and indicate the bearing on a compass dial … How substantial was the contribution of the blind does not emerge from Rawlinson's account; certainly listening posts consisting of stethoscopes attached to wide-mouthed, rotatable trumpets were eventually worked with some success by the sighted.

(Sackville Turner, 1980: 117–18)

4   The students will probably be surprised by the use of the phrase 'concentration camps' being used to describe the imprisonment of German and Austrian citizens in 1914. The term 'concentration camp' was first used to describe camps operated by the British during the Boer War. It became the policy of Lord Kitchener, the commander-in-chief in South Africa to use these camps to defeat the Boers. This strategy was exposed by Emily Hobhouse in a series of newspaper articles between January and March 1901 (www.spartacus.schoolnet.co.uk/Whobhouse.htm).

Hobhouse argued that Kitchener's 'Scorched Earth' policy included the systematic destruction of crops and slaughtering of livestock, the burning down of homesteads and farms, and the poisoning of wells and salting of fields – to prevent the Boers from resupplying from a home base. Civilians were then forcibly moved into the concentration camps. Although this tactic had been used by Spain (Ten Years' War) and the United States (Philippine–American War), it was the first time that a whole nation had been systematically targeted.

David Lloyd George took up the case in the House of Commons and accused the government of 'a policy of extermination' directed against the Boer population. William St John Fremantle Brodrick, the Secretary of State for War argued that the interned Boers were 'contented and comfortable' and stated that everything possible was being done to ensure satisfactory conditions in the camps.

In August 1901 the British government established a commission headed by Millicent Fawcett to visit South Africa (www.spartacus.schoolnet.co.uk/WfawcettM.htm). While the Fawcett Commission was carrying out the investigation, the government published its own report. According to the *New York Times*:

The War Office has issued a four-hundred-page Blue Book of the official reports from medical and other officers on the conditions in the concentration camps in South Africa. The general drift of the report attributes the high mortality in these camps to the dirty habits of the Boers, their ignorance and prejudices, their recourse to quackery, and their suspicious avoidance of the British hospitals and doctors.

(*The New York Times*, 16 November 1901)

The Fawcett Commission confirmed almost everything that Emily Hobhouse had reported. After the war a report concluded that 27,927 Boers had died of starvation, disease and exposure in the concentration camps. In all, about one in four of the Boer inmates, mostly children, died (Pakenham, 1979: 549). However, the South African historian, Stephen Burridge Spies argues that this is an under-estimate of the number who died in the concentration camps (Spies, 1997: 265).

On the outbreak of the First World War the British government decided to establish concentration camps for German and Austrian subjects living in the country. Ernest Sackville Turner has argued:

> It is by now widely believed that Britain invented the concentration camp in the South African War. However, in 1914 the term had not attracted any real measure of obloquy and it was often used to describe the numerous corrals for aliens and internees set up in wartime Britain.
>
> (Sackville Turner, 1980: 106)

One of the first camps established was in Camberley. The camp, that contained 8,000 inmates, had thick barbed wire defences and was patrolled by armed soldiers. Camps were also established in Southend and Tipperary. One of the largest camps was in Knockaloe, near Douglas in the Isle of Man. By November 1914 it housed 3,300 in tents. Unhappy with the conditions in the camp, the inmates started a riot. The soldiers opened fire killing six men. The inquest jury decided that the military had taken justifiable measures.

One also has to realise the class nature of these camps. A camp was established at Donnington Hall for 320 German officers with their servants. One German newspaper, Zeitung am Wittag, pointed out that at the camp 'one can have everything, just as in a hotel' and the 'commandant is very charming ... and permits everything'. One English newspaper reported that Margot Asquith, the wife of Herbert Asquith, the prime minister, had played tennis with the officers. This was untrue and she obtained £1,000 in damages.

The concentration camps were not closed until the end of 1919. Most of the internees were deported, many unwillingly as they had settled in Britain before the war and often had British wives (www.spartacus.schoolnet.co.uk/FWWconcentration.htm).

The final suggested activity is something that might be worth saving for a special occasion. For example, the final lesson before the Christmas holiday. It is a subject that students usually find very exciting. The students are given the following sources concerning ghost stories from the First World War:

1   The *Daily Mail*, quoting an anonymous Lieutenant Colonel who took part in the retreat from Le Cateau in August 1914 (14 September 1915):

> We came into action at dawn, and fought till dusk. We were heavily shelled by the German artillery during the day, and in common with the rest of the division had a bad time of it. Our division, however, retired in good order. We were on the march all night of the 26th, and on the 27th, with only about two hours' rest. The brigade to which I belonged was rearguard to the division, and during the 27th we were all absolutely worn out with fatigue – both bodily and mental fatigue. No doubt we also suffered to a certain extent from shock, but the retirement still continued in excellent order, and I feel sure that our mental faculties were still ... in good working condition.
>
> On the night of the 27th I was riding along in the column with two other officers. We had been talking and doing our best to keep from falling asleep on our

horses. As we rode along I became conscious of the fact that, in the fields on both sides of the road along which we were marching, I could see a very large body of horsemen. These horsemen had the appearance of squadrons of cavalry, and they seemed to be riding across the fields and going in the same direction as we were going, and keeping level with us …

I did not say a word about it at first, but I watched them for about 20 minutes. The other two officers had stopped talking. At last one of them asked me if I saw anything in the fields. I told them what I had seen. The third officer then confessed that he too had been watching these horsemen for the last 20 minutes. So convinced were we that they were real cavalry that, at the next halt, one of the officers took a party of men out to reconnoitre, and found no-one there. The night grew darker, and we saw no more. The same phenomenon was seen by many men in our column.

2   Lance-Corporal Johnstone, letter to the *London Evening News* (11 August 1915):

We had almost reached the end of the retreat, and after marching a whole day and night with but one half-hour's rest in between, we found ourselves in the outskirts of Langy, near Paris, just at dawn, and as the day broke we saw in front of us large bodies of cavalry, all formed up into squadrons – fine, big men, on massive chargers. I remember turning to my chums in the ranks and saying: 'Thank God! We are not far off Paris now. Look at the French cavalry.' They, too, saw them quite plainly, but on getting closer, to our surprise the horsemen vanished and gave place to banks of white mist, with clumps of trees and bushes dimly showing through.

3   *All Saints Parish Magazine* in Clifton reported that two officers serving at Mons told Sarah Marrable about what they saw on the front line (May 1915):

One of Miss Marrable's friends, who was not a religious man, told her that he saw a troop of angels between us and the enemy. He has been a changed man ever since. The other man … and his company were retreating, they heard the German cavalry tearing after them … They therefore turned round and faced the enemy, expecting nothing but instant death, when to their wonder they saw, between them and the enemy, a whole troop of angels. The German horses turned round terrified and regularly stampeded. The men tugged at their bridles, while the poor beasts tore away in every direction.

4   An English engineer who had been serving in the line at Ypres in August 1915 during one of the early German poison gas attacks told his story to an American clergyman from Massachusetts in 1956 and it eventually appeared in *Fate Magazine* in May 1968:

They looked out over No Man's Land and saw a strange grey cloud rolling towards them. When it struck, pandemonium broke out. Men dropped all around him and the trench was in an uproar. Then, he said, a strange thing happened. Out of the mist, walking across No Man's Land, came a figure. He seemed to be without special protection and he wore the uniform of the Royal Army Medical Corps (RAMC). The engineer remembered that the stranger spoke English with what seemed to be a French accent.

On his belt the stranger from the poison cloud had a series of small hooks on which were suspended tin cups. In his hand he carried a bucket of what looked like water. As he slid down into the trench he began removing the cups, dipping them into the bucket and passing them out to the soldiers, telling them to drink quickly. The engineer was among those who received the potion. He said it was extremely salty, almost too salty to swallow. But all of the soldiers who were given the liquid did drink it, and not one of them suffered lasting effects from the gas.

When the gas cloud had blown over and things calmed down the unusual visitor was not to be found. No explanation for his visit could be given by the Royal Medical Corps – but the fact remained that thousands of soldiers died or suffered lasting effects from that grim attack, but not a single soldier who took the cup from the stranger was among the casualties.

After reading these stories the students can try to come up with some logical explanation for these events. Later they can carry out a search on the web for these stories. This will bring them to my website where they can read about the context of seeing these visions. They will also discover that the full quotations reveal that the soldiers themselves were aware that these visions were linked to the fact they were suffering from extreme tiredness and stress at the time (www.spartacus.schoolnet.co.uk/FWWghosts.htm).

Dachshunds have traditionally been viewed as a symbol of Germany. Political cartoonists commonly used the image of the dachshund to ridicule Germany. During World War I the dachshunds' popularity in the United States plummeted because of this association and there are even anecdotes such as a Dachshund being stoned to death on the high street of Berkhamsted, England at this time because of its association with the enemy. As a result they were often called 'liberty hounds' by their owners, similar to 'liberty cabbage' becoming a term for sauerkraut. The stigma of the association was revived to a lesser extent during the Second World War, though it was comparatively short lived. Kaiser Wilhelm II and German Field Marshal Erwin Rommel were known for keeping dachshunds.

Owing to the association of the breed with Germany, the dachshund was chosen to be the first official mascot for the 1972 Summer Olympics in Munich, with the name Waldi. Saying dachshunds, plural, is a bit misleading. As far as I can tell this claim stems from Graham Greene's autobiography, where he describes seeing one dachshund being stoned to death in Berkhamsted. There are other mentions of vague claims of 'streets of London' or even New York, but that is the only first-hand account I have found.

The teacher who wants to use the internet in the classroom has three possible strategies.

1   The teacher can devise activities based on information contained on websites.
2   The teacher can use activities that have been created by others.
3   The teacher can devise activities and create materials and then upload them onto a website.

The problem about using strategies 1 and 2 is that you have only a limited choice of topics and approaches to teaching history. For example, very few teachers have created teaching material for the web. Those that have, especially those employed by large organisations, charge for this material. Even if you find another teacher on the web who shares your approach, unless you live in the same area, you will be unable to use a local history approach to the subject.

My experience of teaching is that my best lessons have been the result of using my own resources. I am sure this is also true of most teachers. Therefore, as most learning moves online, it is vital that teachers embrace this technology to produce at least some of their own teaching resources. One of the most important benefits of ICT is that the internet, and history sites such as *Spartacus* make it easier and quicker for history teachers to do this.

References

Bruner, J. (1960) *The Process of Education*, Cambridge, MA: Harvard University Press.

Greene, G. (1971) *A Sort of Life*, London: Vintage.

Hayward, J. (2002) *Myths and Legends of the First World War*, Stroud: History Press.

Pakenham, T. (1979) *The Boer War*, London: Harper Collins.

Rawlinson, A. (1924) *The Defence of London, 1915–1918*, London: Andrew Melrose.

Sackville Turner, E. (1980) *Dear Old Blighty*, London: Joseph.

Spies, S.B. (1997) *Methods of Barbarism: Roberts and Kitchener and Civilians in the Boer Republics*, Cape Town: Humans Rousseau.

Stenhouse, L. (1980) *Curriculum Research and Development in Action*, London: Heinemann.

Taylor, J. and Walford, R. (1972) *Simulation in the Classroom*, London, Penguin.

United States National Learning Lab (2003) online at www.school-teacher-student-motivation-resources-courses.com/acceleratedlearning.html.

Young, M. (1976) 'The rhetoric of curriculum development', in G. Whitty and M. Young (eds) *Explorations in the Politics of School Knowledge*. London: Studies in Education Limited.

Chapter 9

Signature pedagogies, assumptions and assassins

ICT and motivation in the history classroom

Ben Walsh

Assumptions

Using ICT motivates students. We all know that. Don't we?

It's just common sense. Young people live in a wired, digital world. They are digital natives while we adults, especially older ones, are digital immigrants (Prensky, 2001). Therefore it stands to reason that they will respond positively to using ICT in their lessons, whether they be history lessons or any other subject. With ICT we appear to have, just for once in education, a plain and simple truth – ICT is a powerful motivator and it improves student performance.

Does this perception ring true for history? I wish I could draw on extensive research studies about the impact of technology on students' learning in history in the UK and further afield to illustrate how technology has transformed the teaching and learning of the subject. Sadly, we have relatively little research to draw upon with relatively few researchers showing interest in the subject-specific impacts of technology. In this chapter I will attempt to share some results of my own small-scale study (Walsh, 2010) and then consider ways in which ICT can affect and has been seen to affect student motivation in history lessons.

Promising signs

Some of the responses in my study chimed with the assumptions outlined above about ICT being an effective motivator. For example, ICT seemed to give students a degree of independence or autonomy, one key factor in student motivation (Ryan and Deci, 2000). Typical student comments were:

> In history when we use ICT, we use the internet to research the Transatlantic Slave Trade. It is very interesting and I think that it will help me a lot in history for my notes.

> We do use some ICT in history, but sometimes I think there could be more. ICT keeps my concentration better because I'm really familiar with it because I love computers. I think that ICT in history could be even more useful to find out facts for yourself other than ask your teacher to give you all the answers.

The comments indicate that ICT seems to help students to stay focused but it also makes some students feel they have a degree of independence from the teacher. The comments relating to websites suggest that students are eager to find out more about topics for themselves, a strong indicator that personal control is helping to give rise to personal interest where students are prepared to learn for the inherent interest of the subject matter rather than being motivated by mere novelty value or the fear of being rebuked for not carrying out a task.

Signature pedagogies ... and some reservations

And yet ... It is often the lot of the historian to voice possibilities that run against the grain of what seems like common sense. At the very least, it is the lot of the historian to point out that situations that appear to be cut and dried are often rather more complex. Are these motivational gains brought about by technology? Shulman (2005) contends that certain subject disciplines are founded on signature pedagogies. These are the default approaches to teaching that characterise different disciplines and are generally accepted as the cultural norm for teaching that subject. These pedagogies generally transcend boundaries of language and geography. From Ofsted evidence (2007) and my own experience as a researcher and senior examiner and teacher trainer, the signature pedagogy in the history classroom would appear to be the coverage model – teacher description and or explanation of events followed by work with textbooks and or 'source work' – questions on original sources. Leave aside for a moment the issue of how effective this signature pedagogy is. What is apparent from the student comments we have seen is that they were motivated, but also that the tasks they describe were different from the established signature pedagogy of the history classroom. Either the teacher was doing something different from the norm in these instances or the teacher generally did not adhere strongly to the signature pedagogy. Is it not entirely possible that it is this different pedagogical framework rather than the technology that explains the motivational gains? Or perhaps it lies in some kind of interaction between the pedagogy and the technology, something strongly suggested by Passey *et al.* in their report on the motivational impact of ICT (2004)? The student comment below is a timely reminder of the complexity of the issue at hand.

> At my school we hardly ever use ICT in history. Mr X is a good teacher and we tend to use books; films; PowerPoints; texts and things to learn. Lately we did a student project in groups of 4 where 2 of us went to research and print off pictures to do with the 1970s. This was good because it let us control it. I do like history a lot but art is my favourite topic. History would probably be my second favourite.

This comment shows the powerful motivational effect of using ICT, but this power lay both in the personal control and in the situational interest created by the novelty of using ICT. In addition, these interests were framed within a wider personal interest generated by the quality of the teacher. There is also the rather obvious point that Mr X is regarded as a good teacher even though he hardly ever uses ICT in history. It is hardly consistent with a blanket assertion that, of itself, using ICT motivates students. It would seem to suggest, hardly surprisingly, that quality of teaching and appeal of task are at least as important as the mere fact of ICT usage.

And there is worse news for those who see ICT as a panacea. The picture becomes more complex when we see what this study revealed about amotivation – where students feel that using ICT adds relatively little to their enjoyment or learning. In this cohort levels of amotivation in history were comparatively high. Technical problems usually account for some amotivation but they do not account for the fact that amotivation was relatively high when using ICT in history compared to other subjects. There were a number of student comments that hinted at something deeper:

- I think that history is better without ICT as it is because I can concentrate and I get bored looking at a computer for an hour.
- I think we should use ICT now and again but I prefer not to use it that often.
- I do not prefer using ICT in history because I like writing better.
- I think that learning history in the classroom is much better than using computers as the computer in our school many things are blocked so I think that it's better to do it with your teacher.
- ICT will only be a benefit for history if used properly, if it is not then it may end up being a disadvantage. The teachers have to know the best way to use different pieces of software. If they use PowerPoint by just writing all the information on it then it is no benefit to the students and it would be the same to just print hundreds of sheets and make them read them.
- We rarely use ICT in history. However I still think that most history lessons are interesting. Our teacher is a very good teacher, most other teachers would make the subject sound boring but sir makes it more fun to learn. I think I've learnt quite a lot without using the computers and that. I have chosen history as a subject as I feel I could learn quite a lot more and have a better understanding of it.

The relatively high levels of amotivation may have arisen simply because some students simply enjoy history more without the use of ICT. The departments that contributed to the study were all effective and successful practitioners and the student survey responses indicated that they enjoyed history very much. Harris and Haydn's 2006 survey involving 1,740 student questionnaires and 160 student interviews in focus groups across 12 schools found that the majority of students did enjoy history. The most frequently mentioned activities that students found enjoyable were role plays and debates. The use of computers did not feature prominently in the study. Only 50 students referred to ICT although of these only three made negative comments (Harris and Haydn, 2006).

The levels of amotivation might also be explained by students making judgements about how far they felt ICT actually helped in the learning of history. The comments suggest that the students understand their subject and have considered how they as students learn it, a credit to their teachers. However, through this lens it seems that some students see the use of ICT as less effective than other approaches in achieving their goals in history. There is certain logic to this view. As Deaney *et al.* (2006) show, in Design and Technology it is easy to see how simulation software can help students design virtual electric circuits. In English the word processor helps students to identify key elements of text in a poem. It may be less clear to students how ICT contributes to the core activities that students perceive to be of value in history. Extend this argument further and students may therefore see the use of ICT as a distraction, albeit an interesting and attractive distraction, from the core business of thinking about the individuals, events and developments they have studied, making judgements about them and communicating those judgements. Perhaps this is a speculative thought too far but for some students at least it may be that they feel, albeit instinctively rather than overtly, that technology is a useful tool in low level cognitive operations (initially engaging interest, finding things out, writing) but less valuable as a tool for higher cognitive operations – thinking about concepts such as causes and consequences or the significance of particular events or competing interpretations. It seems plausible that they see teacher–student interaction as the vehicle through which these higher order operations take place.

This would appear to be supported by results from a series of questions that suggested possible uses of ICT in history and then asked whether students and teachers had ever carried them out and also whether they thought the activity was something they liked the idea of doing. It was fascinating to see that there was a disparity between the tasks that teachers and students most commonly carried out (writing up with word processors, searching the internet for information, PowerPoint presentations, projecting images and/or film clips) and the extent to which teachers and students liked the idea of doing these tasks. In short, teachers tended to use ICT for tasks that they did not rate highly. The converse was also true – teachers rarely if ever undertook the activities that they rated highly (for example, creating a historical documentary from a particular perspective or evaluating the accuracy of a computer game). Student experiences reflected the views of the teachers.

A paradox

Of course, it would be unwise to make too many judgements based on this one study, or indeed to regard any conclusions arising from it as definitive or fully representative of existing practice. That said, the phenomenon has been observed elsewhere. Morris' survey of teacher approaches to using ICT (Morris, 2010) suggested that many teachers were unaware or unsure about how to use ICT to do more than engage or demonstrate. Haydn and Counsell describe how some history teachers regarded the activities suggested to them for the use of ICT as low level, meretricious or even pointless (Haydn and Counsell, 2003).

But even if this paradox were limited to the teachers in this study it surely merits some consideration because, in the experience of this cohort, technology is failing to fulfil its potential. Why is this behaviour happening? It cannot be explained away on the grounds of poor teaching. In this study data were collected to show that those involved were successful teachers in successful departments. The teachers recognised activities that were higher order activities and liked the idea of carrying out these activities. So, clearly these teachers were capable of recognising such activities and approved of them and yet apparently they favoured less challenging tasks over them. Why were they unable, unwilling or possibly prevented from stepping up their ambition with technology when they were clearly capable of being ambitious and effective in other aspects of their teaching? Is it that they were not prepared to entrust really serious, high value tasks to approaches that used technology? Did they see technology, in effect, as a solution in need of a question? Many teachers have found themselves in a position where they have been handed technology and tasked to make it work, often being stringently evaluated and implicitly criticised when the rhetoric is not transformed into reality. Citing Cuban (1986, 2001), Reeves reminds us that:

> For nearly 100 years, virtually every new technology to come along has been followed by a shotgun-blast-like surge in studies aimed at finding the educational efficacy of the target of the research. This has not worked in the past and it won't work in the future.
>
> (Reeves, 2011: 6)

Planning for improved motivation

This is not a counsel of despair. Technology can be harnessed with ambition but, as Convery (2009) argues, technological claims need to be looked at from a perspective that represents the interests and concerns of teachers, not the interests and concerns of those with a vested interest in technology.

I believe that this is consistent with my core argument in this chapter. My contention is that improvements in student motivation arise primarily from pedagogical innovation and skill on the part of the teacher. Such a contention makes the issue sound simple which it most certainly is not. Motivation is a complex phenomenon. I would argue that it can be seen as an aim in its own right, alongside developing new knowledge for instance. In practice, and quite understandably, few history teachers plan directly for motivation but perhaps there is a case for factoring into the planning process questions such as: What do we mean by motivation in the history classroom? Is this the same thing as combating de-motivation? Or is motivation something deeper which goes beyond simply engaging attention and develops a genuine personal interest in students so that they want to find out more about a historical topic for its own sake? Should we be pragmatic and be satisfied when an image of film clip about the Treaty of Versailles does not put students off studying the Treaty? Is it realistic for the teacher to try to motivate students so that they want to find out more about the Treaty than the course syllabus requires them to know?

Clearly, motivation and challenge are closely linked. I contend that challenge is a motivating factor, not a demotivating one. Silvia (2005) argues that while the novel is enjoyable, the complex is interesting (and therefore leads to a more sustained motivation). Within a supportive framework, students are generally happy to be challenged. Of course this relationship is tempered by the ability of the individual to cope with the level of challenge that is introduced. Silvia cites a study in which students were looking at a painting. The logical expectation would have been that the image was appealing and that contextual information would be off-putting. In fact, providing extensive information about the painting, such as the artist's biography and the context of the work, had a major effect on the understanding and emotions of the students. Johansen and Spafford (2009) referred to a similar phenomenon in an oral history project in which students commented that after investing many weeks of their own time in a project they now understood what teachers meant when they said hard work could be enjoyable.

So where does technology fit into this picture? Where technology improves motivation, it does so because it supports, to a greater or lesser extent, the core pedagogical aims that the teacher has set out. Haydn makes the point that technology and effective support (such as working in pairs or groups) can create effective high challenge–low threat learning environments and cites one student describing this type of task as 'a lot of fun, but hard fun' (Haydn, 2003: 23). Technology's ability to support students can make the most telling impacts. By making required information quickly and readily available, for example, students can maintain their autonomy in a piece of work without having to refer to the teacher. Alternatively, technology can support students in organising their findings and or presenting their final judgements in a coherent and attractive format. But technology is unlikely to generate significant motivational gains when the challenge that the technology supports is dull or not seen as worthwhile or interesting. Motivational gains are found when students believe in, and are enthused by, the core challenge they have been set.

As an illustration of combining high challenge with technology in support I would like to share observations and experiences based on my own work with students and also on my work with teachers in training events and in observing lessons. I am taking a fairly unscientific and anecdotal approach because I do not wish to make claims that the approaches set out below somehow represent 'how to solve the problem'. I am especially anxious to steer clear of terms such as 'transforming learning' which are used far too liberally in the context of using ICT. I hope that hard-pressed teachers looking for ideas on how to harness the power of technology more fully might be able to relate to some of the events and issues described and take away some elements to adapt to their existing practice.

Is *Assassin's Creed* accurate? Selling the idea of hard work in history to young teenagers

In this instance, hard work meant detailed, meticulous research using secondary and archive sources and an unashamedly intellectual approach in which students tested the validity of historical interpretations and supported their judgements with original sources. In other words, it was a significant motivational challenge! An additional aim was to get students to see that the content of history (i.e. accurate period detail based on research and supported by evidence) and the practice of history (undertaking detailed research and supporting judgements with evidence) could be both relevant and potentially helpful to them in a future job market. The inspiration for this task came from the findings of a survey by Haydn (2005) which discovered that while many students enjoyed history, their ideas about why they had to study the subject, and in what ways it might be useful to them in their lives outside the classroom were quite vague. The context of the activity was the OCR GCSE History Pilot (sadly now defunct). Students were tackling the Multimedia Unit: *Bringing the past to life*. This unit was designed to get students to think about how technology is used to reconstruct the past and make it accessible and interesting to different audiences. This activity was undertaken on several occasions and by several different groups. When I was leading it, it was usually Year 9 or 10 students (14–15 year olds) working for a half day or full day in a City Learning Centre (CLC). I also saw the activity adapted and amended by other teachers in CLCs and in their own classrooms.

Naturally, the primary motive (hard work) was somewhat played down and the emphasis was placed on the fact that students were going to look at the video game *Assassin's Creed I*, a role-player game set in the Holy Land at the time of the Third Crusade (the 1190s). Before I go further, I hope that it is superfluous to say that whole classes of students working their way through the levels of a role-play game involving violence and mayhem is clearly not being advocated here. Most of the big developers publish extensive supporting promotional materials, particularly trailers and developer diaries explaining how games were built, which are easily accessible online. It is these that can be (and were) harnessed.

It is also worth stating at this stage that a reader who might be thinking that what follows is a study of how to use computer games in the history classroom is missing the main point. Similarly, any reader having doubts because they do not teach either the GCSE History Pilot or the Crusades is also missing the main point. At the risk of labouring this form of expression, any reader who thinks that the task could not be attempted without the facilities of a CLC is also missing the main point. Although the facilities at the CLC were good, they were not essential to the task as all that was required was a collection of files, sources and web links. I hope that these points will become clearer as the description develops.

The students had already looked at various ways in which technology had been used to reconstruct the past. This included the use of virtual reality technologies on websites and in feature films and documentaries. It also included interactive displays common in many museums today. Students had written reviews of games of their choice including *Assassin's Creed* but also other games such as the *Medal of Honour* and *Call of Duty* series and strategy games including *1914 Shells of Fury* and *Making History: The Calm and The Storm*. The games were studied on the grounds that they were popular and had sold in large numbers. This very fact had already shifted the opinion of some students about the relevance of history as they could see that even if they themselves were not interested in history or games then a very large number of people were. This activity centred on the key question:

We know it's a good video game, but is it good history?

There is no exact formula for assessing a resource such as a video game. Clearly, the narrative of the game is rarely likely to be historically accurate or capable of authentication. Most students realise this quickly but they concentrate on the game environment. In the case of games such as *Medal of Honour* the game environment can be compared with photographs, letters and a range of other sources to allow students to make a decision about whether or not the game environment constitutes good history.

Ubisoft, the developers of *Assassin's Creed* had taken this a step further which is why this game was chosen. Developers of leisure and video games take the issue of authenticity very seriously. Herrington *et al.* (2010) explore the importance of authenticity in simulation materials designed for learning contexts and, while this is a very complex issue, it is generally accepted that authenticity aids motivation and learning. However, there is a difference between the authenticity of a simulation such as a flight simulator to train pilots or a simulation of heart surgery and a simulation such as *Assassin's Creed*. Apart from the obvious purpose of these different simulations there is the fact that one type is real and designed to impart knowledge that was transferable and useable. *Assassin's Creed* is also dealing with more complex situations that are more fluid and intangible. So, in this exercise one of the aims was to consider the content of the game and assess its authenticity against known references but also to consider the game as a cultural artefact – what can we learn from studying the very fact that the game was produced, its target audience and the attitude of the developers and the audience to history?

In their promotional material and their developer diaries they had gone to some lengths to assert the extent of the historical research that underpinned the game. Students were asked as an initial stage to study these claims.

> Let's look around a little bit. This is the town of Acre. We modelled this based on historical documents from the period of the Third Crusade.
> *Assassin's Creed* demonstration 2007 (www.msxbox-world.com/xbox360/videos/ stream/230/481/assassins-creed/x06-demo.html)

One of our main objectives was of course to make the game as realistic as possible and authentic and as close as possible to the historical references that we found. But the difficulty with a game where guys walk around as knights with armour is that it can feel like fantasy. It was important to us that the game and the feeling was really relevant to people so we played with taking these historical sites: Acre, Damascus and Jerusalem and asked how can we create something which feels cool and relevant and interesting to watch for 40 hours as we play. We have made a huge kingdom, three huge cities and it could easily get repetitive and we didn't want that to happen. These cities in medieval times were bustling with all kinds of people from all walks of life. You have to have the poorer citizens, you have to have the richer class, you have to have the merchants. This amounts to a whole lot of characters you have to create …

Assassins Creed Developer Diary 2 (www.youtube.com/watch?v=CDRBdzlZJ5A)

From the start we worked with one historian and he dug up all this hard to find reference material like plans of all the cities, the way land was used at the time, how people dressed, the types of weapons that were available … This historian got us a huge database of reference art and then I asked him to give a presentation to the team which was really cool. He told us about traditions, what kind of happened in a town of the time and that way the whole team had this basic knowledge of the period … And then we worked with other historians throughout the development of the game at different phases to approve the script, to answer questions that came up, to review the art assets we had created and the layout of the cities. We really went all out in that respect!

Interview with *Assassin's Creed* Producer 2007
(www.youtube.com/watch?v=20e7fuTAT4c)

Bear in mind that these comments are typed extracts from online interviews that liberally interspersed sequences of game play footage. Interestingly, in the course of the task what emerged was a shifting picture in terms of students' thinking about history. In the first instance they were inclined to accept that the game was accurate because of all the claims set out above. However, with suitable prompting they began to examine these claims on the grounds that 'well they would say that wouldn't they?' This led to a process in which they had to decide how the claims were going to be tested. The majority, not surprisingly, opted to compare the representations of the people and places in the game with the available images they could locate in textbooks and online. In the sessions I ran, I attempted to steer students away from Google image searches and encourage them to look at specialist image libraries. This proved easier than expected because in a Google image search a large proportion of the results were stills from *Assassin's Creed*! Students were actually quite impressed with the superior results they gained from using resources such as the British Library Images Online (https://imagesonline.bl.uk) or the Mary Evans Picture Library (www.maryevans.com). A few intrepid souls were determined to go further and located sources of documents such as the Fordham Library. Rather more turned to Wikipedia. However, even this proved interesting as some of the Wikipedia sites were rated as trustworthy whereas some were deemed to be in need of better referencing. This led to an agreed process in which references to Wikipedia in students' final presentations were graded, with 'Wikipedia A' denoting a strong page and 'Wikipedia C' denoting a weak page.

For me, it was clear that students were highly motivated by the task. It would have been possible to use the game footage as a stimulus to generate interest in the Crusades and then pursue a more traditional approach that involved students accumulating information and building a narrative of the events of the Third Crusade. I did not adopt this approach because I was not specifically teaching about the Crusade. However, I was intrigued to find that students were telling me about events they had discovered (most often about Richard the Lionheart and Saladin) and asking why they did not come up in the game.

The technology was supporting the curiosity of these students by making it easy and simple to find out more when they wanted to. I recall working with some Year 9 students in one particular lesson in which students were gradually reaching the conclusion that *Assassin's Creed* was reasonably authentic. But then suddenly, concern ensued. One of the brooding, threatening castles in the game was proving to be a source of contention. It had square towers. Online searches reported that most of the castles in this period in this area had circular towers. The students in this instance were so motivated that they actually wrote to the game designers. To their credit, the developers wrote back and explained that they knew this was an anomaly but that the square towers were more effective in creating the mood they were trying to generate. This brought these students (and others in other events of course) up against some powerful realities. They had been evaluating a historical interpretation – the reconstruction of the Middle East in the twelfth century created by the developers. In the process they became aware of the commercial value of historical content. These developers did not care about authenticity per se. Authenticity is a key selling point in a highly lucrative but very competitive market. So for the first time some students saw actual value in researching history! But they also realised that the developers would prioritise mood, drama and atmosphere over historical accuracy if they felt this was justified. This was a further insight into the nature of historical interpretations – that some interpretations are created not specifically to inform or describe the past but with other purposes as well.

So in trying to sell the value of hard work this task had introduced students to new ways of thinking about history but also about knowledge in general and how it is used in different contexts and for different purposes. If I had set out to provide students with a narrative of the Third Crusade I think much of this thinking would have been bypassed. Nor would technology have added much to the process. However, the nature of this task led students naturally into these types of thinking and it was impossible to do this type of thinking without a strong and secure knowledge. In short, the motivation of the task and the support provided by the technology generated the knowledge and the thinking that we as history teachers are always trying to develop but that many students find hard to carry out.

I indicated earlier that this chapter is not about using computer games, or about the Crusades, or about the GCSE History Pilot. It is about a philosophy and an approach. On various sites that host the output of the now defunct Teachers TV resources you can find Esther Arnott using *Assassin's Creed* as one example of a computer game framed within the enquiry question 'Can computer games tell us anything about medieval warfare?' She describes the impact:

> The really excellent thing about this inquiry based approach is the engagement. They are on tenterhooks, ready and waiting. I've got students coming up to me with computer games saying 'I looked at this again when I was at home last night'. That involvement is fantastic.
>
> (Arnott, 2009)

There are many other games that are applicable to these sorts of approaches. It is a pity that there is such an emphasis on warfare and violence but I for one am not aware of games set in the past that address more peaceful and constructive activities and would love to be told otherwise. Or perhaps this is yet another potential area to exploit. I plan to devise activities in the future that use *Assassin's Creed* as a model and then challenge students to do the necessary research to create a game set in a different time and place, perhaps a nineteenth-century industrial city.

The key remains to see these resources not as a source of information but as a form of historical interpretation to be studied and discussed. The *Medal of Honour* and *Call of Duty* series of games attempt to replicate war theatres in the Second World War. If games are too problematic as a source of study, then reconstructions on websites offer a ready and interesting alternative. The BBC has a suite of resources that attempt to reconstruct various experiences of life in the past ranging from a Viking settlement to life in the trenches on the Western Front in the First World War.

As with *Assassin's Creed*, it is the level of detail and challenge that makes these games and similar resources interesting to many youngsters. Hewson describes the use not of a role-player game but of a strategy game called *Making History: The Calm and the Storm*. This game takes students into extraordinary levels of detail which might have been thought intimidating but turned out to be extremely engaging. Hewson adapted the game to his class and got students working as though they were the British Cabinet in the 1930s:

> We carried out the simulation in lesson time, with the boys sitting around a 'Cabinet' style table arrangement and we discussed each turn what we felt that we, as a nation, should do – there was a 5 minute time limit to each turn, lest we get bogged down in aimless discussion.
>
> ... Now, there are some teachers out there who can teach appeasement with their eyes shut and standing on their heads if need be, and I guess I could too. I had done just that for a decade. But what this activity did more than anything else was light a fire under this class of lads that I never wanted to ever extinguish. Their engagement with history was transformed; all because I had been brave enough to try something that was not safe and didactic. The feedback that I had from the boys was fantastic and all of them wanted to continue to use the simulation (which we managed to do in July after their summer examinations).

Hewson went on to capitalise on this motivation and even got these boys looking at the National Archives Cabinet Papers website searching for actual minutes of the 1930s equivalent of the Cabinet meeting that they had held.

Conclusions

This chapter is partly a call to re-examine rather than abandon the signature pedagogy of the history classroom, at least where technology is being used. A coverage model in which the teacher tells the class the story is a tried and tested approach and for many students it provides what they need. However, for some students it can be confusing or frustrating (the classic enemies of motivation) when they are asked to use textbooks or sources to simply find out again the answer that the teacher provided when he or she gave them the story. Teachers use the coverage model because they are under pressure to cover content and in many contexts this is a sensible solution to the problems they face. And the results of the 2010 study suggest that teachers are probably using technology to the full insofar as it can support a traditional coverage model. Resources such as the video games and websites can be effective means to reinforce this process, if they are seen as sources of information and add to the body of knowledge that students accumulate.

On the other hand, this chapter is also a call to consider whether other approaches are more suited to fully exploiting the potential of technology to support learning in history. I am not going to join the siren ranks who call for learning to be transformed or indeed that technology has transformed learning in history or any other subject. As Convery (2009) has argued, such calls simply put unfair pressure on teachers who are too busy teaching to fulfil the hopes and dreams of technological visionaries or managers looking for an instant solution to deep-rooted problems. However, I hope this chapter has suggested ways in which technology can support motivating approaches to studying history by providing access to content and support for students. Technology can provide the complexity and challenge that students find motivating. If we can use technology to help our students acquire knowledge, think about the nature of that knowledge, reshape that knowledge and articulate their own ideas about the knowledge they have acquired then perhaps the huge investment in technology of the last 15 years or more will start to show more of an impact.

References

Arnott, E. (2009) Online at www.teachersmedia.co.uk/videos/esther-arnott, accessed 26 March 2012.

Convery, A. (2009) 'The pedagogy of the impressed: how teachers become victims of technology vision', *Teachers and* Teaching, 15 (1): 25–41.

Cuban, L. (1986) *Teachers and Machines: The classroom use of technology since 1920*, New York: Teachers College Press.

Cuban, L. (2001) *Oversold and Underused: Computers in the classroom*, Cambridge, MA: Harvard University Press.

Deaney, R., Ruthven, K. and Hennessy, S. (2006) 'Teachers' developing "practical theories" of the contribution of information and communication technologies to subject teaching and learning: an analysis of cases from English secondary schools', *British Educational Research Journal*, 32 (3): 459–80.

Harris, R. and Haydn, T. (2006) 'Pupils' enjoyment of history: what lessons can teachers learn from their pupils?', *Curriculum Journal*, 17 (4): 315–33.

Haydn, T. (2003) 'Computers and history: rhetoric, reality and the lessons of the past', in T. Haydn and C. Counsell (eds) *History, ICT and Learning*, London: Routledge, pp. 11–37 .

Haydn, T. (2005) 'Pupil perceptions of history at Key Stage 3: Final Report', online at www.uea.ac.uk/~m242/historypgce/qcafinalreport.pdf, accessed 23 February 2012.

Haydn, T. and Counsell, C. (eds) (2003) *History, ICT and Learning*, London: RoutledgeFalmer.

Herrington, J., Reeves, T. and Oliver, R. (2010) *A Guide to Authentic e-Learning*, New York: Routledge.

Hewson, J. (Forthcoming) 'A pilgrim's progress: my travels and travails with ICT', in E. Arnott and B. Walsh (eds) *Teaching and Learning with ICT: History*, London: Continuum.

Johansen, M. and Spafford, M. (2009) 'How our area used to be back then: an oral history project in an east London school', *Teaching History*, 134: 37–46.

Morris, D. (2010) 'Are teachers technophobes? Investigating professional competency in the use of ICT to support teaching and learning', *Procedia Social and Behavioural Sciences*, 2: 4010–15.

Ofsted (2007) *History in the Balance: History in English schools 2003–07*, London: Ofsted.

Passey, D. and Rogers, C. with Machell, J. and McHugh, G. (2004) *The Motivational Effect of ICT on Pupils: A Department for Education and Skills research project* 4RP/2002/050–3. Nottingham: DfES.

Prensky, M. (2001) 'Digital natives, digital immigrants', *On the Horizon*, 9 (5): 1–6. MCB University Press, October.

Reeves, T.C. (2011) 'Can educational research be both rigorous and relevant?' *Educational Designer*, 1 (4): 1–30.

Ryan, R. and Deci, E. (2000) 'Self determination theory and the facilitation of intrinsic motivation, social development, and well-being', *American Psychologist*, 55 (1): 68–78.

Shulman, L.S. (2005) 'Signature pedagogies in the professions', *Dadalus*, 134: 52–9.

Silvia, P. (2005) 'What is interesting? Exploring the appraisal structure of interest', *Emotion*, 5 (1): 89–102.

Teachers TV (nd) 'From good to outstanding: Esther Arnott', online at www.teachersmedia.co.uk/videos/esther-arnott, accessed March 2012.

Walsh, B. (2010) 'The motivational impact of ICT in the secondary classroom: is history different?' Unpublished MA dissertation. Lancaster University.

Chapter 10

Immersive learning in the history classroom

How social media can help meet the expectations of a new generation of learners

Johannes Ahrenfelt

Introduction

A new generation of learners is emerging. Many of these students are equipped with complex skills and have expectations that can sometimes be challenging to match. They are looking for more than a narrative. They want exploration, material and social interactivity, constant reinforcement and problem solving in an immersive environment. In many respects, education is the last institution to adapt to their world. This chapter explores how new technology such as social media and mobile technology can help history teachers bridge the gap between students' expectations and the reality of a twenty-first-century classroom. It will also examine how new technologies such as Augmented Reality and Quick Response Codes (QR codes) can help connect the real world with the virtual world and provide opportunity to engage this new generation of history students.

A new generation of learners

> Teenagers do not wear wristwatches. I don't mean they can't or they're not allowed to, they just often choose not to… They see no reason to do this. And by the way, you don't need to do it either; it's just that you've always done it and you carry on doing it. My daughter never wears a watch… she doesn't see the point. As she says, "It's a single function device."
>
> (Robinson, 2010)

If you ask young students in your own class how many of them wear a watch you might be surprised to hear that only a fraction do. The reason they will give is that a watch is only providing one feature but that their mobile phones do not. In their view, watches tell time, possibly the date and some provide an alarm feature, but can you update your Facebook status, send Tweets on Twitter, update your blog or interact digitally with other people and physical items with a wristwatch? The answer is of course – no.

Students born in the 1990s and in the new millennium have become more involved with technology than their older siblings. In fact, they are using the tools popularised by their older counterparts. These young adults have not experienced a world without the World Wide Web or mobile phones. New Media such as Social Networking and Augmented Reality such as QR codes are becoming the norm for these youngsters and the way they communicate, establish friendships and use technology have transformed the way they learn – outside of school. This has therefore created a gap between their expectations about learning in their everyday lives and the reality of the classroom.

Professor Mike Sharples makes the point that schools might consider how they might constructively integrate mobile phones into their practice, rather than banning them:

> It makes no sense for schools to pay for rooms full of desktop machines when children have more powerful computers in their pockets. The new smartphones are scientific instruments, with built-in e-book readers, cameras, voice recorders, timers, web browsers, accelerometers, position locators and tilt sensors. Children can use them for research, creativity, and project work. Instead of banning mobile phones, schools should be training children in how to use them properly.
>
> (Sharples, 2011)

What is 'immersive learning'?

The idea of 'immersive learning' has become influential in language teaching in recent years (see, for example, Pachler *et al.*, 2008). The idea is that the best way to learn a language is to live in that country with people who speak the language using all the senses to integrate the words themselves. Ideally, students will talk in the 'target language', perhaps videoconference with pupils in French schools, read French newspapers and magazines, watch French television programmes, absorb French culture, sample French cuisine, go on French websites and so on. This approach is called *total immersion* (Rosen, 2010).

The idea is that we will not truly develop a 'rich associative network' until we immerse ourselves in the culture where the language is spoken. This means that we will learn more if we are exposed to other 'realistic' sensory stimuli that cannot be provided by materials such as books and PowerPoint. According to Rosen (2010), 'realism is the key'. The idea is that the closer an activity is to reality (sometimes termed 'authentic tasks'), the more students feel a sense of connectedness between themselves, the teacher and the subject. Based on this, consider how far the following teaching tools simulate a real-life event that students will connect with:

- books
- worksheets
- listening to the teacher
- audio (CD, podcasts)
- watching films
- engaging in virtual worlds.

Consider the way students learn history in school. Would you say that it echoes a total immersive approach? Perhaps not. How can we change the way we teach to develop a sense of 'immersion' in learning about the past? The nature of the subject does raise questions about immersion given that many concepts involved in learning history are 'abstract', and much of it is of course 'in the past'. However, as Faulkner famously said, 'The past is not dead, it is not even past' (quoted in Haydn *et al.*, 2001: 13). History is about the relationship between the past, the present and the future (Aldrich, 1997), it is 'an argument' (Arnold, 2000), and the arguments, debates and discussions about the effect of the past on the present are a constant presence on television, the newspapers and the internet. There is some evidence to suggest that pupils want to be actively involved in these arguments and debates, and to learn through participation, dialogue and active contribution to discussions and arguments about the past, rather than simply 'receiving the past' passively from their teachers (QCA, 2005).

My experience of working in schools over the past decade suggests that the actual experience for a pupil in a secondary classroom can be quite different. They attend their lessons sitting in rows facing the front, most of the time. If they are lucky and they have a wacky, cool, progressive classroom practitioner they might sit in a horseshoe shape. Alas, this only happens to the lucky few. The main bulk of their day can involve listening and looking at PowerPoint slides, lesson after lesson. Traumatised, they arrive back home when they carry on learning outside of the classroom. Regretfully, learning beyond the classroom does occur but may not necessarily be linked to what we consider is the curriculum. Instead, they learn about their friends, clubs, artists, idols, sporting stars; they interact and learn via Facebook, Instant Messaging, micro-blog on Twitter, play online games, engage in Virtual World – the list is endless. They return to school the following day and continue to sit in rows, patiently listening to us. The contrast between their expectations about learning and the reality of the classroom is not met. In fact, education is the last institution to adapt to their very different world.

Fortunately, we are history teachers, and building stories to help understand the past is what we do best. New technology can help to enhance our teaching further and bridge the gap between the past and the present, and challenge students to think. I have tried to provide some examples of how the use of social media in school history can help to involve students more actively in their learning and to provide the 'immersive' learning environment that will help to persuade them that history is relevant to their lives outside the classroom.

How can Social Networking provide for enhanced and immersive learning?

Case-study: The Gun Powder Tweeting and Plot, 2010

In 2009 Chris Leach, a Primary school teacher, and his Year 6 class used Twitter to create an environment where the events of the Gunpowder Plot of 1605 could unfold as if it was happening at the time. Groups in the class were given one of the key characters to research and once the class and Chris had gained an understanding of the background and individuals involved they each 'took control' of one of the historical personalities connected to the plot (http://chrisleach78.wordpress.com/2010/03/18/the-gunpowder-plot).

Twitter is a micro-blogging site where you are only able to send messages (Tweets) with 140 characters. This means that students must be succinct and carefully select the information they want to send in each Tweet. (Twitter is a very simple tool to learn how to use, and there are several excellent guides and ideas for using Twitter. Start by looking here: http://goo.gl/FQfvj (a part of my website devoted to social media issues – see http://www.johannesahrenfelt.com).) Chris and his class managed to use Twitter as a means of creating a digital role play and, where possible, the chronology of the plot including the lead up to Fawkes' and Catesby's capture. Hundreds of teachers and pupils followed the drama live on Twitter and the feedback Chris received was very positive (see http://www.wallwisher.com/wall/rcatesby).

The power of using a tool such as Twitter is its immediacy. Students are used to receiving feedback from their friends when they partake in online games, connect via Instant

Messaging or when communicating via Facebook. Being part of class with 30 other students makes it difficult for any teacher to give each individual this immediate feedback they are so familiar with. Micro-blogs such as Twitter can help bridge this gap.[1]

Further ideas for using Twitter in the classroom to promote immersive learning

- Chat and discussions during the lesson.
- For homework the class send in a Tweet which classmates can critique.
- Feedback during or after presentations: the open backchannel which fellow students can use to ask questions, mention points of interests, all of which can be referred back to after the presentation.
- Inter-lesson activities: provide additional tasks or use as opportunity to challenge those very able or support those that need extra help.
- Simulations and Alternate Reality Games.

Alternate Reality Games – when online Social Networking becomes 'real'

An Alternate Reality Game (ARG) combines real-life items and people with clues and puzzles hidden online. Players follow a sort of narrative that contains a series of clues, puzzles and events developed by a 'puppet master', the person who guides the players. ARGs are not computer games, although players tend to use handheld devices to access clues online. Nor are they role-playing games as players represent themselves. ARGs tend to happen within a fictitious world based in a real environment. So, clues can be found anywhere from books, cafés, bus stops, websites, Facebook wall, QR-Codes and so on. As not one player is likely to find all the clues, the real solution is in the collaborative process between those involved.

A game can have several entry points or 'rabbit holes' where users join the game. For example, a new player is suddenly given a specific clue such as a text message on their mobile, which 'invites' them to investigate an odd occurrence, and they find themselves drawn into an interaction with another player before they even enter the game properly. The vast majority of ARGs have a definite conclusion.

Why use it in learning and teaching?

As ARGs involve a strong element of collaboration as well as social exploration and discovery, their potential to enhance learning is immense. Students' involvement in ARGs will not only help to enhance their problem-solving skills but will also encourage collaboration, provide scholarly research opportunities and experiential learning. ARGs can also provide students with a toolbox of functional skills that can help in their professional lives where they will be expected to solve problems by using different materials from various resources, thinking critically and analytically as well as placing their individual skill-sets, interests as well as abilities at the disposal of a group dedicated to a common goal. Most significantly, the use of ARGs is a move towards an immersive curriculum. See Figure 10.1 for an extract from an ARG.

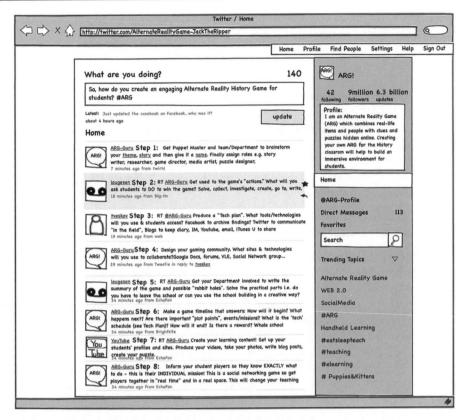

Figure 10.1 How to create your own Alternate Reality History Game

Scan! Tap! Learn!

Bridging their real and virtual world using mobile phones

Imagine if you could share any online information, music, images, text messages and videos with your students when they interact with your classroom, school signs, books or any other physical items by scanning them with their mobile phone? Well, you can achieve that with QR codes.[2]

There are no real technical skills involved in creating a QR code as all of the tools required are available online. You only need access to a QR code Generator and have a QR code Reader installed on the mobile phone.[3] Most QR code Generators allow you to create or 'hide' a number of different resources within the QR images, for example:

- website URL
- vCard
- text message
- phone number
- email address.

Here follows a few practical examples of how you can quickly use QR codes to enhance learning outside of the classroom.

The hook

Before students enter your room there tends to be a few minutes when they wait patiently (or not so ...) outside. Why not get them involved in their learning even before the lesson begins?

Visit one of the QR code Generator websites that you found from your search earlier and create an image that links to a YouTube video or image, quote or cryptic comment that relates directly to what they will be taught in the lesson. For example, a Year 10 History class waited outside my classroom and were able access the image in Figure 10.2, scan it, and see what we investigated in that lesson.

Using PowerPoint interactively

I had a really enjoyable opportunity to showcase some creative ideas for using ICT in the classroom to a group of History PGCE Mentors at the University of East Anglia. I asked how many of them used QR codes. No hands went up. Nearly all of them used PowerPoint, but they had not come across the idea of embedding QR codes within PowerPoint to make PowerPoint presentations more interactive. QR readers have become very sophisticated so students can actually scan images from the back of the classroom. This means that your expositions and student presentations can now be more engaging than ever. For example, if you are teaching a group of A-Level students and you want them to become more actively involved in your presentation, then try inserting QR images on particular slides containing links to further reading or a documentary you want them to watch on Teachers TV or Archive.org. Similarly, if you get used to adding a 'Think about this ...' image in the bottom right-hand corner of a slide that takes students to a question you want them to consider, then this will help generate discussion and also allow them thinking time. See Figure 10.3 for an example of what this looks like.

Figure 10.2 Year 10 lesson hook

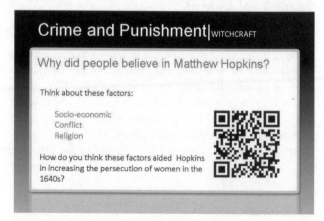

Figure 10.3 Using QR codes within PowerPoint

You could also have two codes and students scan one for YES and the other for NO (or similar outcomes). Then you just see the reports about the scan to gauge the end result (requires an account to SQUARE:CODE see. www.squarecode.biz).

Why did Eric leave the classroom? Or, how to use social learning games

Rarely do students have the opportunity to collaborate and work together as well as they do in physical education where team work really is important to winning a game. There are ways where this mentality and methods of working can be used in history by playing social learning games. In such games students have to work in teams to find clues to a problem and they receive rewards if successful. The most favourable social learning games involve careful planning so that students take them seriously, otherwise they are likely to fail. This particular example also involved using a SQUARE:CODE which allows the teacher to place codes around school but then change the message of each code without having to replace them like they need to with a conventional QR code. Here follows one example:

- Students in a middle ability Year 9 class were informed that they were to work in teams to solve a mystery and that it would be time limited (20 minutes). The mystery contained keys that were scattered around the school and they would unlock further keys and ultimately the solution to the mystery. Each key was worth five points. There were ten keys in total but the mystery could be solved with a minimum of seven keys. The winning team was the one that had solved the mystery, runners up were based on the number of points accumulated.
- The mystery was to find a solution and to be able to explain and answer the question: *Why did Eric leave the classroom?*
- The question dealt with how children from the school were affected by the Second World War. 'Eric' was forced to leave the classroom together with his classmates to enter the bomb shelter when the air raid siren was set off. No one was hurt but Eric kept a diary so his reactions to the event could be used by our students.
- Students were given five minutes to get into groups of four. They were then asked to think of a good team name (five minutes) – this was essential for motivation before the task. Each team were given a map of the school with four visible QR code images displayed. They had to get to one of the images before the other groups as each image contained various levels of difficulty in decoding the message (*you could differentiate this by giving them direction to the image you want them to look at first*) and would therefore take them to different areas of the school as the first QR code would establish which pattern they followed on the map. Groups now had 20 minutes (exact time was set) before they had to be back to the classroom. Failure to arrive before the set time would result in disqualification.
- The four sets of ten keys (QR code images stuck onto walls, trees, windows, ceilings, doors, etc.) contained information from primary evidence: diary extracts, newspaper clippings, video clips and MP3 tracks, as well as messages typed up by their teachers, all of which linked to another location on the map where they could find the next key.
- If groups were particularly sharp they would also realise that each 'pattern' on the map, the directions they walked, resembled a shape of where Eric walked to, namely, the bomb shelter.

One major difference with the QR codes used in this game was that they had the ability to change content any time we wanted without replacing the QR code image. For example, one code was placed outside the canteen but the message changed every ten minutes with new information. This meant that students had to return to this particular message regularly to discover more about what happened to Eric at this location. To give you a practical example, the image below will automatically change content each day at 8.25am. Some content may be text, another day a video clip and so on. This freedom allowed us to create a very unique experience for each group as it enabled us to personalise the content for each SQUARE:CODE. See Figure 10.4.

Revision

Getting some students to revise can be difficult at times and those who do want to spend time on their work may lose sight of what they are doing or just run out of steam. The latter can be attributed to revision material and activities that essentially are note-taking tasks and can therefore fail to engage even the most industrious of students. Here are a few ideas that work well to encourage revision and engagement:

- *The revision board:* create a series of QR images that contain links to subject-specific video clips that students can download to their iPods/mobiles. Then place these images on the department's revision board in the corridor. You will be surprised how often students come back to check on updated resources.
- *Top-tips:* images containing revision tips, tools for learning or exam techniques you feel that they would benefit from looking at. You could place one of these codes by the school's front door for students to scan when they arrived at school – hooked into learning as soon as they arrive.
- *Revision QR stickers:* provide classes with stickers that contain a RSS feed to the department or team's blog. Alternatively, use codes you can update again and again. This ensures that the content is always updated. Stickers are very reasonably priced nowadays; alternatively, buy business cards with the image on them.

Figure 10.4 Using QR codes

Scan this image with i-Nigma (in your app store) every Monday at 8.26am and you'll see a different message each day. This was put up outside my classroom for students to scan before their lessons started.

So, can history teachers help bridge the gap between students' expectations and the reality of today's classrooms?

Students do face a very different way of learning when they walk through the school gates. Their learning experiences will also vary significantly from subject to subject and teacher to teacher. Whether we as history teachers are able to replicate the 'perfect lesson' by using Twitter or QR codes is perhaps not the point. If some of our lessons challenge students' way of thinking, which includes the opportunity for them to be swept away into an all-embracing world where education meets their expectations of learning using New Technology, then we have done a pretty decent job as teachers. It is worth making the point that many of the Web 2.0 and social media apps and programs come 'cost free'. One example of this is the *Poll Everywhere* app (www.polleverywhere.com), which enables pupils to vote electronically in the classroom with mobile phones, without the need for expensive voting/response software.

Using technology is of course not the sole solution to bridging the gap between what they expect and what we as educators can actually offer them. It is, however, a step in the right direction. Building, creating and planning immersive environments do not have to include technology, but it can help.[4]

Notes

1 Before you set up your Twitter account that you will use with a class it is worth pointing out that Twitter is public. This means anything you write and share can be seen by millions of others. However, if you 'protect your tweets' and all the students do the same then the problem is solved. See this link for a helping hand using Twitter: http://goo.gl/pJDV.
2 For more information about QR codes, its history and usage please read the Wiki entry: http://goo.gl/kTn2.
3 See this link for all the resources you need: http://goo.gl/ogDdu.
4 For more information on these ideas, see the 'using social media' section of my website, www.johannesahrenfelt.com.

References

Aldrich, R. (1997) *The End of History and the Beginning of Education*, London: Institute of Education, University of London.

Arnold, J. (2000) *History: A very short introduction*, Oxford: Oxford University Press.

Haydn, T., Arthur, J. and Hunt, M. (2001) *Learning to Teach History in the Secondary School*, London: Routledge.

Pachler, N., Barnes, A. and Field, K. (2008) *Learning to Teach Modern Foreign Languages in the Secondary School*, London: Routledge.

QCA (2005) *Pupil Perceptions of History at Key Stage 3*, London: QCA.

Robinson, K. (2010) *Bring on the Learning Revolution* (TED website), online at www.ted.com/talks/sir_ken_robinson_bring_on_the_revolution.html (07.43min), accessed 18 January 2012.

Rosen, L. (2010) *Rewired*, Basingstoke: Palgrave Macmillan.

Sharples, M. (2011) Quoted in J. Friedberg, 'Good things are happening all around you Mr Gove', *Cribsheet* (Guardian Blog), 6 April 2011.

Chapter 11

What can you do with an interactive whiteboard?

Alf Wilkinson

Introduction

I have heard it said, with regard to interactive whiteboards (IWBs), that 'Never, in the field of Educational Technology, has so much equipment been used so effectively by so few.' It is now six years since I helped produce an article for the Historical Association journal *Primary History*, 'Questions you have always wanted to ask about using a whiteboard' (Fewster, 2005). This article was published at a time when policymakers and manufacturers were making strong claims that 'the use of IWBs can transform teachers' practice', and when the then Secretary of State for Education, Charles Clarke, was associating IWBs with 'a learning revolution' (Gillen *et al.*, 2006: 1). IWBs thus had a considerable burden of expectation placed on them even as they were beginning to be installed in UK classrooms. Everyone, it seemed, was either getting an IWB in their classroom, or wanted one, among claims that teaching and learning would never be the same again.

So, in the meantime, what has changed? The hype was extensive, but what is the reality? And what impact have IWBs had? Anecdotal evidence suggests very little, in some cases. On a recent 'New pupils Open Day' visit I made to a brand spanking new Academy, every single classroom had an IWB. Only three of them were switched on. Two had lesson objectives boldly listed, and the third had a 'fill in the blanks' type 'Word' worksheet displayed. And this was when the school was on show to the world and trying to attract pupils. Clearly in this case the revolution has passed them by – or was it just a 'bad day at the office?'

Research evidence paints a mixed picture of the impact of IWBs (see, for example, Smith *et al.*, 2005: Moss *et al.*, 2007; Ofsted, 2011), including suggestions that IWBs may actually be an impediment to learning rather than an asset. A recent teacher blog argues that we should be 'switching off the whiteboard for good' (McLoughlin, 2011). The author suggests rather tongue in cheek that IWBs are mostly used just like normal whiteboards, only with the internet on them, and the sooner they are removed from classrooms the better, as far as most teachers are concerned. He argues they are rarely used in an *interactive* manner, and that the money could be spent better elsewhere. Many of the contributors to the blog agreed, and argued that there should be much more emphasis on teaching and learning methods and less on the technology.

Other studies are just as critical: IWBs can slow the pace of whole class learning, a study commissioned by the Department for Education and Skills suggested, as pupils took it in turns to use the board. They can also lead to relatively mundane activities being over-valued, the Institute of Education study found (Moss *et al.*, 2007). The research was carried out in 2004–5 as part of a project to put IWBs in London schools in three core subjects. Admittedly, the research was carried out within 12 months of the boards being installed, so it was perhaps a little early to expect outstanding progress in their use having been made.

The Schools Minister of the time, Jim Knight, added 'Only when teachers have the skills to use it properly can we expect them to use the technology to support and transform traditional teaching methods' (Knight, 2007). As Haydn and Barton have argued (2008), teachers need time to think and develop their own ideas when offered new technology. They need to be able to decide how the new technology, in this case, interactive whiteboards, fits into their own style of teaching.

This is not to suggest that the evaluation of IWBs has been unremittingly negative. According to the British Educational Communications and Technology Agency (Becta), the now defunct ICT government quango, some of the key benefits of using interactive whiteboards in the classroom include:

- encouraging more varied, creative and seamless use of teaching materials;
- engaging students to a greater extent than conventional whole-class teaching, increasing enjoyment and motivation;
- facilitating student participation through the ability to interact with materials.

Dr Mary Ann Bell (2002) offers us a personal perspective. In a list of reasons for using an IWB she includes:

> It is interactive. Users can be contributing directly by input both at the computer and at the board. The combination I liked best was for the teacher to be stationed at the computer, with students at the board and in the class offering suggestions and physically contributing ideas and actions. The interaction that transpires between the person at the computer, the users at the board, and the computer itself is a unique and very adaptable arrangement.

In *Interactive Whiteboards and Learning – Improving student learning outcomes and streamlining lesson planning*, Smart Technologies, a leading interactive whiteboard manufacturer and retailer, concludes:

> The interactive whiteboard has been incorporated into learning environments for over a decade, and an increasing flow of research into its impact is emerging from the United States, the United Kingdom and Australia. From the available body of research, several themes and patterns have emerged, including the positive effect interactive whiteboards have on student engagement, motivation, the ability to accommodate a variety of learning styles (including special needs students) and the capacity to enhance student understanding and review processes. Observations also indicate that designing lessons around interactive whiteboards can help educators streamline their preparations and be more efficient in ICT integration, thereby enhancing their overall productivity.
>
> (Smart Technologies, 2006)

A TechLearn (nd) briefing argues that interactive whiteboards can be used primarily as presentation devices. It then goes on to argue that the key pedagogic aspects of IWBs are:

- their size, which facilitates collaborative group working;
- their interactivity, which facilitates active learning, not just passive reception of information;

- their accessibility, for learners with visual or physical impairment;
- their recordability, so that an end product can be emailed, stored for subsequent re-use, or deconstructed to analyse a process.

Much of the discourse on IWBs advances the idea that (*interactive*) whiteboards aid learning by making it engaging and active, rather than passive. Remember the saying, that we retain approximately 10 per cent of what we read, 20 per cent of what we hear, 30 per cent of what we see, 70 per cent of what we say and 90 per cent of what we say we do (see Chapter 8). How can we encourage pupils to both say and do in the history classroom? This chapter will explore how we might use interactive whiteboards in history classrooms, under four main headings – as a presentation tool; as an organising tool for teachers and pupils; as an assessment tool; and, perhaps most importantly of all, as an interactive tool for learning.

Interactive whiteboards as a presentation tool

Let's not underestimate the impact of the IWB as a presentation tool. I know it might not be using the full power of the technology, but it is impressive when compared to a blackboard or non-interactive whiteboard, and it has lots of useful features. When I first started teaching, textbooks were illustrated – if at all – with simple black and white drawings, or indistinct 'grey' photographs. Older readers may remember that duplicating was done on a 'Banda' spirit duplicator, and we had just managed to figure out how to use two colours. Otherwise it was 'chalk and talk'. The ability to project a full colour high-density image four-feet square is a powerful tool. Students can see the detail, and explore an image as evidence in a new way. For example, you might take an old newspaper or Trade Directory. They contain lots of advertisements, but they are often very small, perhaps 10cm square. Scan them into your computer and enlarge. Then project onto your whiteboard. It is just the same with sound and moving images, and there are some superb animations on the web. Try the 'Animations' on the BBC website as a good source (www.bbc.co.uk/history/interactive/animations). It is much easier to understand how a steam engine, for example, works after watching it on 'the big screen'. At a simple level it is much easier to watch film clips on a large screen, and size does seem to have an influence on learner attention.

Ask students to present their work on the whiteboard. If I am feeling mean I will ask them to present a key idea on one screen with three bullet points and one image. If I'm feeling generous I allow them five bullet points. That is quite a challenging activity. Any activity that makes pupils select and discard from a pool of information forces them to think about content, one of the factors that Willingham (2009) argues contributes to knowledge retention. The link to the internet is crucial for presentation, making finding and collecting images much easier. Keep them in clearly labelled galleries where they will be easily accessible in the future. Think carefully about the filing system you use – make it logical in terms of your teaching. As a starter, try presenting students with a selection of eight or ten images of the same person – not a common activity in textbooks – and ask them to select the one they think sums up that person in whatever context you are talking about them. Save the screen. Ask two or three others to do the same, then get the whole class to decide which image the class thinks best sums up that individual. By the end of the activity you should have quite a selection of images that students have chosen. Get them to 'drag and drop' them into a sequence – chronological, importance, whatever. They are using the IWB as a presentation tool, but the historical thinking involved in such activities can be at quite a high level.

Of course there are endless variations for presenting material. You can record a commentary to your presentation – ideal for poorer readers – or present discordant and conflicting evidence on your soundtrack. A favourite activity of mine is to show a film as sound only, then as vision only, then both together, with questions and discussion between each showing, helping students build up a picture of how the film clip is leading them to a certain conclusion. It is much easier to do this with an IWB than any other way I know. And of course you can stop the action at any time and use the highlighter tools to annotate/graffiti the scene – a powerful way to make a point.

Students always find it difficult to explore images, especially cartoons which are often used in examinations. They tend to see the obvious, but not the detail. Whiteboards have a variety of tools that make it easier to develop visual literacy. You can use the 'blind' tool to obscure most/all of the image, and 'reveal' it bit by bit. You can use the 'circle' tool to focus on one part of an image. I remember one activity like this very well. A cropped photograph of Emily Pankhurst, all dressed up in furs and a smart hat, smiling and walking towards the camera, suggesting a stroll in the park or a night out on the town. A second, fuller, version of the photograph showed she was being marched away firmly in the arms of two tall Metropolitan policemen. Another technique is to 'hide' information and/or pictures behind white pen marks, so they appear, when the white pen is erased, as if by magic. The IWB gives us lots and lots of opportunities to easily 'manipulate' images to make our students look carefully at them, to initially draw the wrong conclusion, and then to see something very differently as content or context is revealed.

Another history skill students find difficult to develop is the ability to extract data and information from graphs. The IWB makes it easy to present graphs in a variety of ways and colours. Again, they can be 'revealed' bit by bit to make it easier for students to interpret them. None of these suggestions necessarily use the full functionality of the interactive whiteboard, but they can all enhance history lessons. They can present evidence, detail, information, problems and conundrums for students to solve. The best lessons, of course, are not purely 'chalk and talk', or totally teacher led. All the suggestions in this section can lead to 'closed' activities or 'open' ones. It is in the pupil interaction with the ideas and materials on the interactive whiteboard as a presentation tool that effective learning will take place.

Interactive whiteboards as an organising tool for teachers and pupils

One of the biggest changes an IWB made to my teaching was in terms of organisation. Everything could now be in one place and readily accessible. Film clips were instantly available – no need to scroll though a video that someone had forgotten to rewind to the correct place, no need to rush off to duplicate more worksheets that someone had used up and not replaced. No need to chase up that 'lost' or misplaced resource. I was in control! Once found and used, images were stored in the appropriate gallery and were instantly available to call up and use when an unexpected question or point arose during a discussion or debate. Equally, students' work was easily available, pulled out of the appropriate file, for reference or use with another class as required. And all at the click of a mouse or the tap of a board. It did not in itself make my teaching any better but it was certainly more efficient. Similarly with students' work – it was on tap and accessible from the VLE whenever they – or I – wanted it. Savings in my time were not unappreciated. Counsell (1997) has made the point that one of the things that pupils find difficult about history is its sheer vastness. Huggins (2006: 1) argues that one of the most useful affordances of the IWB is the facility it offers for pupils to organise their thinking and marshal information on the whiteboard using what he terms 'graphic organisers', a range of layouts that help pupils to sort information, to experiment with it, move things around, test out different ideas through the use of visual frameworks such as 'skill triangles, venn diagrams, chain of events, reliability squares, zones of tolerance, idea showers and a host of other organising tools' (these ideas can be accessed at www.e-help.eu/seminars/huggins.htm).

Whiteboards as an assessment tool for teachers and pupils

Assessment should, in my opinion, be an integral part of teaching and learning, not a bolt-on. Students need to know what they can do, but also what they need to be able to do to get better at history. One often overlooked aspect of IWBs is their use as an assessment tool. 'Save' a screen of a student's work to refer to later. It is really simple to use the 'record' function to record discussions, debates, or a student's presentation or line of argument. This can be used by the teacher to mark a piece of work, or to ascribe an end-of-key-stage Level of Attainment, or as a basis for later discussion between teacher and student. It can also be kept and replayed later in a topic/term/scheme of work to allow students to see just how much, or how little, progress they have made in developing a skill or concept. In addition to providing a potentially useful contribution to portfolio collections of pupils' work (Freeman and Philpott, 2009), it can also provide a useful means of recap, revisiting and 'overview' perspectives of topics and themes that span several terms, so that pupils develop an understanding of 'the big picture' which is so important to their historical understanding (Counsell, 2000; Howson, 2007; Ofsted, 2011).

IWBs are also helpful for modelling answers to examination questions or activities. You can scan in one of your answers as an example, or, better still, type it in to your computer using word processing software. Or, use the handwriting recognition software – if your handwriting is good enough – and let the IWB software turn it into text. Students can then discuss the merits of your specimen answer and suggest improvements. As with a paper version of this activity, colour coding can be used to highlight strengths and weaknesses, words, phrases, etc., but with the IWB the specimen answer can be endlessly modified – each version saved for later if you wish – until both you and the group are totally satisfied with what has been developed. You or they can input the changes as and when required. No messy piece of paper, just a deliberated and collaboratively produced answer that does exactly what you want it to – and each student can have a copy if they wish. It is not just the final product that matters, but the process pupils have gone through in reaching that answer. The interactivity of the whiteboard makes the whole process easier and much more satisfactory than any other way of doing this. A modification of this activity is to use student answers – not necessarily examination-type questions – as a starting point for any discussions.

Peer assessment is increasingly used in history classrooms and can be a very effective way to help students develop an understanding of what they can, and cannot do. As Black and Wiliam (1998) have argued, if formative assessment is to be productive, pupils should be trained in self-assessment so that they can understand the main purposes of learning and thereby grasp what is to be achieved. It often takes a lot of time to develop effective peer assessment. Students frequently respond better to criticism from peers than from teachers, so effective peer assessment is worth the time and effort involved. (For a useful resource on the use of peer and self-assessment and its impact on pupil attainment, see Highland Council, nd.) By modelling the process on the whiteboard, it is possible to help students become more confident in being positively critical about other students' work, thereby improving their own performance.

A widely used strategy for peer assessment is to get students to make a presentation to the class and invite comments. Many students will be familiar with this way of working. Using an IWB, as in the first example cited above, makes the process more accessible, and gives an 'on-the-spot' result. It allows instant recorded feedback and shows students how to get better. Nothing is lost, as often happens with oral feedback. It also gives the teacher the opportunity to stand back and decide what steps it is necessary to take next lesson. There is nothing technologically difficult here, but a very simple and effective, way to develop peer assessment in your classroom.

Interactive whiteboards as an interactive tool

The clue really is in the name – an *interactive* whiteboard. Many reports of whiteboard use show it being used as a closed presentation tool by teachers, rather than as a tool used by both teachers and students on a joint journey of learning and discovery. Too often teachers talk, or lead, and expect students to follow. Teachers need to be prepared to stand back at times and not be in control of everything. This is scary for many of us, but absolutely essential if we are to make maximum use of the potential of an interactive whiteboard. This does not mean to abrogate responsibility for what goes on in the history classroom. It requires a detailed and carefully thought out plan of action taking students from where they are to where we hope they can get, but also taking into account students' ideas and responses to the teaching. So how can we do this?

The whiteboard allows us effortlessly to manipulate a wide range of resources, from a wide range of sources. History is really well served with digital collections readily available for educational use (see Chapter 1). It allows us to start with a 'fact' or opinion; add photographs, documents, maps, film or sound archive, in a limitless combination, all pre-placed in a gallery waiting to be called into play as and when required as the lesson unfolds. Of course this could still be in a teacher-led 'closed' sequence of activities, but is much more powerful when teacher and students together set out on collaborative enquiry. We all know from experience that quite often the most rewarding of lessons happen in a way, or end up in a place, we least expected, because we have followed discussion, ideas or debates arising from student comment or curiosity. The whiteboard makes it easier to follow these thoughts, trends and ideas effectively and immediately.

Education outside the classroom is again in favour – not that it went out of favour in many schools. Careful preparation and follow-up is essential to make the most of the time on site. Old maps, photographs, memoirs, trade directories, census details are among the myriad of resources now readily available for most areas and all can be used to pose questions about a site before a visit. IWBs can be used to explore all this. Mobile technologies such as smartphones and digital video cameras allow data from the visit to be sent back to school in a variety of ways, so the detailed discussions on site can be recorded and built upon back in the classroom. The whole process can be integrated much more effectively than in the past when the visit was often seen as a one-off in isolation to events in the classroom.

(An interesting example of integrating digital resources into a visit can be found at 'What was Vintner's Park like in 1890?' at https://shareweb.kent.gov.uk/Documents/leisure-and-culture/heritage/heritage-education-packs/vinters-park.pdf.)

Other ways to make lessons more interactive with a whiteboard include moving images, ideas or evidence around the screen to give a chronological sequence to show change over time – a kind of 'card sort' approach. You can do this in PowerPoint, but it is easier and more effective with a whiteboard.

Variations on this approach include plenary tables, with headings such as 'what do we definitely know/what do we probably know/what do we still need to find out?' to encourage reflection on learning and set goals for future actions. 'Drag and drop' is a relatively simple technique with infinite variations that can be very effective in promoting dialogue between student and student, as well as between teacher and students. Partial selection of data and asking 'what is missing?' is another useful approach, as is prioritising activities of one form or another. A simple selection of a jumble of material/events/actions/opinions/viewpoints into two columns can be very effective. Most of these work more easily on a whiteboard because they allow for extended discussion and debate as to the preferred answer or option. And let's not forget the ability to write/annotate on a whiteboard – to graffiti ideas, thoughts and first impressions onto/next to other views and opinions, helping to build up a 'mind map' of a topic, or build up students' understanding of the topic.

Change over time and chronological understanding are concepts that many students find difficult to get to grips with. Geographical Information Systems are widely used to capture data and display it as maps in the geography classroom – why not in the history classroom too? Many systems, such as Google Maps or Infomapper are widely used both commercially and in schools. By superimposing old maps on modern equivalents, or by superimposing old photographs and new, by appending photographs of the area both old and new, by using aerial photographs as well as maps, it is possible to explore effectively how an area or site has changed over many years.

Perhaps one of the most underused aspects of IWBs is the 'save' function. Summarise the discussion/where the argument is at the end of a lesson and save the screen. Before the next lesson, jumble up the arguments and use that as a starter. Or add another aspect or two to the discussion. The important history skill at work here is the idea that much historical thinking is provisional and subject to change through the discovery of new evidence or the addition of a differing viewpoint. Students find it hard to get their heads around this idea, but it is crucial to a complete understanding of history as a discipline. You can extend this by re-introducing a screen saved much earlier in the scheme of work, based on less evidence and understanding. Ask if students still agree with their earlier conclusions, and if not, why not. Of course you can do this activity in many different ways, but the interactive whiteboard encourages review of thinking and rewriting, precisely because it is so easy to do: you do not have to 'dig things out' or start all over again.

Conclusion

A lot of writing about IWBs has been about the technology – what the boards can do; for example 'drag and drop', 'hide' and 'reveal', 'spotlight', and so on. But for me the crucial aspect of the IWB is the way it can be used to generate meaningful dialogue between teacher and student, as they both embark on a (carefully controlled by the teacher) historical enquiry, responding to inputs easily and effectively. These are the aspects I have tried to highlight in this chapter. It is not what you do with the interactive whiteboard in terms of technical sophistication that is important, it is *how* you use it to make pupils think, talk, discuss and contribute that matters.

A recent paper 'Using interactive whiteboards to orchestrate classroom dialogue'(Mercer *et al.*, 2010) calls this type of teaching and learning 'dialogic interactivity'. It is dependent on open-ended tasks and higher-order questioning, all things that we are familiar with in the history classroom. The paper provides an interesting history case study using a First World War poem ('Dulce et decorum est', by Wilfred Owen) as part of a sequence of activities to try to understand what it was like being in the trenches. The authors conclude:

> [T]he effective use of the IWB as an educational tool is not inherent on the hardware, software or even the materials it displays. It is predicated upon the teacher's practical understanding of how to engage students and to help them learn.
>
> (Mercer *et al.*, 2010: 207)

This brings us back to the quote I used in the introduction from Jim Knight (2007), when he said 'Only when teachers have the skills to use it properly can we expect them to use the technology to support and transform traditional teaching methods.'

The IWB was perhaps afflicted by the hyperbolic claims that accompanied its introduction into UK classrooms. It is unusual for new technology to provide an instantaneous transformation or revolution in learning, but over the past decade, increasing numbers of history teachers have worked out some useful things to do with the whiteboard; it is a useful tool.

There is evidence to suggest that given time to explore what IWBs might do to enhance learning in history, and the opportunity to share ideas and good practice, some teachers are using IWBs in ways that involve pupils more actively in their learning and that encourage them to participate more fully in lessons (Moss *et al.*, 2007). There is also evidence to suggest that the use of IWBs has a positive effect on pupil motivation and engagement, if used in ways that actively involve pupils in learning (see, for instance Wall *et al.*, 2005). A history teacher educator recently told me that whereas a few years ago, many mentors were quite sceptical about the potential benefits of IWBs, more and more of them are now talking positively about their benefits. There is a need to invest some time in becoming 'fluent' in using the whiteboard, but the benefits or 'payoff', particularly in terms of active pupil engagement in learning, can be considerable. If you have not yet delved into the world of the IWB, I would urge you to at least give it a try.

As Terry Haydn argues in Chapter 7 of this volume, good teaching is primarily about the quality of ideas, resources, pupil activities, and the teacher exposition and questioning that teachers bring to a class. Some new technology applications can help the teacher to work with these things in a more effective and productive way. I hope that I have persuaded you that IWBs are one of the developments in ICT that can help you to do this, and that if you have not thus far engaged wholeheartedly with IWBs, you will at least give some time and thought to exploring their possibilities.

References

Becta (2004) *What the Research Says about Interactive Whiteboards*, London: DfeS.

Bell, M. (2002) *Teachers.Net Gazette*, 3 (1), January, online at http://teachers.net/gazette/JAN02/mabell.html, accessed 18 February 2012.

Black, P. and Wiliam, D. (1998) *Inside the Black Box*, London: NFER/Nelson.

Counsell, C. (1997) *Analytical and Discursive Writing at Key Stage 3*, London: Historical Association.

Counsell, C. (2000) '"Didn't we do that in Year 7?" Planning for progress in evidential understanding', *Teaching History*, 99: 36–41.

Fewster, S. (2005) 'Questions you have always wanted to ask ... about using a whiteboard', *Primary History*, Spring: 18–20, Historical Association, London.

Freeman, J. and Philpott, J. (2009) '"Assessing pupil progress": transforming teacher assessment in Key Stage 3 history', *Teaching History*, 137: 4–12.

Gillen, J., Staarman, J., Littleton, K., Mercer, N. and Twiner, A. (2006) '"A learning revolution?" Investigating pedagogic practices around interactive whiteboards in British primary classrooms', paper presented at the AERA Conference, April, San Francisco, online at www.educ.cam.ac.uk/research/projects/iwb/AERA2006.pdf, accessed 14 March 2012.

Haydn, T. and Barton, R. (2008) '"First do no harm": factors influencing teachers' ability and willingness to use ICT in their subject teaching', *Computers and Education*, 51 (1): 439–47.

Highland Council (nd) *Learning and Teaching Should Be Flexible: Peer and self assessment, Highland Learning and Teaching Toolkit*, online at www.highlandschools-virtualib.org.uk/ltt/flexible/peer.htm, accessed 18 February 2012.

Howson, J. (2007) 'Is it the Tuarts and then the Studors or the other way round? The importance of developing a usable big picture of the past', *Teaching History*, 127: 40–7.

Huggins, R. (2006) 'How to develop interactive teaching and learning styles using an interactive whiteboard', presentation at e-help seminar, Toulouse 8–10 June, online at www.e-help.eu/seminars/huggins.htm, accessed 18 February 2012.

Knight, J. (2007) BBC News Channel, 30 January.

McLoughlin, K. (2011) *Switching off the Interactive White Board for good*, online at www.ictsteps.com/2011/05/switching-off-the-interactive-white-board-for-good, accessed 19 February 2012.

Mercer, N., Hennessy, S. and Warwick, P. (2010) 'Using interactive whiteboards to orchestrate classroom dialogue', *Technology, Pedagogy and Education*, 19 (2): 195–209.

Moss, G., Jewitt, C., Levaãiç, R., Armstrong, V., Cardini, A. and Castle, F. (2007) *The Interactive Whiteboard, Pedagogy and Pupil Performance Evaluation: And evaluation of the Schools Whiteboard Expansion Project, London Challenge*, London: Institute of Education.

Ofsted (2011) *History for All*, London: Ofsted.

Smart Technologies (2006) *White Paper, Interactive Whiteboards and Learning: Improving student learning outcomes and streamlining lesson planning*, online at http://downloads01.smarttech.com/media/research/whitepapers/int_whiteboard_research_whitepaper_update.pdf, accessed 18 February 2012.

Smith, H., Higgins, S., Wall, K. and Miller, J. (2005) 'Interactive whiteboards: boon or bandwagon? A critical review of the literature', *Journal of Computer Assisted Learning*, 21 (2): 91–101.

TechLearn Briefing (nd) *Interactive Whiteboards in Education*, online at www.jisc.ac.uk/uploaded_documents/Interactivewhiteboards.pdf, accessed 18 February 2012.

Wall, K., Higgins, S. and Smith, H. (2005) '"The visual helps me understand the complicated things": pupil views of teaching and learning with interactive whiteboards', *British Journal of Educational Technology*, 36 (5): 851–67.

Willingham, D. (2009) *Why Don't Students Like School?* San Francisco, CA: Jossey-Bass.

Chapter 12

Tools for the tech savvy history teacher

Nick Dennis and Doug Belshaw

A key question is how to harness the potential of ICT to deliver what is pedagogically useful in day-to-day history teaching, rather than what is technologically impressive in terms of 'what can be done'.

(Haydn, 2000: 99)

Principles behind effective use of ICT – why learning comes first

Despite the explosion of investment in ICT in UK schools over the past two decades, there has been a general acknowledgement that ICT has not always had the revolutionary impact that was hoped for in educational contexts. Even some of those at the forefront of ICT innovation and development – including Steve Jobs and Bill Gates – have expressed disappointment about the outcomes of investment in ICT (Isaacson, 2011). In the most recent report on school history in England, Ofsted (2011) notes that the use of new technology to improve teaching and learning in history is uneven and at times disappointing. And yet, most of us know some departments and some teachers who are doing interesting, worthwhile and at times inspirational things with new technology. In some cases, this is by using comparatively straightforward and 'low-level' ICT applications, and in others, history teachers are using quite new and 'cutting-edge' ICT applications.

In this chapter, we argue that whether you are using new or established ICT applications, there are some fundamental principles involved in the effective use of new technology. We then go on to provide some examples of the use of new developments in ICT that may be of interest to history teachers who want to explore some of the applications that have recently emerged.

Gillespie (2011) argues that in relation to ICT, teachers can be divided into three broad categories: a large group that stands in the centre, who are open minded but not messianic about ICT, and two smaller groups – 'resistors and sceptics' on the one hand, and 'early adopters' on the other. This chapter is for those on the far left of the normal curve of distribution of innovation, 'the outliers', who are keen to explore new possibilities, in search of new tools to 'amplify their intelligence' (Lucas and Claxton, 2010: 98).

This status does come with a warning: being innovative with new tools does not mean that the work your students will produce will be inherently more analytical or more detailed despite it looking more impressive (initially). This is something Christine Counsell (2000: 2) identified over a decade ago in *Teaching History* in relation to the use of technology at a very good school. Counsell explained that the use of technology in Hampstead School was neither good nor bad but fed off and fed into some deep, shared professional thinking about the sorts of historical knowledge and reflection they wanted to develop over time. Counsell was pointing to the importance of the principles driving the use of technology in the lesson to support historical learning, and what Hampstead were clearly able to demonstrate in their use was clear and context-specific guidelines to help with planning. In essence, clear principles create the means to use a range of technological tools to create outstanding learning. In other words, technology is best thought of as an amplifier and in the hands of a skilled history teacher; the effects can be amazing (although we often seem to think the technology is doing the work rather than the teacher). In the hands of someone who does not share these deep professional principles, the technology will be used, but the outcome will be less than satisfactory in terms of learning.

Simon Sinek in his book *Start With Why* (2011) suggests that to really provide something of excellence, outstanding leaders start with the 'why' and not the 'how' and 'what' and his idea also explains why the effective use of ICT in schools is poor – they often start with the 'what' and then 'how'.

This is not the fault of teachers, because most people communicate from the outside in. In schools, the use of ICT in this way can be likened to the 'Pot-noodle' approach where the technology is simply added to the learning (the 'what') and the method is 'how' it is done, but not really thinking about whether it helps the learning or not. For example, using electronic representations of traditional card sort activities does not improve the outcome of the essay by itself but it tends to become the focal point rather than the historical reasoning needed to produce a good essay. By adding ICT to the 'what', the technology becomes the main focus and the learning takes second place. To overcome this problem, you need to plan or think from the inside of the 'Golden Circle' outward, using these principles to decide whether the use of technology is right for the learning task and provides the most appropriate tools (which can mean not using technology at all). Being clear about these principles removes the possibility of becoming distracted by the latest innovation and moves you towards examining its usefulness in relation to the information and skills you want to teach.

A more technologically focused way of thinking about the correct use of technology is Rueben Puentadura's SAMR model, which can be accessed from: www.hippasus.com/rrpweblog/archives/2012/01/19/SAMR_GuidingDevelopment.pdf. Puentedura's model presents a simple checking system for the use of technology to support historical learning, with each level clearly indicating the opportunities available within each half of the model. If the planned use of technology merely replicates something you can already do, then it is merely a substitution and questions should be asked about its effectiveness. Going back to the card sort example to illustrate, an electronic version used in class offers nothing more than the normal paper-based version. Clearly, the use of technology offers no tangible benefit over traditional methods. Where it can provide some value is if the technology allows you to do something you could already do and add an additional feature, such as create a timeline but with interactive content that provides context. In this instance, the technology is augmenting the understanding of chronology that would occur through a paper-based approach. If the use of technology allows you to redesign the task significantly for the benefit of the learning process, then it really is worth pursuing and, finally, if the technology allows you to create new tasks that were previously inconceivable without the technology, it is redefinition.

To sum up, the use of technology in the SAMR model can enhance or transform the learning experience although the technology itself is not the learning – the device or application is not the pedagogy – the learning drives the use of technology and the technology supports this. This may seem fairly straightforward in terms of history teaching but it is harder than it looks. Finding the 'why' that drives historical learning in the classroom or checking on what level of the SAMR model your use of technology is placed at is a time-consuming and iterative process that requires constant attention and refinement. It necessitates a deeper and sharper argument for historical learning that goes beyond the need to 'provide an understanding of the past' (Husbands *et al.*, 2011: 20). To this end, the examples below arise from a particular conception of 'why' which has been honed through an adherence to the second order concepts, clear guidelines about what progression means, and making learning visible (Counsell, 1997). Moreover, the examples also suggest that instead of merely viewing students as receivers of ICT content, they can be creators of content.

Example 1: Thinking about change and continuity using comics

Change and continuity are, for Counsell, 'elusive prey' (Counsell, 2011: 109), as students can be lured into the trap of seeing historical change as an event rather than a process (Shemilt, 2000: 87). This is a particular problem when teaching social change in Nazi Germany for GCSE, as students are assessed on both the range of changes and the extent of change. Enabling students to discern these types of change and continuity presented in the GCSE question demands a clear focus and one that sometimes presents problems for pupils. In the long-term plan for this topic, the need for overviews was built into the scheme of work at the start and at the end of the normal teaching with a particular focus on the extent of change. However, this still meant that there was an outstanding issue with regard to the types of change that a six-mark question would represent. Robert Marzano's work on effective teaching strategies suggests that students can increase their performance by almost two GCSE grades if they use 'compare and contrast' activities and graphic organisers to help structure their work (www.marzanoresearch.com/research/meta_analysis_database.aspx). Mindful of the demands of the examination in terms of describing the *type* of change related to a particular group but also the *extent* of change, by comparing different social units, comics seem to be a natural fit as they would allow the students to have a graphic representation of the different types of change but also allow them to think about the extent of change by comparing the different groups. There are a number of comic book applications that exist but the one used for this activity is called *Comic Life* by Plasq. What makes this a particularly useful application is that is available on the Mac, PC and iPad.

The interface is designed around three steps. Once you have selected a theme for the comic you can select the layout of the panels. The second step is to add content, and you can add pictures from iPhoto on the Mac, the file browser or via the webcam. Once you have the image you want, it can be dragged onto the page and positioned to suit the style of comic. The final step is to add titles or text that can be accessed through the tray and the bottom of the screen by selecting speech bubbles, text boxes and different types of lettering. For the purposes of the unit, the outcome of the work was to create a graphic novel that would be around eight pages long with each page representing a particular social group or form of change. Each page was divided into two halves and the instructions were:

- to revise the work and think of creating two contrasting images that could describe changes between 1933 and 1939 in Nazi Germany;
- to use a limited amount of text to explain the image;
- to complete the task within one lesson;
- to make sure that, despite the use of comics, the work must be historically rigorous and treat the subject sensitively.

In the following lesson, students brought a variety of props to create their comparisons of change between 1933 and 1939. Using the webcams on the computer controlled through the program, the students took pictures of their props or themselves to illustrate the changes with plenty of discussion about whether the image was appropriate and whether the text they had thought about before was indeed necessary. Once they had selected the images they required, they were placed within the pre-selected template. They then added or pasted the images into the pre-selected template and worked on the text to make sure it gave adequate information as a reminder. The result of one of the pages can be seen in Figure 12.1.

What was interesting about the images produced was how evocative the comparisons were (and the students' use of colour), which were entirely the students' choice in terms of representing, for them, what was a negative change for women. This is a good example of Mishra's argument that if it is to really add value to learning, ICT needs to be used in a way that enables learners to 'share, explore and create' (Mishra, 2012).

Figure 12.1 Pupil created images

After the class completed their comparison, they were printed out and given to the students as a comic, which was to aid the revision process in terms of making clear the different changes but also, through the collation of work, the extent of change. Aside from the outcome, it is worth going through the learning steps necessary to create the comic to think about change and continuity:

- The students had to revise the material.
- They then had to find/create something visual to represent the material before they came into class, which involved them thinking about change between 1933 and 1939 carefully.
- The text was intended to only be a supplement to the main image and this also required careful thinking.

To reiterate the point, using *Comic Life* was not the 'Why' of the lesson but the 'How' and the 'What'. The end product was impressive itself but the real goal of the work was the learning process. Anecdotally, the students said that it helped them remember the key changes during the period, a good example of the use of ICT to promote 'stickiness' – pupils remember what they have learned because of the way they learned it (Heath and Heath, 2008). Another measure of success was the examination – over 50 per cent of the class gained full marks on the external GCSE unit.

Example 2: Using chronology to help provide an overview and targeted feedback

The second example of a tool to help improve understanding is Beedocs Timeline 3D. The 'driver' in this case was not the second order concept of chronological understanding but the desire to provide feedback on students' work. According to the research of Black and Wiliam (2006) and Hattie (2009, 2011), feedback is one of the most effective ways to raise achievement but the time devoted to feedback can be fleeting owing to perceived constraints (syllabus/curriculum coverage, behaviour management issues or lack of time). Convinced of its necessity and mindful of wasting curriculum time by keeping students busy while others received feedback, an opportunity presented itself as a result of the natural rhythm of teaching where the assessment (the essay) falls at the end of the topic and unit. Following Dawson, Moorhouse and Banham's ideas about the usefulness of overviews to provide hooks for historical learning (see, for example, Dawson *et al.*, 2009), it seemed sensible to use this opportunity to create a framework for future learning and use the time to provide feedback, but it needed to be structured in such a way that once the student was in discussion about their work, they would be able to return to the lesson and pick up where they left off.

Using Beedocs Timeline 3D provides a timeline that is a little more than just a simple chronology. In their timeline, you can include audio files, pictures, text and video, all the things necessary to provide a framework for further development. See Figures 12.2 and 12.3.

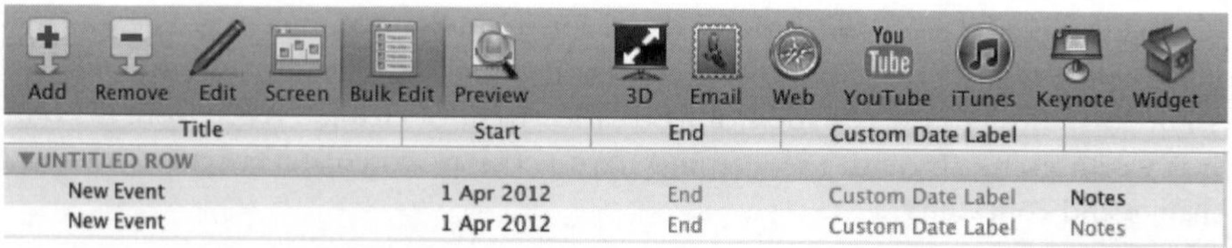

Figure 12.2 A digitally constructed timeline

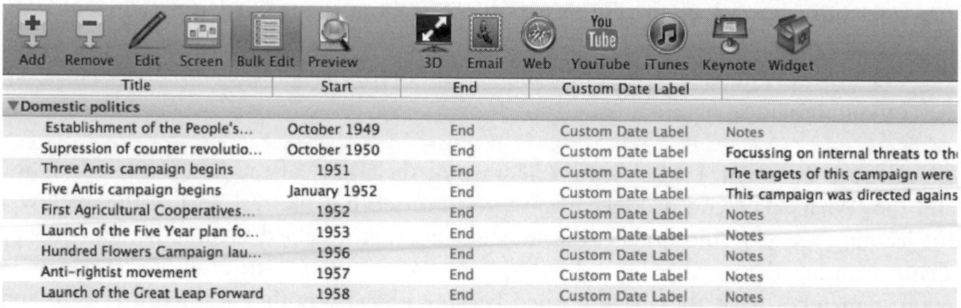

Figure 12.3 Timeline: bulk edit option

There are two ways of entering information – the screen above is the bulk edit option which can be easier to use when creating the timeline in the first instance.

The bulk edit view above shows the title of the event to be displayed, the start date (where it will be placed in the timeline), the end date (if you want to give more detail) and the notes. It is worth keeping these notes brief as they will appear in your event display.

Once you are happy with the events in bulk edit mode, you can switch to screen edit mode (see Figure 12.4). As you can see, the events placed in the bulk edit view are now spread across the line from left to right and the notes appear under the titles. You can also see some images – these are media files that can be inserted if you double click the event.

The box labelled 'Media', shown in Figure 12.5, is where you can add video clips (.mov or MP4), audio (MP3) and images (jpegs and tiffs), giving the ability to illustrate or explain in more detail the events in the timeline. For the purpose of the lesson, video clips from a documentary about China were included (no more than five minutes) and brief comments from podcasts by historians giving their interpretation of events. What makes this application particularly engaging is its ability to present the content in 3D and export its timelines into YouTube videos and MP4 files which can be added to other content (as will be explained in the next section).

When the timeline was finished it was copied over to a class set of iPads (although it could easily work if it was available on YouTube or placed on a laptop computer) and I supplied the class with comprehension questions. As they watched the timeline, I was able to discuss with the students individually their work using the following prompts:

- How well did you do? The students are asked to fill in a self-assessment form when they submit work.
- What aspects did I like?
- What could be improved?

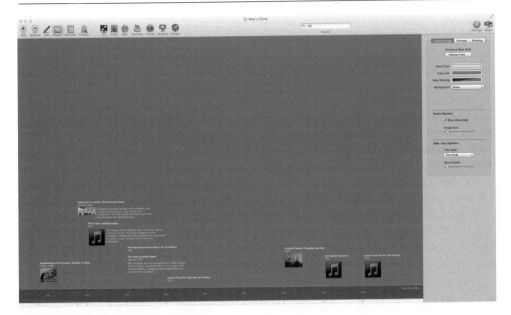

Figure 12.4 Timeline: screen edit mode

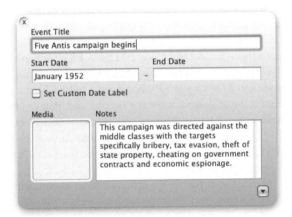

Figure 12.5 Timeline – options

The students responded positively to the feedback, but what was particularly interesting were the observations that:

- students could pick up their learning where they left it after discussing their work and they did not feel disadvantaged by spending a few minutes in the corridor discussing their work;
- the ability to 'scrub' through the clip allowed them to replay important points at their own speed and to reduce the friction between moving between the questions and the resource.

Although the use of the technology may seem pretty mundane, the results were impressive on two fronts. First, the students had an in-depth discussion about what they needed to do to improve their next piece of work. Second, they were able to return the following lesson and relate the overview of events to the abstract discussion on Mao's political ideology and gave them a richer understanding of the period.

Timeline 3D is an impressive application but it is only available on an Apple Mac. However, there are a number of web-based timeline applications that can be used to enhance chronological understanding at the same time as giving feedback. Tiki-Toki (www.tiki-toki.com) is impressive in that it is web based and allows you to embed YouTube videos, images from the web and audio. Dipity (www.dipity.com) also allows you to create timelines and allows multiple people to edit the timeline (Timeline 3D is limited to a single user). It works on a variety of devices and has a range of subscription modules. In both Timeline 3D and Tiki-Toki, you can create timelines with different categories within the same timeline looking at social, economic or political changes over the same period of time. These types of timelines can be used to help support multidimensional narratives of time that move beyond the simple causal explanation that timelines can create (Shemilt, 2000).

Example 3: Putting it all together – creating an ebook

One of the most frustrating aspects of using new technology to enhance history teaching is the inability to put all the resources in one easy-to-access place. Virtual Learning Environments (VLEs) can do this but they are often glorified file storage systems with little more than a heading for a page or section to keep the content together. Moreover, the VLE keeps the content on the web and the files often need to be downloaded one at a time and then put into a folder structure (although this can be done via the VLE). One solution to keep content together and unify the learning experience of students is to create basic ebooks to use on the Kindle by converting files to PDF or the EPUB format. Calibre (http://calibre-ebook.com) can help you do this but it is not able to utilise the rich content that can be created as outlined above and does not take into account the interactive nature of devices such as the iPad. Apple has recently released a free authoring program called iBooks Author which allows you to create content for the iPad and to include the content you or your class have generated, as well as link to a number of web applications.

iBooks Author is interesting in that it is a cross between a word processor and a presentation tool (http://itunes.apple.com/gb/app/ibooks-author/id490152466?mt=12). You are given options to help construct your book by including an opening clip, a table of contents and a glossary. Underneath, you are given page layouts that you can change or delete. On the top of the menu, you are given basic word processing design features and on the right you are given the options to add content you already have on the computer.

Adding text

If you want to start your ebook from scratch, you can select one of the layouts and start typing. If you already have notes written in a word document, you can however simply add them to the publication by dragging them into the page layout sidebar and it will automatically format your content to fit the style of the book. Once you drop the Word file in, you will be prompted with a choice of page layouts. Select the one you would like and it will import the word file although you will need to make some adjustments to make sure there is a consistent feel with the rest of the layout. Once you are happy with the text, you can then begin to add some of the content you have created.

Widgets

Widgets are the main tools that allow you to add a number of interactive features to your digital textbook. By clicking the widget button on the top of the menu bar you are given a few choices:

- You can add images such as sources and add text explanations that are revealed when you zoom in by tapping the screen.
- Images can also be used in an interactive gallery where they can be viewed by swiping across the screen.
- Videos that you own can be included and you also can add audio files such as podcasts. You can also link to web pages in the text or through images so students do not need to type in web addresses.
- Review questions allow you to check for comprehension within the book itself. These review questions can either be a form of multiple choice or alternatively drag and drop activities that are similar in most interactive whiteboard software from educational publishers. The scores are displayed within the ebook and are not saved anywhere else.
- If you have coding skills, you can create HTML widgets that can be placed within the textbook. If you do not have the skills, you can add widgets such as an interactive timeline and live polls, and embed YouTube at Classwidgets (www.classwidgets.com). This is currently free.

There are a number of ways an electronic textbook can be useful in the history classroom. In its simplest form as just a book with text, it enables students to carry course/subject notes with them. A more effective use is that it can mirror, develop and extend the learning within the classroom by offering additional information or enquiries, and by placing all the necessary content in one place and if you have created podcasts, comics and want to incorporate links to blogs, you can add them into the text of the ebook. If a link was to become redundant, it could be easily removed or a new link or resource could take its place and the book can be 'republished' either through the iTunes store or as a download to replace the current version on the device.

Conclusion

Technology serves to amplify the intentions and knowledge of the user. If there is a lack of clarity or an ambiguity about the principles driving the use of technology, the use of the technological tool only serves to augment the confusion for the students and negates the focus on learning. The only way to make sure the tool is used appropriately is through a careful application of professional knowledge and being 'tool-minded' enough to seek and experiment with technologies to amplify historical learning. By adopting what Dweck (2007) has called a 'growth mindset' towards our own professional thinking and the use of ICT, we can indeed fulfil the golden principle that drives us as teachers – to help students enjoy and achieve in our lessons.

References

Black, P. and Wiliam, D. (2006) *Inside the Black Box: Raising standards through classroom assessment*, London: Granada.

Counsell, C. (1997) *Analytical and Discursive Writing at Key Stage 3*, London: Historical Association.

Counsell, C. (2000) 'Editorial', *Teaching History*, 102: 2.

Counsell, C. (2011) 'What do we want students to do with historical change and continuity?' in I. Davies (ed.) *Debates in History Teaching*, London: Routledge, pp. 109–23.

Dawson, I., Moorhouse, D. and Banham, D. (2009) *Medicine and Health through Time*, London: Hodder.

Dweck, C. (2007) *Mindset: The new psychology of success*, New York: Ballantine.

Gillespie, H. (2011) Presentation at *ICT in Teaching* symposium, University of East Anglia, 1 November.

Hattie, J. (2009) *Visible Learning*, London: Routledge.

Hattie, J. (2011) *Visible Learning for Teachers: Maximizing impact on learning*, London: Routledge.

Haydn, T. (2000) 'ICT in the history classroom', in J. Arthur and R. Phillips (eds) *Issues in History Teaching*, London: Routledge, pp. 98–112.

Heath, D. and Heath, C. (2008) *Made to Stick: Why some ideas take hold and others come unstuck*, London: Arrow.

Husbands, C., Kitson, A. and Steward, S. (2011) *Teaching and Learning History: Understanding the past 11–18*, Maidenhead: Open University Press.

Isaacson, W. (2011) *Steve Jobs: The exclusive biography*, New York: Little Brown.

Lucas, B. and Claxton, G. (2010) *New Kinds of Smart*, Maidenhead: Open University Press.

Mishra, P. (2012) 'Creative Teaching with Technology', keynote address at the Technology in Education and Society Conference, University of Barcelona, 1 February, online at http://ties2012.eu/en/pg-videos.html, accessed 2 April 2012.

Ofsted (2011) *History for All*, London: Ofsted.

Shemilt, D. (2000) 'The caliph's coin', in P.N. Stearns, P. Seixas and S. Wineburg (eds) *Knowing, Teaching and Learning History*, New York: New York University Press, pp. 83–101.

Sinek, S. (2011) *Start with Why: How great leaders inspire everyone to take action*, London: Penguin.

Chapter 13

History webquests

Janos Blasszauer

Introduction

Thousands and thousands of schools are now connected to the internet all across the world and more and more history teachers are trying to explore the educational possibilities of the internet for improving the quality of their teaching, and pupils' learning.

Bernie Dodge, an American professor from San Diego State University has focused on the design, implementation and evaluation of computer-based learning environments since 1995 and created a learning model that is now one of the most popular and effective ways of using the internet to teach and learn history. Webquests allow students to develop their historical knowledge and understanding of particular aspects of the past by working through a teacher-constructed web-based enquiry. It can involve pupils working individually, or 'sub-contracting' elements of the enquiry, working in collaborative groups, taking on the roles of historical figures, and presenting the outcomes of their enquiries. It is important to note that there is no requirement for webquest resources to be limited to internet sources; often a mixture of resources are used. Dodge (1997) defines a webquest as 'An inquiry-oriented activity in which some or all of the information that learners interact with comes from resources on the internet, optionally supplemented with videoconferencing'.

Tom March, who has also been working to develop the webquest as a strategy for effectively integrating the web into classroom instruction, after nearly a decade conducting workshops, writing articles and developing many webquests, found it necessary to offer a refined definition as follows:

> A Webquest is a scaffolded learning structure that uses links to essential resources on the World Wide Web and an authentic task to motivate students' investigation of an open-ended question, development of individual expertise, and participation in a group process that transforms newly acquired information into a more sophisticated understanding. The best Webquests inspire students to see richer thematic relationships, to contribute to the real world of learning, and to reflect on their own metacognitive processes.
>
> (March, 2007)

It is important to note that the distinguishing point between webquests and other web-based activities in this definition is that the webquest prompts students to 'transform newly acquired information into a more sophisticated understanding'. Therefore the outcomes of a webquest can't be copied and pasted; it is not a scavenger hunt. The use of 'Why...?' 'How...?' and 'To what extent...?' questions, when formulating the questions posed by the webquest, rather than 'What...?' and 'When...?' questions can help in this respect, as can keeping in mind the 'hierarchy' of questioning outlined in Bloom's Taxonomy (for a succinct summary/reminder about Bloom's Taxonomy, see Andrew Church's diagram at http://edorigami.wikispaces.com/file/view/bloom%27s+Digital+taxonomy+v3.01.pdf).

A webquest activity should foster the development of higher order thinking and the products of webquests are ideally subjected to critique or 'put out' to other participants for feedback, discussion and debate. Of course, much depends on the skill with which the webquest has been constructed; the appropriateness and quality of the resources selected, and the quality of questions and sub-questions posed. A webquest is not an easy or time-free enterprise for the teacher, as good ones take time to put together, although older pupils may be able to put together their own webquests if they have had experience of doing well-constructed webquests lower down the school.

It should be stressed that the students themselves are not responsible for going out onto the internet to find quality resources; this is something the teacher must accomplish and present to them at the start of the webquest activity. The main mission of the students is to investigate the task presented.

Why use webquests?

A well-constructed webquest has some of the benefits of active, enquiry-based learning, often involving elements of project-based and cooperative learning. Students not only access, consider and deploy information that they are directed to on the web, they work in groups and often take up different roles modelled from the real world. For example, a webquest exploring views about the Gallipoli campaign of 1915 has students playing the roles of two historians with differing views on the campaign, a journalist who has been covering the campaign in the newspapers, a soldier (preferably one of the Australian and New Zealand troops, or perhaps an Allied and a Turkish soldier) participating in the battle, Winston Churchill explaining the rationale for the campaign and defending it, and a judge on the committee of enquiry into the campaign, reporting the verdict of the committee. Similar personnel equivalents are also invoked for webquests on General Haig on the Battle of the Somme, and the Appeasement Crisis of 1938 (examples formulated by the *Lycee Edmond Perrier*, Limoges). The webquest lends itself to the study of any historical event or person where there are differing interpretations of events or reputations. It is a helpful way for students to learn that slavery and the Holocaust are not the only controversial issues in history: much of the past is contested (Arnold, 2000). This model does not just involve students working on the computer, exploring, analysing and summarising web-based sources, it can be combined with techniques such as role play and debate, in which students are expected to work in groups and explore the different opinions and perspectives of the historical 'stakeholders' involved in the event being studied.

Students have to participate actively in the enquiry structured by the webquest, and they are usually given a degree of autonomy in some aspects of the process through which the webquest will be conducted. One of the aims of the webquest is that pupils will learn to conduct a historical enquiry that places some responsibility for learning on them, rather than them being expected to be 'spoon-fed' by the teacher. As they become more experienced in working with webquests, they can also learn to generate some of their own questions, and it can be helpful for the structure of the webquest to be crafted so that there are some gaps in terms of 'what questions might be asked...?' This is something that has been suggested as an important element of progression in pupils' study of the past (Ofsted, 2011).

With the proper guidance and scaffolding, students can learn a lot in terms of their depth of historical knowledge and understanding of particular aspects of the past (students often do substantial amounts of work on the webquest outside lesson time), and in terms of their ability to conduct a historical enquiry.

The webquest also provides a degree of 'scaffolding' in terms of teaching pupils to use the internet in a mature and effective way. It can make an important contribution to 'a historical education' appropriate to the twenty-first century by showing pupils what the internet is good for, and what its limitations and dangers are, and webquests can empower them with the right strategies and skills to take advantage of the educational power of the internet. Most history teachers are aware that just giving pupils an enquiry question and telling them to 'find out about it on the internet' is not a rigorous, appropriate or time effective way for them to learn history (see, for instance, Walsh, 2008). However, as Moore (2000) argues, in the longer term, we *do* want pupils to be able to use the internet autonomously and intelligently outside the classroom, and when they leave school. The webquest is a useful stepping stone on the path towards intellectual maturity in the use of the internet.

Another potential benefit in using webquests is the effect it can have on pupil motivation. Students often find it intrinsically motivating to use 'real' resources on the internet, rather than being confined to the resources available in textbooks. Using the internet also provides an element of 'authenticity' to pupils' work. We invite our students to get involved in controversies and contested issues that are currently being debated live on the internet, using sources that are usually more up-to-date and informed by current scholarship than the coverage afforded by the average history textbook.

The internet is also a rich resource for engaging pupils in constructivist learning through multiple representations of a topic – it enables them to see that 'different stories can be told' about the past, and can develop an understanding of the relationship between 'stories' and 'sources', and lay the ground for getting them to understand why some stories might be better founded than others. One additional advantage of having resources in an electronic format is that it can help with differentiation. There can be differences in the resources used by pupils in different sets. The more able students can be provided with additional challenge, while the less able students can be given additional support.

The webquest model allows teachers to focus students' attention on a specific goal, and provides students with the resources and guidance that enables them to reach that particular goal. As they work through the webquest, students' understanding of the 'key concepts and processes' of the National Curriculum for History (QCA, 2007) can be developed, at the same time as they are developing their depth of understanding of the substantive historical knowledge that the webquest asks them to explore. The author of this chapter has found it worthwhile to make good use of webquests in the long-running pan-European citizenship project called Spring Day in Europe (Blasszauer, 2003, 2004).

In terms of the learning theory underpinning the use of webquests, Barron and Darling-Hammond (2008) argue that:

- students learn more deeply when they can apply classroom-gathered knowledge to real-world problems, and when they take part in projects that require sustained engagement and collaboration;
- active-learning practices have a more significant impact on student performance than any other variable, including student background and prior achievement;
- students are most successful when they are taught how to learn as well as what to learn.

Thomas has argued that project-based learning, such as webquests, help to address problems of knowledge retention and knowledge application (see Chapter 1), because it encourages a degree of involvement and ownership of the learning process, 'helping move students beyond surface learning, beyond learning held in short-term memory, learned for the test and then dropped … because the learner sees the information as important to him' (Thomas, 2000).

This aligns with Bruner's argument (1990), that learning is an active process in which learners construct new ideas or concepts based upon their current/past knowledge. Pupils have to work hard in webquest lessons, fulfilling Wiliam's suggestion that in 'a good lesson', the pupils should have to work at least as hard as the teacher (Wiliam, 2011), and that pupils should not be able to get away with not engaging and participating in the learning by simply pretending to listen to what the teacher is saying and playing 'truant in mind', and responding with minimalist compliance to requests for oral contributions. Of course, as with other forms of groupwork, the teacher needs to check whether all members of the groups are contributing, but much of the teacher's work has been done in designing the webquest, which should give the teacher time to support groups and undertake 'light touch monitoring' of their progress in the webquest, as well as chairing debate, discussion and feedback elements of the webquest.

Other desirable characteristics of webquests are that students should feel comfortable and confident in posing questions on aspects of the problem that they do not understand, and that they see during the course of the webquest that learning is an ongoing process, and that there will always be (even for the teacher) new angles, perspectives, and problems to be explored.

The structure of the webquest model

Introduction

The first decision to make in creating a webquest is that of the topic. A good topic is one that fits these criteria:

1   It is clearly tied to the curriculum standards.
2   It makes good (though not necessarily exclusive) use of the web, and could not be taught as well without the web.
3   It requires a level of understanding that goes beyond mere comprehension.
4   It is challenging, motivating and suits students' interest.

Task

Describe clearly what the end result of the learners' activities will be. The task could be:

- a problem or mystery to be solved;
- a position to be formulated and defended;
- a product to be designed;
- a complexity to be analysed;
- a personal insight to be articulated;
- a summary to be created;

- a persuasive message or journalistic account to be crafted;
- a creative work, or anything that requires the learners to process and *transform* the information they have gathered.

If the final product involves using some tool (e.g. Audacity, the web, video) you should mention it here.

Process

Describe briefly how the lesson is organised. Does it involve more than one class? Is it all taught in one period per day, or is it part of several periods? How many days or weeks will it take? Is it single disciplinary, interdisciplinary, multidisciplinary or what?

If students are divided into groups, provide guidelines on how you might do that. If there are misconceptions or stumbling blocks that you anticipate, you should describe them here and suggest ways to get round them.

Resources

Describe what is needed to implement this lesson. Some of the possibilities are:

- class sets of books
- email accounts for all students
- specific software (how many copies?)
- specific hardware (what kind? How many?)
- specific reference material in the classroom or school library
- video or audio materials.

If the lesson makes extensive use of specific websites, it would be appropriate to list, describe and link them here. Describe also the *human* resources needed. How many teachers are needed to implement the lesson? Is a field trip designed in as part of the lesson?

Evaluation

How will you know that this lesson was successful? Describe what student products or performances you will be looking at and how they will be evaluated.

Teachers have found *rubrics* to be very useful in providing guidance and feedback to students where skills and processes are the targets being monitored. Examples of skills or processes that adapt well to being measured by rubrics are the following: the writing process, the application of the method of scientific inquiry, thinking skills (i.e. constructing support, comparing, problem solving, analysing and synthesising information). Methods other than rubrics are aimed at measuring information known by a learner. These methods may include tests, quizzes, checklists, etc.

Rubrics have the potential for helping a teacher assess a student performance during the teaching/learning process by clearly establishing the standards and quality expectations. It assists in customising the student feedback: what a student has done well; what weaknesses exist; and how or what might be done to correct or improve the performance. It assists students in the fair and honest opportunity for self-assessment of their work and allows them the opportunity to set, monitor and achieve their personal learning goals. It helps students and parents in understanding the tasks and the standards by which the progress will be measured.

Conclusion: evaluation and summary of what has been learned

Make some kind of summary statement about the worthiness of the webquest and the importance of what has been learned. This section reminds students about the most important points they have learned, in terms of the topic that has been studied, the implications of working with internet resources, and their own ability to learn things in history.

Some examples of history webquests

It can be helpful to 'see what one looks like'. It is of course not 'cheating' to use or adapt someone else's webquest, but it can be rewarding and interesting to develop one that is designed for your own interests and enthusiasms, and your own teaching groups. I have made my own webquests (Blasszauer, 2003, 2004) but do not want to suggest that these are the best examples available.

The 'Gilded Age webquest: documenting industrialization in America' is an exceptionally well-designed example of a webquest. This is how John F. Lyons describes it, and the description gives some indication of the criteria for a good webquest:

> The term 'Gilded Age' comes from a Mark Twain novel that described the corrupt nature of American politics during industrialisation. In the webquest, students are required to produce a documentary about the period. Students are divided into groups, and each group is asked to produce a segment of the documentary, in PowerPoint, using images and voiceover. Each group is required to design one of the following segments: technological innovation; big business; urbanisation; immigration, and reaction to the period... Navigation is seamless, the introduction is engaging, the task is well explained and doable, suitable resources are indicated and a rubric is provided to guide the students. The webquest encourages cooperative learning and higher level thinking skills. However, The Gilded Age has its limitations. The webquest needs to have a longer introduction, with a little bit more background information for the students. The guiding questions need to be a bit more focused. There is no mention of historiography and the opposing views of historians on the period.
>
> (Lyons, 2009)

A British equivalent, asking the overarching enquiry question, 'Did life became better as a result of the Industrial Revolution or not?' can be found at http://mhslibrary.org/Teacher%20Projects/Teacher%20Projects/Social%20Studies/D%27Acquisto/Industrial%20Revolution/homepage.htm. Students consider the question from a range of perspectives, including an industrialist, a Luddite, and (perhaps anachronistically) a representative of a human rights organisation, a consumer and (interestingly) Lord Byron (letter to Lord Holland, 25 February 1812, http://orion.it.luc.edu/~sjones1/byrlett.htm).

A webquest that has been widely used in the UK is Dan Lyndon's webquest, 'Black and Asian soldiers of the First World War' (www.comptonhistory.com/ww1webquest.htm). There is also a useful 'gateway site' for history webquests at https://sites.google.com/

site/442webquests/system/app/pages/subPages?path=/high-school/history, although as with several such resources, in terms of content, there is an emphasis on American history. The nine national museums in Great Britain have a nice collection of webquests (www.npg.org.uk/webquests). At Bestwebquests.com webquests are arranged by content area and learners' age. You'll be able to read what the site developers think makes a good webquest and can submit yours for consideration, and get tips on webquest design (see http://bestwebquests.com/bwq/listcrosstab.asp?wqcatid=6&edid=4). Other interesting examples are 'All men are created equal...?' at http://kathyschrock.net/webquests/LAMB/index.htm, and 'Rome: The past is present' at http://kathyschrock.net/webquests/FOULKE/rmindex.htm.

Recommended webquests for History and Social Studies can be found at the Center for Teaching History with Technology (http://thwt.org/index.php/discussion-collaboration/webquests); Questgarden (http://questgarden.com) and Zunal (www.zunal.com) are also useful sites where one can search for ready-made history webquests.

Some tools to support webquest work

There are several free online tools and templates that help teachers to create their own webquest. Thus, creating a webquest is not only for 'tech-savvy' educators. It should also be pointed out that pupils undertaking a webquest do not spend all their time at the computer. Some time is usually spent comparing findings, sharing information and discussing and debating emerging findings. With this in mind, as well as suggesting resources for constructing webquests, I have suggested links to some sites that are designed to help pupils with the processes involved in marshalling information and discussing and debating issues.[1]

The first step for a teacher who would like to give a webquest a try with his/her students is to search the internet for an already existing webquest related to the topic currently covered by the class. If the project is well-received by the students and the teacher finds it rewarding then the educator should start planning his/her own webquest.

Webquest check list

http://Webquest.sdsu.edu/processchecker.html

Webquest design process

http://Webquest.sdsu.edu/designsteps/index.html

Webquest example

www.teacherWebquest.com/WQ/HighSchool/CollegesWQ/index.html

Webquest search

http://Webquest.org/index-research.php

Webquest taxonomy

http://Webquest.sdsu.edu/taskonomy.html

Webquest templates

http://Webquest.sdsu.edu/templates/lesson-template1.htm

The best way to use webquests

www.thirteen.org/edonline/concept2class/Webquests/demonstration.html

Webquests course map

www.mapacourse.com/Webquesthtml/

Webquests evaluation rubric

http://Webquest.sdsu.edu/Webquestrubric.html

Webquests for the classroom

www.readingonline.org/articles/art_index.asp?HREF=/articles/stinson/

Webquests learning environment

http://eduscapes.com/sessions/travel/index.htm

Webquests lesson plan

www.thirteen.org/edonline/concept2class/Webquests/demo_sub1.html

Webquests in the classroom

www.readingonline.org/articles/art_index.asp?HREF=/articles/stinson/

Building blocks of a webquest

http://projects.edtech.sandi.net/staffdev/buildingblocks/p-index.htm

Receptive scaffolding
http://eduscapes.com/distance/course_guides/reception.htm

Transformation scaffolds
http://eduscapes.com/distance/course_guides/transformation.htm

Production scaffolds
http://eduscapes.com/distance/course_guides/production.htm

Filamentality

www.kn.pacbell.com/wired/fil – Filamentality is a fill-in-the-blank interactive website that guides you through picking a topic, searching the web, gathering good internet sites, and turning web resources into learning activities.

Zunal webquest maker

www.zunal.com – This is a web-based software for creating webquests in a short time without writing any HTML codes. You may also find examples and plans on how to begin writing a webquest.

Questgarden

http://questgarden.com – QuestGarden is an online authoring tool, community and hosting service that is designed to make it easier and quicker to create a high-quality webquest. No knowledge of web editing or uploading is required. Prompts, guides and examples are provided for each step of the process. Images, worksheets and other documents can easily be attached or embedded in the webquest, and users have complete control over the appearance of the final lesson.

Templates

www.educationaltechnology.ca/resources/Webquest/templates.php

http://Webquest.sdsu.edu/LessonTemplate.html

www.babylonia-ti.ch/Webquesten.htm.

Bloom's taxonomy and digital tools

Bloom's Digital Taxonomy – http://edorigami.wikispaces.com/Bloom%27s+Digital +Taxonomy

Bloom's Digital Taxonomy Pyramid – www.usi.edu/distance/bdt.htm

Bloom's Taxonomy Blooms Digitally – www.techlearning.com/article/blooms-taxonomy -blooms-digitally/44988

Kathy Schrock's – Google Blooms Taxonomy – http://kathyschrock.net/googleblooms.

Recommended tools, sites and ideas for discussing different historical perspectives

Pro-con lists (http://proconlists.com)

The site enables students to collect together the advantages and disadvantages of a particular subject and create a list of each to see how they balance out.

When creating the list students can also add to or reduce the influence of some factors and balance emotional and rational factors of each too. It sounds complicated, but these are very easy to produce. Just register and log in and go to 'Create a list'. Give the list a title, select the topic and add a description. You are then ready to start adding the pros and cons. Each of the pros and cons added has a default weight of three in both the emotional and rational settings, but students can click on the numbers to increase or decrease the weight if they think the pro or con is more or less significant.

Once they have completed their lists they can publish them or share them through a range of social media platforms. Visitors to the lists can then leave comments or agree or disagree with each of the individual pros and cons in the list, simply by clicking on them and voting.

Mashpedia (http://mashpedia.com)

This is a combination of a search engine and an encyclopaedia. It's very simple to use, you just type in a search query and hit search. The site will then generate a page of information links about your search topic. It collects information from multiple media and different sources from books, blogs, text images to video and even Twitter references.

Here are some possible research tasks you could use that would work for most topics:

- Get students to look at the information and use it to create a quiz on the topic. They find information that interests them and write questions to quiz the rest of the class.
- Set students to find 5–10 facts about a topic. You could stipulate some of these need to be negative aspects and some positive to make it more challenging.
- Get students to search the page and decide which of the sources it links to is the single most informative or interesting.
- Get students to research a topic and create a multimedia poster about it using text, images and video embedded. You could use something such as Glogster (www.glogster.com) for them to show their results.
- Get students to research a topic and create a short documentary or news report about it. If you have access to a video camera you could video their presentations.

(Peachey, 2010)

Debating online

Forumotion (http://forumotion.com)

I'm not sure how many people still use text-based threaded discussion forums, but if you do, Forumotion is a pretty powerful tool with some nice features that you can use to set one up for free. It's very quick and you don't need any technical skills or hosting.

You simply go to www.forumotion.com and click on 'Create a free forum'. You'll then be able to select from a range of different template designs. Once you've chosen the one you want you fill in the details of your forum and create a password. You'll then be ready to activate your forum and start using it. The best place to start is on the Administration Panel. Here you can get some tips on how to get started and how to get your forum registered with search engines etc. If you want to see what a forum can look like and try it out, there's one here that I created as an example: http://nikpeachey.forumotion.net/index.htm. Forumotion has some nice features and is pretty simple. There is also a newsletter function so that you can send messages to all the members of your forum. This is a handy tool if you are teaching distance classes, or would just like to set up some simple online discussion topics for your students. It also looks like they are taking their responsibilities seriously regarding e-safety too, though you should still read the terms of use, as there is some sharing with third parties of non-personal information (Peachey, 2009).

Debate (www.debate.org)

www.debate.org is a membership-based online debating service designed to provide an easy and free system for our members to intellectually challenge, debate and communicate with each other on the web. Members create their own unique profiles and our technology provides a 'ratio of disagreement' with the other members based on the information that each member provides, making it easy to select an opponent or to build group of friends. Members can challenge existing members or invite anyone to come and debate them on a topic of their choice selected from a wide range of categories including politics, sports, the arts and entertainment. A formal debate is between two members, the instigator and contender; but every member can participate in the debate by posting comments and voting on the winner once the closing arguments are presented. www.debate.org launched its third generation in August of 2008 which includes a laundry list of new features including new voting technology, debate and member ranking, photo albums, messaging, advanced searching, YouTube video integration, demographic charting and a friends and networking system. www.debate.org is evolutionary in nature and will continue to add new features to encourage further education, discussion and communication among the members.

Idebate (www.idebate.org)

Today, from Haiti to Serbia, from The Netherlands to Mongolia and beyond, IDEA debates are gaining ground as forums for promoting democratic values. And just as Socrates spurred his listeners to examine their assumptions 2,500 years ago, IDEA is today encouraging students around the world to question, to listen to each other, and to explore even the most volatile subjects openly and in the spirit of tolerance and cooperation.

Convince me (www.convinceme.net)

www.convinceme.net is the ultimate debating website. It is free to join. There are three main debating sections: Open, Battle, and King of the Hill (KOTH). Open debates can have endless debaters all competing for their side. In open debates, if your argument convinces someone, then you gain a point. It's your chance to convince the world that you are right! Fight for your side! Battles are one-on-one debates with another member of convinceme.net. You can create a general challenge, or challenge an individual. Then you argue, add evidence, and convince other members to give you their vote. The winner takes all. KOTH is a little like open debates, except that you get one main argument, and your goal is to convince members to give you the points. The first person to get ten points wins, and is crowned king of the hill.

Debatewise (http://debatewise.org)

Debatewise was created around the idea of trying to encourage people to make informed decisions. This is a place where the best possible arguments for one side are listed next to the best possible arguments against. These arguments aren't created by one person, but by like-minded individuals collaborating to form the strongest case. This allows people both to easily compare the pros and cons and also to come to a decision safe in the knowledge they have the best information to hand. (As an example, see http://debatewise.org/debates/1831-are-cellphones-safe.) This can easily be adapted for use with historical debates.

Truthmapping (http://truthmapping.com)

TruthMapping.com is a free tool that provides a focused, rational method for adversarial discussion that overcomes the limitations of standard message boards, email and even conversation; it is a site for persons who believe that reasoning should be at the heart of public debate.

Argumentum (http://arg.umentum.com)

The goal of Argumentum is to provide a better way for people to argue online. In most digital discussion mediums, such as forums, blogs or email, the arguer is forced to respond to an entire argument all at once. While this may be OK in an email, since there are usually only a few parties involved, this method of responding (all at once) is responsible for the chaos and disorder that is clearly evident in the forums, message boards and the like. On Argumentum, you can address multiple points, one by one, by posting multiple follow-up arguments. This naturally breaks down the original argument into a set of propositions, thus making the system much more logical, scientific and stimulating.

Tools for debates

Compendium (http://compendium.open.ac.uk)

Compendium is a hypermedia software tool, providing a visual interface for mapping the connections between people, ideas, multimedia documents and websites, to support the analysis of socio/technical problems. You can customise the icons and links to anything you want, but it comes preloaded with the visual language for IBIS (Issue-Based Information System), which supports the mapping of debates in terms of issues, ideas, pros/cons/arguments and decisions. Students could use Compendium to manage the digital information they harvest from the internet, since they can drag and drop in any document, website, email, image, etc., organise them visually, and then connect ideas, arguments and decisions to these and present them in the classroom.

Visual Understanding Environment (http://vue.tufts.edu)

At its core, the Visual Understanding Environment (VUE) is a concept and content mapping application, developed to support teaching, learning and research and for anyone who needs to organise, contextualise and access digital information. Using a simple set of tools and a basic visual grammar consisting of nodes and links, faculty and students can map relationships between concepts, ideas and digital content.

VUE is a flexible tool to help students integrate, organise and contextualise electronic content in their work. Digital content can be accessed via the web, or using the VUE's 'Resources' panel to tap into digital repositories, FTP servers and local file systems.

Sharing and presenting information are important aspects of academic work. VUE's pathways feature allows presenters to create annotated trails through their maps, which become expert guided walk-throughs of the information. The pathways feature also provides a 'slide view' of the information on the map. The power of VUE's slide mode is the ability for presenters to focus on content (slide view) while preserving the information's context (map view), by way of a single toggle between the two views.

SciPlore mindmapping (http://sciplore.org/about_en.php)

SciPlore (originally *Scienstein*), a non-profit project, aims to support researchers in searching and evaluating scientific publications and offers tools to ease their daily work. SciPlore MindMapping is the first mind-mapping tool focusing on researchers' needs by integrating mind mapping with reference and PDF management.

Nestor (www.gate.cnrs.fr/~zelinger/nestor/nestor.htm)

If a teacher wants to keep track of students' research work then I can highly recommend the use of a free software called Nestor. A quote from their site:

> Promoting constructivist learning: in education, when the web is used as a source of information, Nestor maps provide a kind of 'notebook': teachers can ask their students to search the web for documents relevant to a given theme ... and ask them to provide the results as a Nestor map: the students are encouraged to add their personal annotations, personal texts and information structure to the maps (and not merely pure web resources!). Nestor philosophy is to encourage users to evolve from web readers to web writers, from navigation experience to abstraction, from individual work to collaborative work and thus from raw information access to knowledge construction. Nestor is intended to be used as a constructionist environment.

Conclusion

To sum up the benefits of webquests, I have tried to summarise some of the benefits that can accrue from taking the trouble to explore with this online learning model:

- Like any carefully planned lesson, a good webquest can make learning interesting and engaging for students.
- Webquests let students work at their own pace, either individually or in teams.
- They also let students explore selected topics in more depth, and in their own time, but within the limits that the teacher selects. This makes webquests ideal for mixed-ability classes.
- Webquests offer a way of 'modelling' a historical enquiry, and teaching students about the value of research.
- Webquests can increase the 'comfort level' of students using the internet for learning activities. A properly designed webquest can help students become effective researchers rather than simply 'pinball browsing' from one site to another.
- It enables students to develop critical thinking skills and 'internet literacy'.

- It provides students with the opportunity to interact with a wide range of different sources related to a particular topic.
- It can develop pupils' willingness to read and work with extended texts, and their active literacy skills (writing, debating, public speaking). It provides a mode of text production that they find more congenial than some 'traditional' writing activity in school history.
- Some of the outcomes of webquest enquires can be digitally 'showcased' on the school VLE, or on the internet.

Note

1 URLs sometimes change, are moved or deleted. Apologies if some of these links are no longer valid when you read this chapter, but hopefully you will be able to access most of the sites mentioned by use of keywords and Google searches.

References

Arnold, J. (2000) *History: A very short introduction*, Oxford: Oxford University Press.
Barron, B. and Darling-Hammond, L. (2008) *Powerful Learning: Studies show deep understanding derives from collaborative methods*, online at www.edutopia.org/inquiry-project-learning-research, accessed 12 January 2012.
Blasszauer, J. (2003) *Tolerance Webquest*, online at www.reocities.com/bjohnnyus/myWebquest, accessed 12 January 2012.
Blasszauer, J. (2004) *Enlargement Webquest*, online at www.reocities.com/bjohnnyus/Enlargement.htm, accessed 12 January 2012.
Bruner, J. (1990) *Constructivist Theory (an overview)*, online at http://tip.psychology.org/bruner.html, accessed 12 January 2012.
Dodge, B. (1997) *Some Thoughts about Webquests*, online at http://Webquest.sdsu.edu/about_Webquests.html, accessed 12 January 2012.
Lyons, J.F. (2009) *Teaching History Online*, London: Routledge, online at http://schoolnet.org.za/PILP/themes/trainer_offline/waw/gilded/student.htm.
March, T. (2007) 'Revisiting Webquests in a Web 2 world: how developments in technology and pedagogy combine to scaffold personal learning', in *Interactive Educational Multimedia*, 15: 1–17, online at www.ub.edu/multimedia/iem, accessed 12 January 2012.
Moore, R. (2000) 'Using the internet to teach interpretations in years 8 and 12', *Teaching History*, 101: 35–9.
Nestor Map (free software) www.gate.cnrs.fr/~zeiliger/nestor/nestor.htm.
Ofsted (2011) *History for All*, London: Ofsted.
Peachey, N. (2009) *Create a Quick Discussion Forum*, online at http://quickshout.blogspot.com/2009/04/create-quick-discussion-forum.html, accessed 12 January 2012.
Peachey, N. (2010) *Create Authentic Web Based Research Tasks With Mashpedia*, online at http://quickshout.blogspot.com/2010/04/create-authentic-web-based-research.html, accessed 12 January 2012.
QCA (2007) *The National Curriculum for History: Key Stage 3*, London, QCA, online at www.education.gov.uk/schools/teachingandlearning/curriculum/secondary/b00199545/history, accessed 12 January 2012.
Thomas, J.W. (2000) 'A review of project based learning' (prepared for *The Autodesk Foundation Online* 2000), online at www.bie.org/research/study/review_of_project_based_learning_2000, accessed 12 January 2012.
Walsh, B. (2008) 'Stories and their sources', *Teaching History*, 133: 4–9.
Webquest materials Online (nd), online at http://Webquest.sdsu.edu/, accessed 12 January 2012.
Wiliam, D. (2011) *Embedded Formative Assessment*, Bloomington, IN: Solution Tree Press.

Index